C000278871

BIG MAL

BIG MAL

THE HIGH LIFE AND HARD TIMES OF MALCOLM ALLISON, FOOTBALL LEGEND

DAVID TOSSELL

MAINSTREAM
PUBLISHING

EDINBURGH AND LONDON

Copyright © David Tossell, 2008
All rights reserved
The moral right of the author has been asserted

First published in Great Britain in 2008 by
MAINSTREAM PUBLISHING COMPANY
(EDINBURGH) LTD
7 Albany Street
Edinburgh EH1 3UG

ISBN 9781845963309

No part of this book may be reproduced or transmitted
in any form or by any other means without permission
in writing from the publisher, except by a reviewer
who wishes to quote brief passages in connection
with a review written for insertion in
a magazine, newspaper or broadcast

The author has made every effort to clear all copyright permissions,
but where this has not been possible and amendments are required,
the publisher will be pleased to make any necessary
arrangements at the earliest opportunity

A catalogue record for this book is available
from the British Library

Typeset in Big Noodle and Palatino

Printed in Great Britain by
Clays Ltd, St Ives plc

CONTENTS

	Acknowledgements	7
1	Man and Boy	9
2	Tactics in the Teacups	25
3	Hammer Horror	41
4	Running Wild	55
5	Part-time Love	71
6	Pilgrim's Progress	81
7	Whines and Women	99
8	Made in Manchester	111
9	Anatomy of a Championship	131
10	Paradise City	147
11	Cup Kings	165
12	The Birth of Big Mal	181
13	The End of the Affair	197
14	Sinking Feeling	215
15	Out of the Blues	223
16	Crying Game	235
17	Cat in the Hat Meets the Bird in the Bath	247
18	You Can't Go Back	261
19	North-East Frontier	281
20	Rovers Return	297
21	No More Games	317
	Bibliography	335

ACKNOWLEDGEMENTS

Many people's memories and opinions have helped to shape this story, so I am greatly indebted to all those with whom I have discussed Malcolm Allison during my research: Mark Allison, Colin Bell, John Bond, Tony Book, Alistair Brownlee, John Cartwright, Terry Cochrane, Joe Corrigan, Paul Crockford, Steve Daley, Derek Dougan, Don Howe, Gordon Jago, Stewart Jump, James Lawton, Francis Lee, Stuart Lee, Eddie Lewis, Graham Little, Terry McDonald, Bob McNab, Peter McParland, Gary Megson, Ian Mellor, John Newman, Bob Nichols, Ian Niven, Frank O'Farrell, Jeff Powell, Norman Piper, John Radford, Nicky Reid, Don Rogers, Lynn Salten, Dave Sexton, Nigel Sims, Roger Spry, Mike Summerbee, Peter Taylor, Andy Tillson, Mike Trebilcock, Derek Ufton, Ron Walker and Alan Whittle.

I am particularly grateful for the support and assistance that was forthcoming from James Lawton and from Malcolm's long-time partner, Lynn.

Tony McDonald, publisher of the retro West Ham magazine *Ex*, allowed me to make use of interviews appearing in his publication. If only every club could boast such an admirable journal. Richard Whitehead was his usual source of contacts and sound advice, while Phil Tanner went beyond the call of duty to provide information about Malcolm's time at Bath City and Ian Whittell opened up many important doors in the Manchester area. Others who have assisted me in many and varied ways are: Phil Alexander, Derek Armstrong, Mike Blackstone, Mal Butler, Tony Ellis, Colin Ewenson, Peter Hall, Steve Harris, Shaun Keogh, John Ley, John Little, Paul Mace, Barry

Mead, Ken Nicholl, Jim Platt, Neil Rioch, Haydn Parry, John Richards, Derek Robinson, Jonathan Sides, Brian Spurrell, Alan Stewart, Fred Street and Dave Thomas.

Thanks to Bill Campbell, Iain MacGregor, Graeme Blaikie and all the staff at Mainstream for their professionalism and support and to Andy Cowie at Colorsport and the staff at Getty Images and Rex Features for their assistance in sourcing photography for this book. I am grateful, as always, to all those writers and authors whose material has formed an important part of my research. I have endeavoured to acknowledge them in the bibliography.

Final thanks once more to my family, especially Sara, Amy, Sarah and Laura, for all their love and encouragement.

A percentage of royalties from this book has been donated to the Alzheimer's Society (Registered Charity: 296645), which continues to research into all forms of dementia, offering care to sufferers and their families. Further information can be found online at www.alzheimers.org.uk.

1

MAN AND BOY

'What would big Malcolm Allison do in a situation like this, eh?'

'Smack [him] over the head with a bottle of champagne and stub his Cuban out on his hand'

– Manchester CID members discuss how to deal with a 1970s criminal (*Life On Mars*, BBC 1, February 2007)

It was still only late August, the opening weeks of the 2006–07 season, but the familiar pattern had been re-established already. Even on their own ground, little consideration had been given to the likelihood of Manchester City achieving victory against a multi-national, multi-talented Arsenal team whose ambitions of winning another Premiership title contrasted starkly to the home club's more modest aspirations for the coming campaign. A penalty scored by City's Joey Barton appeared merely to be delaying the inevitable. For most fans in the City of Manchester Stadium, games between these sides had usually conformed to this recognisable blueprint.

Spotting a recognisable face in the crowd, the Sky Sports cameras homed in. Here was a man whose influence almost 40 years earlier had made things very different. A man whose vision, planning, motivational powers and, often, sheer force of personality had made Manchester City the team against whom the likes of Arsenal measured themselves. The graphics operators hurriedly got to work. Up went the caption, 'Malcolm Allison, former Manchester City coach'. Commentators were sufficiently distracted from the latest piece of Thierry Henry trickery to purr at the memory of Allison's achievements at the club: four major triumphs in a three-year span, including a complete set of domestic trophies and a European success.

Young viewers knowing only of life in the glossily packaged days of endless live televised football – even those who had flown in the face of the modern trend by following City instead of rivals United – blinked unknowingly at their screens. Those a little older might at least have been somewhat familiar with the name, perhaps heard some of the outrageous stories with which it had become associated. Anyone who had been watching football when Allison was in his glorious, exaggerated prime in the 1960s through to the '80s, was shocked by what they saw, even those who had heard the stories of his mental deterioration. The imposing physical figure was still evident under his grey jacket, even if it was hunched forward in his seat, but the eyes that used to sparkle with a potent mix of charm, wit and cunning seemed glazed and distant. The expression behind which a thousand schemes used to play, whether planning the next big game or deciding where to dine with his latest female companion, appeared bereft of any indication that he was aware of his surroundings.

On one hand, it was painful to see how one of the most expansive minds and sharpest personalities in football's recent history had been diminished by the illness of dementia, into whose grip he had been slipping more completely over the previous five years. At the same time it was a chance to turn to younger companions and say, 'See that guy there? Well, let me tell you . . .'

Preparation of this book was already well under way at the time of Allison's televised visit to the club where he had written himself into football's lore. Those interviewed in the aftermath shared those mixed feelings: sorrow at Allison's plight; pride that their careers, and lives, had been touched by him; and gratitude that, at least fleetingly, he had emerged from a regimented existence in his council-run nursing home and was back in the public eye, being acknowledged for something more than the fedora hat and fat cigar that had become the enduring image of the man they called Big Mal.

The ravages of his illness were something that Malcolm was powerless to prevent, although reports have suggested that his excessive alcoholic intake over the years contributed to the onset of his Alzheimer's-type affliction. His achievements in the game should, however, have afforded him the ability to live out his years in a little more physical comfort than has been the case. Scarcely any personal possessions survived the excesses of a man who placed no import on the accumulation of long-term wealth. Instead, his idea of being rich in his final days, he used to tell friends, was to be able to sit in a rocking chair with a big smile on his face, remembering – without regret – all the good times: the on-field success, the cigars, the best wines and all the beautiful women he had bedded. The cruel irony is that not only did the money all go, but many of those precious memories were eventually taken from him as well.

Yet the sad final chapter should not dominate the story of a life lived so fully. In Allison's case it would be impossible for it to do so anyway. A pioneer of modern football techniques while a player at West Ham, his loss of a lung to tuberculosis at the age of 31 ended his on-field career, but his recovery from the depression that followed implanted a passion and a zest for living that, for most of the time, survived the highs and lows that were partly thrown at him by fate and frequently self-created. When life kicked Allison, his response was to kick back. Having reached the peak of the English game with City, he set himself up for a fall by describing how he would conquer Europe. When the boast came crashing around his ears, he simply picked himself up and did it the following year instead.

It is interesting that the man with whom Allison was most often bracketed at the peak of his career – in terms of coaching ability, achievement, outspokenness and, ultimately, human weakness – was another whose playing days had been cut short by circumstance: Brian Clough. 'One of the aches in Malcolm's life was that he wanted to be a better player than he was,' says friend and journalist James Lawton. 'He marvelled at the young Brian Clough and envied his talent. That created a little tension in him. He wasn't as good a player as he wanted to be and his career ended prematurely, and I think in the early days it was what made him such a dynamite coach.'

There was a time when Clough and Allison were the 'people's champions' of English football, the men the fans wished to entrust with the task of guiding the fortunes of the England team. Of course, the Football Association would no more appoint one of them to the post of England manager than the various governments would think to name either on any kind of honours list.[1]

Allison was a man of extremes. When talking about his burning desire to create the best football team in the country, Manchester City players glow with their descriptions of the fanatically driven coach who inspired them to collective achievement and personal overfulfilment of potential. Virtually every player interviewed for this book believes that on a one-on-one basis Allison improved them – from members of the West Ham youth team to experienced men like Tony Book, who was turned from a bricklaying non-League footballer into a trophy-winning First Division captain. Then there were lower division signings such as Colin Bell, Mike Summerbee and Francis Lee, who were moulded into England players within a few months of each other.

'Malcolm rubbed off on you,' Bell explains. 'You might have been a half decent player, but he gave you an extra 10 per cent, added something to your game and gave you a cutting edge. Those of us who were connected with him know it was a great thing that he has been in our lives.'

Away from football, Malcolm was no less committed. Michael Parkinson once described him as 'possibly the least tranquillised Englishman alive'. Enjoying life was something he did to the limit – whether it was ordering the best champagne for everyone or taking home the prettiest girl. Money meant nothing, as long as he had enough to order the next round. Even if he didn't, he would still insist that the drinks were on him.

With the extremes came the contradictions. He was generous to a fault with his friends and he embraced and trusted his fellow man. That was why he got on so well with a number of criminals. It was not just circumstances that made that happen – notably his spell as a nightclub owner in London – but his willingness to identify good in others. It showed in his approach to football. His personality was to see the best in people, which was why he preferred to concentrate on getting the maximum out of his own players rather than become a fearful coach in the manner of Don Revie.

---

[1] Clough had to wait until 1991, almost two decades after winning his first League title and more than ten years after back-to-back European Cup success, before being made an OBE.

Yet he also embraced more than his fair share of females and often overlooked his obligation to those women who were closest to him. The fact that he was open and honest about his affairs, confessing to his weaknesses and never seeking to justify them by blaming those behind whose backs he went, contains a certain honesty and virtue. But that is of little comfort to those hurt by his actions: the wives left waiting at home, the children denied the presence of their father.

Tales relating to that aspect of Malcolm Allison's character form an undeniable part of his story and are present within these pages. Insight is offered where appropriate by those close to the source, yet the intention is to relate such stories without celebration or condemnation.

Another contradiction: Malcolm was a physically imposing man, with an aura of confidence that merely added to the force of his presence. Former City player Ian Mellor tells a story to illustrate that. 'I remember being in the players' lounge after a game and it was packed shoulder to shoulder, with twice as many people as should have been in there. Malcolm walked in and said something simple like, "Is Glyn Pardoe in here?" The whole place just stopped dead. You could have heard a pin drop. That was the power of the man: to walk in a room of a hundred people and silence them with one question.'

And Rodney Marsh remembers becoming the biggest signing in Manchester City's history when he was bought for £200,000, yet as he walked to the ground with Allison at his side it was Malcolm to whom the autograph hunters flocked.

Privately, however, Allison went through periods when he felt anything but big. He was racked by doubt bordering on self-loathing. When, having moved on from City, he suffered successive relegations as manager of Crystal Palace, he spent tortured nights in his London flat looking for answers that had previously seemed to come to him so effortlessly. Thoughts of suicide invaded his moments of sleeplessness.

Malcolm had truly turned into Big Mal when he became a nationally recognised figure during his irreverent, outrageous television appearances during the 1970 World Cup finals. He had become the voice of the common man. The showman within his psyche, never far from the surface, developed an addiction to the spotlight. He was no longer content to be second in command at Maine Road and he plotted to dissolve the partnership with manager Joe Mercer that had brought such success. Yet Allison without the presence of City's senior citizen was like a lead guitarist without the grounding influence of his rhythm section. Lacking someone to provide a framework for his genius, his work became a series of tuneless flights of fancy. Even before Allison helped to engineer the departure of the man who had taken him to City in 1965, leading football writer Ken Jones was commenting:

> Talented, magnetic but intolerant to the point where football management was always likely to blow up in his face, Allison found at Maine Road the perfect level at which to work, the ideal man to work with. He could unroll the full scope of his talent yet there was always a voice to utter a warning when the steam was building up to a head.

Having decided to go it alone, first at City, then at Crystal Palace and various other teams, success in England deserted him, his only achievements of note coming on the foreign fields of Portugal and the Middle East. And so his personality had to work even harder to maintain his celebrity profile. What other explanation could there be for stunts like that which found soft-porn star Fiona Richmond naked in the bath with Allison and his Palace players. Had he achieved more at Palace, perhaps the Big Mal persona that eventually took over and helped to undermine his football endeavours would have been kept in check. Allison became a modern-day football Jekyll and Hyde, trapped in a vicious circle from which there was apparently no escape.

Such a flaw prevented him from creating a long-term legacy of on-field achievement. Instead, most of his employments ended in acrimonious sackings, the result of failure on the field, confrontation with the board or lurid stories of his private life – and often all three. Francis Lee, who has known Allison as well as anyone over the past four decades, suggests, 'When you look at people like Alex Ferguson, Bill Shankly and Arsène Wenger, the great thing they have had is consistency. They have been in one place for a long time and generated success. That was something Malcolm couldn't achieve.

As soon as things started going well, he would create trouble, just because he wanted to.'

For all the importance to this story of the gambler, the womaniser, the party animal and the personality, it is Malcolm Allison the football man that remains at its heart. Before there was the champagne, there was the young player who, inspired by the great Hungarians of the 1950s, sought to drag football single-handedly into the modern age by changing the way of life at West Ham. Before the fedora, there was the budding coach who came back from two years outside football to prove his potential during an apprenticeship with Cambridge University, Bath City and Plymouth Argyle. Before the cigar-smoking TV pundit, there was the man who helped lead Manchester City from the Second Division to the League Championship inside three years and spent the next two seasons winning just about every cup competition on offer. And before the man who lurched from one professional and personal disaster to another, there was the dynamic, energetic, groundbreaking coach whose methods helped to inspire a paradigm change in English football.

Without him there would have been no Big Mal.

The formative years of one of the most colourful characters to inhabit British sport in the second half of the twentieth century were spent in and around the London of the Second World War. Born in Dartford on 5 September 1927, Malcolm Alexander Allison would recall much of his childhood having consisted of 'drab, grey days filled with ration books and demob overcoats'. He seemed determined to spend the rest of his life compensating.

Allison's youth, however, was a long way from the kind of deprivation endured by many of his contemporaries. His parents, Charlie and Doris, while not rich, were comfortable, thanks to Charlie's job as an electrician, which often forced him away from home on contract work. With brothers Roy, Clive and Morris, and sister Pauline, Malcolm was moved, shortly after his birth, to the south-east London suburb of Bexleyheath.

Until the Enclosure Act passed through Parliament in the early nineteenth century, giving landowners the right to secure their property from squatters and beginning a programme of town development, Bexleyheath had earned notoriety as a raw, open stretch of land patrolled by highwaymen. They picked off their victims as they travelled along Watling Street, the old Roman road between London and Dover. Given the company he would keep at various stages in his later life, it is easy to imagine Malcolm, had he grown up in such times, being attracted to the glamour and bravado of such men.

By the time the Allison family arrived, a period of concerted development throughout the 1930s had seen the now respectable market town expanding away from the immediate surrounds of Watling Street, offering Malcolm a semi-detached upbringing that was, notwithstanding the disruption of the war, contentedly unremarkable. His academic achievements fell into the same category. 'My schooldays, affected by war-time evacuations, had been sketchy as legally possible,' he confessed.

One of his earliest reports said that he was 'good at sport, but uses his mouth too much' and Allison would claim to have deliberately failed the entry examination for the local grammar school – much to his father's disapproval – because he didn't want to be stuck anywhere they played only rugby. In Brian Belton's book, *Days Of Iron*, Allison explained:

> All I wanted for Christmas as a kid was football gear, boots and so on. I just loved the game. My mother's family was very football orientated. Her two brothers both played good amateur football. They used to give me a lift on the handlebars of their bikes to go with them to different matches.

Attending Central School in Bexleyheath, Allison played in the football team as an 11 year old against boys three years his senior. Teachers and parents gradually came to accept that football was the most potent force in his life and training with a young professional called Alf Rosier, who was on Fulham's books, enriched his education in the game. 'We used to practise things together,' Allison said. 'He was a big influence on me.' Malcolm's competitive nature made an early appearance when he won the school's Victor Ludorum sports trophy, but only after he tripped his closest rival in a vital race. He at least had the decency to feel ashamed when he collected the award from his headmaster.

His appearances as a scheming inside-forward for the St John's Boys Club team in the Dartford Minor League were good enough to earn him selection for the league's representative team. It was there he teamed up, for the first of many times, with Derek Ufton, who had achieved his call-up while playing for rival team Borough Juniors. 'We were boys of 13 and 14 playing against 18 year olds,' Ufton explains. 'Malcolm was always going to be the great player. He had marvellous skill on the ball at a young age. And he was taller than most of us so he always seemed to have that swagger about him.'

After giving polite consideration to following his father into an apprenticeship in electrical engineering, Allison began work as a messenger for a Fleet Street photographic agency and was thrilled to be given an assignment at one of the wartime FA Cup finals played at Wembley. The glamour of the job quickly faded, though, when he was sent from the stadium with only a few minutes played to get some plates back to the office for developing.

As it turned out, Allison was becoming a good enough footballer that he was not going to have to satisfy his dreams vicariously by witnessing the feats of others. Charlton Athletic had noted his prowess and at the age of 15 he was offered the chance to play in a trial game. Nervous and short on confidence, he was instructed to line up at centre-forward, from where he proceeded to score a hat-trick of goals to earn an invitation to sign for the club as an amateur. Various accounts have Allison playing games for non-League Erith and Belvedere around that time, although the club's own records suggest that a few wartime reserve games might have been all that he managed. At 17, however, he reserved a place for his name in the official annals of the sport when he signed as a professional for Charlton.

It was February 1945, with the war in Europe entering its final phase, when Allison reported to The Valley as an apprentice. The often-haphazard nature of football during those years of conflict meant that he was soon given his first experience of big-game nerves. Teams rarely knew their line-ups until moments before kick-off, often relying on players securing military leave or guest performers turning up from their local postings. The late arrival of George Green for a game against an Arsenal team that included the great Cliff Bastin meant that Allison was told to get undressed. Gripped by 'terrible fear', Allison felt a wave of relief when the face of Green at last appeared round the changing-room door.

Allison spent most of his opening months at The Valley – which he called a 'vast scruffy bowl of concrete' – in a state of excited awe. He would rush to the newspaper stand to see his name printed in the junior team line-ups, saying that 'it filled my whole body with a sense of achievement'. The inferiority complex that he carried around with him in those teenage years would provide him with an empathy in later life when, as a coach, he was confronted by nervous young players about to be thrown in at the deep end. Allison would attempt to retain a sense of that frightened boy who'd thought he was facing Bastin. 'I have never tried to lose the memory of how difficult it could be to play well,' he would say.

There was little opportunity for Allison to become more comfortable in his surroundings. His national service papers dropped through the letterbox in the autumn and he was off on a journey that would open up a whole new world of football.

A dreary day in Maidstone in December 1945 held little promise of the range of experience that lay ahead of Private Allison as he reported for duty with his fellow conscripts. The next three years, much of it spent in Austria, would be at times eye-opening, and at others heart-rending. All of it would broaden Allison's mind, leaving him to report, 'Though I never lost my ambition to make the game my life, the army did teach me that football was no more than an aspect, perhaps a reflection, of the hard business of life.'

Allison witnessed the misery of those stationed at a camp in Klagenfurt – Czech, Ukrainian and Russian refugees whose plight tore at his spirit. One night, as he sat in a truck that was driving past the camp, a woman threw herself and a baby in front of the vehicle. Such despair in others seemed to show Allison that life was for living. In future years, the image would come back to him when he saw fellow managers so racked with fear and anguish over a mere game of football.

Yet the military also helped to lay out in front of Allison the rewards that life could offer. A two-week visit to Cortina in the Italian Alps to compete in the army skiing championships transported him into a colourful world of capitalism, the black market, a thriving café society and beautiful women. After the grimness of wartime Britain, this was Allison's first taste of the high life – even if he was, on this occasion, more observer than consumer. 'I absorbed the pattern of these extraordinary lifestyles, and the feeling came to me very strongly that I could never be content with an ordinary life. I had to have all this colour, all this exhilaration for myself.'

There were the inevitable scrapes, most notably when he escaped with a week's fatigues after he and a prisoner he was guarding stole and killed a chicken to supplement their rations and ended up pulling a gun on a pair of Yugoslav border guards. And there was the introduction to the joys of female company, a force that was to run so powerfully through his future life.

And of course, there was football. Allison was in the habit of hitting the parade ground at 5 a.m. every day to go through his daily training routine, a discipline that so impressed his commanding officer that the rest of the camp was ordered to rise an hour earlier to join him. Asked to organise the battalion's football team, he led them to victory in the Regimental Cup and also played some games for a local team, FC Wacker Innsbruck.

The most important part of Allison's military football education came at the Prater Stadium in Vienna, a venue that was to feature large in his future career but for now was where he took the opportunity to watch the training sessions of the young players of the Austrian national team – including the elegant midfielder Ernst Ocwirk. 'I liked the way they enslaved the ball. They made it do all the work. They were neat and controlled. There was nothing haphazard or crude about their work and I thought to myself, "Surely this is the wave of the future. This is what we have to do in England."'

Allison was struck by the 'purpose and knowledge' demonstrated by the trainers, the variety of the routines. Every player was kept interested. Everything was done for a reason. It left him feeling excited about his own football future as the end of his national service approached. In the hands of professionals in England, coupled with what he had learned from the Austrians, he felt sure that his game would develop at a great rate. He was soon to learn that others did not share his vision.

Demobbed and back at Charlton, Allison – not for the last time in his career – felt immediate discontent with his surroundings. Charlton were a First Division club and had been in two FA Cup finals while Allison was in army uniform, losing to Derby in 1946 and beating Burnley a year later. Yet he could not help but be hugely disappointed at the approach of the club compared with what he had witnessed overseas. 'It was like getting in a time machine and finding yourself travelling in the wrong direction.'

Life in post-war Britain might have been moving forward at a significant pace but football was showing little inclination to keep up. While the introduction of the National Health Service and the nationalisation of major industries were shoving the country into a new age of social responsibility, the keepers of the national sport remained mired in pre-war complacency. So eager had the country been for the return of major sports events that all club directors had to do was throw open the doors of their often derelict and unsafe grounds and sit back and count the cash. Little of it found its way into the pockets of players who, even with appearance money and win bonuses, were picking up less than £10 a week. As more than 40 million spectators a season turned out for Football League matches in the late 1940s, English football patted itself on the back and kidded itself that everything was just grand.

Few professional players, whose relatively glamorous existence offered some release from the post-war austerity suffered by the average working man, were ready to question the health of their sport. Allison was one of the minority. What he experienced at Charlton had the genteel, civilised feel of a tea dance rather than the vigorous, challenging ambience he expected of a professional football club. Charlton goalkeeper Sam Bartram spoke of the 'wonderful atmosphere' at The Valley, adding, 'the club has been a supremely happy one and because of that, it has enjoyed success on the field. There has been a minimum of bickering and a maximum of helpful cooperation.'

Eddie Firmani, the South African forward who made his name in

English football at Charlton in the 1950s, offered a similar description. 'Charlton possessed something neither money nor the honours of the game could secure for us: a wonderful family spirit; an atmosphere in which every fellow trusted the other chap; a club-spirit which meant every player would fight his heart out for the good of Charlton Athletic.'

But Allison was no longer the awestruck kid checking the newspapers for mention of his name, content just to be part of the professional game. He had grown into a cynical, disillusioned young man. All this talk of 'jolly good chaps' meant nothing to him. As he looked around he saw no one who shared his view of the way football should be played or operated. Where were the men from whom he could learn, who were willing to nurture a young talent?

He certainly didn't feel that Jimmy Seed, the manager who had led the team from Third to First Division in the 1930s, was such a man. 'To me he didn't grasp the essentials of the job,' was Allison's damning verdict.

What he encountered, however, was largely symptomatic of the era. Tactics, coaching and thoughtful preparation were still new concepts for most teams – totally alien to many more. English football had barely progressed over the previous half-century. The only widespread on-field advance had been when Herbert Chapman, the innovative former Huddersfield and Arsenal manager of the '20s and '30s, moved back his centre-half to play as a dedicated defender between the two full-backs, creating the classic 'WM' formation. Until the Second World War, most Football League teams had still been overseen by a 'secretary-manager', who was often regarded as little more than an office boy by the club directors. His administrative duties were frequently considered more important than getting the players ready to win games. Only relatively recently had realisation dawned on the managers that, if directors were happy to calmly toss them aside when results went against them, perhaps they ought to think a little more deeply about ways of influencing events on the pitch. Even the concept of the manager having sole responsibility for picking the team was considered newfangled.

'Managers at that time were not used to bringing in fresh ideas,' says Dave Sexton, a striker who would become a teammate of

Allison's and go on to be one of the most respected coaches in English football. 'It was like they were forbidden to do anything new.'

Derek Ufton, soon to join Allison at Charlton, adds, 'There wasn't coaching in those days. You ran round and round the field, had a practice game on the Tuesday but never really saw the ball after that for the rest of the week. Wednesday and Thursday would be strength and running and on Friday you had a massage and waited for the team to go up on the board. All my life I had played up the street with a ball every day and once I became a professional I hardly saw it. The view was that you would be hungrier for it on Saturday.'

Bartram, who had been at the club since 1934, was typical of the older generation of players who happily accepted that the manager knew all there was to know. He certainly held a very different view from that of Allison, and his description of Seed in his autobiography suggests that the manager would not have expected to have his knowledge and authority challenged by a young upstart. 'No man in the game, I think it is safe to say, knows more about football, footballers and football tactics than he,' Bartram gushed, adding, 'It is an unwritten law at The Valley that the boss must never be let down.'

Yet Allison found Seed to be a remote figure, with whom he had virtually no personal contact. There was no explanation of why he was left in the third team on an occasion when injury to centre-half Harold Phipps left everyone at the club expecting a first-team call-up for Allison – a snub that left him feeling 'discarded'.

A frequently recounted tale was that of Seed trying to impress a visiting member of the South African FA by shouting encouragement to Allison as he lapped the field during a training session. Allison resented the fact that he had said nothing to him for years but was now trying to appear like a father figure to impress a visiting dignitary. He was even angrier the next day when Seed picked him up on not having responded by saying, 'When I speak to you I expect a reply.'

Allison detested what he saw as an old-boys' network of former players staying in the game to earn a living as trainers without showing the least interest in doing the job with any degree of professionalism. He had little regard for the football knowledge of Charlton trainer Jimmy Trotter, who also filled that role with the England team, and whose sessions amounted to little more than tedious amounts of jogging. Even the training kit appeared designed to sap the players' enthusiasm, consisting as it did of a pile of shirts and shorts that were thrown on the floor, prompting an unseemly scramble for items that were clean, undamaged and came close to fitting properly.

Ufton had followed his friend's path from the army to Charlton, thanks to a chance meeting at a dance on the day he was demobbed. Having informed Allison that he was about to sign for Cardiff, he was told, 'You don't want to go all that way. Meet me on Wednesday and I will see if I can get you a trial.' Ufton took his opportunity, signed for the club and, ironically, made it into the first team before Allison.

He clearly remembers Allison's discontent at The Valley. 'The thing that upset him was that he had been an inside-forward with great skills as a young player, a craftsman who could bamboozle the opposition. Now he had gone back to centre-half and he couldn't understand why Jimmy Seed didn't put him straight in the team. Malcolm was outspoken and was a very popular member of the club. He was a bit different and had a more flamboyant style than most of us. He liked the West End and the rest of us liked to stay in suburbia. I think it became a bit of a personal thing with him and Jimmy. He always had this feeling against authority and that would be why Jimmy turned against him. It would get to his ears that Malcolm would be saying things and then Malcolm would argue the point instead of accepting that Jimmy was manager.'

Despite being out of the first team, Allison had no fear of challenging the senior players, even though the strongly held views of a lad barely out of his teens could on occasions be greeted with ridicule by elders who felt Allison's opinions had no basis in experience. He had sufficient self-awareness to realise that his own ability as a player left something to be desired, yet felt there was no one to whom he could turn for advice. The one player with whom he did bond was Scotland international forward Tommy Brown, who had been bought from Millwall and made no pretence of having any respect for the manager. It was the sharp-dressed Brown who took Allison on his first night out in the West End.

In the days when low salaries meant clubs could afford to stockpile players in their second and third teams, Allison's Football League debut did not arrive until the age of 22, in a 2–0 defeat at Manchester City on Christmas Eve 1949. He played his second, and final, game for Charlton three days later in a 2–1 home defeat against Portsmouth. 'Jimmy didn't contemplate him again for some reason after that,' says Ufton, who had already established himself at left-half. 'Harold Phipps was the regular centre-half and Jimmy brought him back. Then after Malcolm left Charlton I moved over to centre-half, which was always a bit of a bone of contention between us.'

The early seeds of Allison's coaching career were planted in that first game in Manchester, where he realised he had 'burned myself out on the training ground' and was shattered physically and confused mentally. He was surprised at the lack of instruction coming from the Charlton bench, recalling, 'It seemed like madness in this ultimate team game to send out men with no clear idea of how they related to each other.'

He took the opportunity to take part in some basic coaching at The Valley, working on the technique of shooting, heading and kicking, but he had long since realised that there was a strict limit on how far he could progress his career without moving away from Charlton. In February 1951, a day after he had told Seed how bad he thought the training was at the club, he was sold to West Ham for £7,000. The move owed much to the presence on the Charlton staff of Benny Fenton, who recommended Allison to his brother Ted, manager of West Ham, as a possible long-term replacement for stalwart centre-half Dick Walker. It was with no regrets that Allison turned his back on The Valley – and walked into one of the most significant phases of his career.

2

TACTICS IN THE TEACUPS

'Frequently the more trifling the subject, the more animated and protracted the discussion'

— nineteenth-century US President Franklin Pierce

The Upton Park at which Malcolm Allison arrived in February 1951 was not exactly thriving. Relegated from the First Division in 1932, West Ham United Football Club's biggest annual achievement was simply keeping its head above the deep financial waters that constantly threatened to pull it down.

It was a struggle, however, that was borne with a smile. Maybe it was something to do with London, the spirit of the Blitz and all that chirpy Cockney nonsense, but – just like Charlton – the Hammers were a happy-go-lucky club who placed more emphasis on fun than professionalism. Irishman Frank O'Farrell, who had arrived from Cork in 1948, explains, 'It was a laid-back family club. They hadn't been anywhere in football terms for years but it was a nice club to play for, full of nice people. There was not the ruthlessness that there is in modern football.'

Since the summer of 1950, the burden of improving the team's fortunes on meagre resources had rested on the shoulders of Ted Fenton. Born in the Forest Gate area of east London, Fenton had become an effective wing-half for his local team, playing 176 games for the Hammers before the war and appearing in their 1940 War Cup final victory over Blackburn Rovers at Wembley. Having served as a physical training sergeant major during the Second World War, Fenton had gone into management at Southern League Colchester United, where he captured national attention with some notable FA Cup results. Rejoining West Ham as assistant manager in 1948, he had to wait only two years before ascending to the position of manager in place of Charlie Paynter, a Hammers servant for 50 years as player, trainer and, since 1932, manager. Fenton had been seen all along as Paynter's successor and the serious prospect of demotion to the Third Division had made it clear that the time had arrived to effect the handover.

Fenton quickly fell in love with the cut and thrust of transfer market negotiation, but it was his very first signing, Allison, who was to remain his most significant piece of business. Even the official club history acknowledges that the capture of Allison 'represented a watershed in the history of the Hammers'. Full-back John Bond, who was to become one of Malcolm's best friends at the club, says, 'He made a big impression on most people as soon as he arrived from Charlton. He was a big, brash good-looking fellow who had plenty to say for himself and was mad keen on football.'

For Fenton, it was an important symbolic signing as the physically imposing 6ft 1in. Allison, named as team captain, was bought to take over the shirt of Dick Walker, the strongest link to the Paynter era. 'It was difficult for Malcolm,' says O'Farrell. 'He was replacing a very good and very popular player who was reaching the end of his career. Dick had a great rapport with the fans, had a proud record as a paratrooper in the war and was very personable. He was one of those characters who can say anything and get away with it. Malcolm was obviously brought in to replace him so it took him a while to sell himself to the crowd.'

Allison happily accepted the challenge, relieved to have escaped the retarded footballing environment of The Valley, and for a short while he was far happier with his lot at West Ham. At least he was in the team. But it did not take long – approximately six months – for him to be afflicted by the same old frustrations with English football. The pastoral air that surrounded the East End club was, according to O'Farrell, 'the sort of thing Malcolm saw as a hindrance to progress'.

Allison discovered that West Ham was even more backward than Charlton – 'a feat which I would have believed impossible', he said. Training had no more purpose than at The Valley and being even shorter, necessitated less commitment from the players. The sessions took place on a scrub of land at the back of the stadium, where clusters of trees offered the players the chance to break off from their runs for a crafty cigarette.

For Allison, the important difference between Charlton and West Ham was that, as an older player and a more confident personality, he felt able to effect some kind of change – and he had the single-minded determination to do so. He admitted, 'I'm amazed how one-dimensional I was in those days. My dedication was absolute. I didn't smoke, I didn't drink and I never had sex within three days of a match. Incredible!'

O'Farrell adds, 'Malcolm arrived at the club just when more people in English football were beginning to say that we should be looking at ourselves and the way we approached the game. He brought that sort of attitude with him.'

Allison began to draw up his own practice schedules for the team, finding allies for his methods among the other players. Eddie Lewis, a forward who would join West Ham after spells at Manchester United and Preston, had been used to training that consisted of little more than laps of the pitch followed by 15-a-side free-for-alls. 'Under Malcolm everything was so organised. One small group would be playing six versus six, another playing head tennis, another doing weights, another running. The whistle would blow and the groups would change. You didn't see any clubs doing that at that time.'

Fenton – who Allison felt had been 'promoted out of his depth' – might not have been much of a tactician, but his wheeler-dealing meant there was a steady influx of new players throughout Allison's time at West Ham. It was Malcolm's good fortune that so many of them responded to his football philosophies and the force with which he indoctrinated them. The list of Hammers colleagues who went on to managerial and coaching careers at the highest level – men such as Bond, O'Farrell, Noel Cantwell, Ken Brown, Dave Sexton, Malcolm Musgrove, Jimmy Andrews and Andy Nelson – is the most obvious testament to Allison's influence and the open-minded atmosphere that pervaded the Upton Park dressing-room during the 1950s.

A tight-knit group, they loved nothing more than to gather after training in Cassettari's, a Barking Road café just round the corner from the stadium, where they would talk about the game. And talk and talk. Even after evenings of greyhound racing, usually at Hackney or West Ham, several of them would regroup in the café's upstairs room to continue their debates, pushing salt cellars, cups and ketchup bottles around the tables like chess pieces as they discussed tactics. Bond recalls, 'We used to come out of that café smelling of egg and chips. Loads of the other lads would go to the pictures or snooker but Malcolm, Noel, me and a few others would go back to the ground. Malcolm was a big influence on people who wanted to know and listen.'

Sexton says, 'I don't know if it was Malcolm's idea originally, but he was in charge. Those meal times were very important because we used to explore different subjects and that was when people would come out with any ideas they had. As well as a working team, we were a talking team.'

O'Farrell remembers most players being 'in tune' with the mood of self-improvement. 'We would talk mostly about how English football could change. But we put into practice the things we spoke about. We trained with a ball more, varied the times at which we trained. We were trying to improve the game and we were maturing as people as well as players. I remember that Dave Sexton was a bit of an intellectual and could discuss lots of topics. Some players, all they knew about were horses – they didn't even know who the Prime Minister was. During pre-season training we would have a quiz during our lunchtime break. Dave would buy *The Times* coming up from Brighton and he would set the questions. It made people think and kept the brain active.'

Allison described his band of followers as a 'revolutionary group' and explained, 'We used to fill the room with our theories and disputes. We had opened our minds and declared ourselves willing to try new things and be prepared to make mistakes on the way.'

Cantwell, who joined West Ham as a 19 year old from Cork United in September 1952, quickly became an Allison disciple, even though he was aware that not all at the club were happy with the influence being exerted by the skipper. Before his death in 2005, he explained to *Hammers News* how Cassettari's had become the home for Allison's think tank. 'West Ham decided to give us two shillings and sixpence so you could go and have lunch there. We all had vouchers and that was abused because some guys did without lunch and copped the money instead to go to the dogs. But the café used to be packed upstairs with a stream of players – who weren't always well behaved, I promise you.

'We were a nightmare for George, the groundsman. He would prepare his pitch for Saturday on Wednesday afternoon, but we'd go out there training on a Thursday or Friday for hours, cutting the whole thing up. George would go and see Ted, but there was nothing he could do because Malcolm would have gone mad.'

When, in 1995, the BBC made its *Kicking and Screaming* series, charting the progression of professional football, Cassettari's was considered important enough to merit an interview with Philip Cassettari, whose father Phil was in charge of the café in the Allison era. He told the TV crew, 'At the time I didn't realise how important it was. They were just footballers that came in to the shop and in those days footballers didn't earn fantastic livings and they were quite glad to come and eat in the café and have somewhere to stay. A lot of them were living in digs.'

Allison's group established a pattern of morning training, lunchtime tactical seminars and frequent additional afternoon practice sessions, in which Allison was often assisted by Bond and Cantwell. 'They used to talk about the ABC of West Ham – Allison, Bond and Cantwell,' says Lewis. 'I wasn't mad about moving to London but I joined West Ham because they were a forward-thinking club. When I got there, it was clear that Malcolm, along with the others, was in charge.'

Lewis even remembers seeing Allison preparing his great friend, Cantwell, to play for the Republic of Ireland against England. 'He took Noel out one afternoon and kept pushing the ball past him and running because Noel, at left-back, was going to be up against the great Tom Finney.'

Allison would be back at the club a couple of evenings every week to coach the schoolboys and junior players. The opportunity to imprint his vision of the game upon impressionable young minds was more important to him than the additional one pound and ten shillings he earned for his extra duties.

John Cartwright, a future England youth-team coach, was one of those who were quickly hooked on the passion that Allison radiated. 'We were his protégés, if you like,' he explains. 'We used to train with him on Tuesday and Thursday nights. We had all learned the game in the streets – there was no coaching for young kids in those days. But then we started working with Malcolm. In the summer holidays, several of us used to go to his house and he would take us over to the local sports area to train with him. When we left school all of us could have gone anywhere, to be honest. I could have gone to Arsenal or Chelsea, but we picked West Ham, even though they were in the Second Division, because of Malcolm Allison. Me and guys like Bobby Moore all went there because of him. He was just mad about the game and was very inspirational in everything he said. Even as young players on the ground staff, we used to go upstairs in Cassettari's and he would talk to us about the game.'

Terry McDonald, a winger who joined the Upton Park ground staff in 1954, admits, 'Malcolm was massive to us, awesome. We looked up to him as an icon.'

If there was one event that coloured in the sketches of modern football that Allison had drawn for himself during his time in Austria, it was the game played at Wembley Stadium on 25 November 1953. That was the day the Hungarians tore down the smug superiority of English football with a 6–3 victory, becoming the first team from outside the British Isles to win an international on English soil and providing Allison with his 'eureka' moment. Already Allison had been disturbed that nobody in the sport had acknowledged a need to examine its structure following the debacle of England's 1–0 defeat to the USA during the 1950 World Cup finals in Brazil. Now he was captivated by a team that 'arrived from another planet'.

Allison, who travelled to the game with teammate Jimmy Andrews, was initially unimpressed when he saw the Hungarians practising outside the stadium, pointing to the obviously overweight man in the number 10 shirt. But once Ferenc Puskas began exchanging 25-yard volleyed passes with colleagues during the pre-game warm-ups, Allison turned to his colleague and said, 'Tell you what, Jim. These aren't bad.'

From their lightweight boots and shorts cut high on the thigh to the skilful expertise and tactical fluidity of their play, the Hungarians were, in Allison's words, 'so bright, so brilliant' that 'even the walls of complacency in English football began to crumble'.

Only days after witnessing Hungary's brilliance, Allison's despondency deepened further with West Ham's 6–0 Upton Park thrashing by a technically overwhelming AC Milan team, led by Swedish centre-forward Gunnar Nordahl. Years later he was still discussing that match. 'Nordahl gave Malcolm such a hard time,' recalls Eddie Lewis. 'He was always talking about it. Those kinds of games, and the Continental style – which was so far ahead of England – were a big influence on him.'

Confirmation of Allison's growing feeling, that coaching could hold the key to his long-term football future, arrived at the FA's training centre at Lilleshall, in the Shropshire countryside. Having seen details of off-season coaching courses pinned on the Upton Park notice board, Allison had eagerly signed up in the hope that such activity would improve him as a player. 'I had abandoned hope of getting any meaningful help from the club,' he admitted.

Once there, he devoured every piece of information offered by the likes of England manager Walter Winterbottom, future Burnley, Sunderland and Sheffield Wednesday boss Alan Brown and Tottenham manager Arthur Rowe. It had been Rowe's 1950–51 League Championship winners, with their groundbreaking 'push-and-run' style, who had been the first English side to stress the importance of the movement of players without the ball. Allison believed that Winterbottom, hamstrung by the archaic hierarchy of the Football Association, was a far more enlightened thinker than his record with the England team suggested, referring to him as 'the messiah'. Derek Ufton, whose one cap for England was earned a month before the Hungary game, recalls, 'Walter wanted things to happen and he started people thinking about the game. He had a lot of disciples all around the country.'

Allison wrote of his visits to Lilleshall, 'In that atmosphere I sensed that I could make an impact.' And it was there where he encountered another coach who was to have a massive impact on his career, Argentinian-born Helenio Herrera, who would enjoy success with numerous teams in Spain and Italy, most notably Inter Milan. Described by Allison as 'a Svengali with a whistle', Herrera borrowed some of his coaching methods from army manuals, and his spectacularly choreographed routines would go over the head of uninitiated observers. Allison observed that 'there was precision, but also a rich dash of imagination' and noted Herrera's ability to make his sessions intense and thorough without becoming monotonous.

Allison, whose enthusiasm had initially been checked by Winterbottom's warning not to bite off more than he could chew, passed a considerable personal test when he took a group of players under the watchful and intimidating eye of Herrera. The master visited him in the dressing-room to deliver the verdict, 'You can be a great coach.'

Back at West Ham, the atmosphere of learning and debate perfectly complemented the ideas Allison had picked up at Lilleshall and gave him the opportunity to put his theories into practice. Finally, he was enjoying and achieving fulfilment from life as a professional footballer. The dark, tedious days of Charlton were far behind him, prompting him to say, 'I used to get up in the morning and feel like singing.'

An interest in discussing and dissecting the game was unusual enough in the 1950s; it seems even more so in these days when players disappear to their country mansions as soon as training finishes. They certainly wouldn't be congregating in the local greasy spoon café. But Bond, who went on to win medals under Ron Greenwood and credits Allison with taking him from 'a naïve little kid to some sort of manhood', says, 'We were conscientious and knew what we wanted. I would come home at five o'clock completely knackered but I learned so much. I always had tea and toast on a Saturday morning until Malcolm told me I shouldn't drink tea on the day of a game.'

Colleagues recall that it was Allison's own opinions that were voiced loudest during the players' discussions and Malcolm himself said, 'I just told them what to do. It was my determination and aggression that made other players fall into line and realise there was more to the game than they thought.'

Dave Sexton's memory is, 'Malcolm listened to others and it was good to be there with them. But he was the one who prompted us more than others and his personality was such that we followed. He felt that we should be a modern team. We wanted to play football at all times and we did.'

However, O'Farrell believes that Allison often overdid the dogma. 'His problem was that he wanted to impose his view of football. He didn't try to sell it; he just told us that this was what we should do. He could be a bit autocratic in that respect. You can't always have a consensus, but he wasn't prepared to listen to other people. His ambitions were noble in lots of ways – he wanted to take football forward – but he didn't carry everyone with him, which could make people feel disenfranchised.'

Wing-half Tommy Moroney was a popular foil for Allison and the Irish international would often be heard yelling, 'Fucking hell, Malcolm, what are you talking about? You're talking a lot of bollocks, aren't you?' O'Farrell continues, 'You had to say, "Malcolm, I don't agree with you." You had to stand up to him or else he would ride all over you. There were two or three players he could influence but I was a bit older, was independent and could hold my own in a discussion and argue that there was another way of doing it.'

The press latched on to what was happening and christened the 'West Ham Academy', but not every member of the Hammers squad bought into Allison's ideology or sought a place in his clique. John 'Jackie' Dick, the joint third-highest scorer in West Ham's history with 166 goals, mostly kept himself away from Cassettari's and liked to play without referral to tactics. He would be the only Hammers player in the early '60s to absent himself from a Ron Greenwood-led coaching course at Lilleshall. Sexton recalls, 'Not everybody was involved because, at any football club, there are degrees of enthusiasm among the players. What we were doing was enjoyed by those who were keen on becoming better players and there were more who wanted to do it than those who didn't.'

Lewis looks back on his experiences with Allison with 'mixed feelings', his emotions reflecting the extremes of Malcolm's personality. 'If you add up the pluses when talking about him, they outnumber the minuses. His passion was football, but sometimes when he was having a go at people he went over the edge and got too personal. I remember a number of times when you saw him spitting out insults. If he'd had a little more compassion he could have had more success.

But he had this aura and I wanted to impress him. I remember being in the gym in a group that had to bench-press a certain weight 15 times. I had nearly finished but when Malcolm came over I went back to counting "two, three, four" because I didn't want him to think I was cheating and was making out I had done more than I had. Unfortunately there were two camps at West Ham. I can't say for sure, but if you were in Malcolm's band then it appeared that he would look out for you and influence Ted Fenton to get you in the team. I wasn't a big fan of his socially and some of his off-field behaviour nullified my feelings for him, but I felt I was one of those who were on his good side and he liked me as a player.'

Meanwhile, Musgrove called Allison, 'a very strong character – too strong for some I suppose'. In Brian Betton's *Days of Iron*, he said, 'I didn't like [Malcolm] for what he could do to people he didn't like.' But he added, 'If he liked you as a person and footballer he'd go through a brick wall for you. But he would crucify those he didn't get on with.'

Cantwell saw the resentment some players held towards Allison, who he felt 'didn't like people who didn't like football'. He noted, 'Some people got fed up talking about the game and there were those who weren't keen on learning.' Of those people, Allison would sneer, 'We can do without them.' Cantwell admitted, 'Malcolm wasn't popular with everybody. A lot of people don't like change and he did lots of things that weren't popular with the manager.'

Which prompts the most obvious question about this period in West Ham history: who the hell was running the place – Malcolm Allison or Ted Fenton?

'Eventually I began to run the team, with his tacit agreement,' is Allison's description of the arrangement with his boss. 'I was able to bring some variety to our training. And Fenton allowed me to get on with it.' Allison described the relationship with his manager as 'scarcely satisfactory'. Even though it didn't sink as low as the frosty non-communication of his experience with Charlton boss Jimmy Seed, manager and captain could hardly be called bosom buddies.

Allison felt that the club directors' loyalty in appointing an old Hammers stalwart proved that they 'had no sense of how to achieve anything or to be successful'. He believed they would rather appoint someone unsuitable than bring in a thrusting, forward-thinking outsider who might show up their own lack of football knowledge. The might of Allison's personality inevitably caused friction with Fenton, but the manager at least appeared to appreciate that those issues were born of a desire to see the club progress. And as long as Allison's influence was dragging the club in the right direction it seems that Fenton was happy to indulge such a brazen show of player power.

Sexton explains, 'Ted didn't interfere. He was very in love with football and so were we. If it was going to make us better, then Ted let us do it. Coaching was a new scene for most people, but we were lucky to have Ted because he could have put the boot in, as some managers would have. He was as keen as us.'

Bond states, 'Ted used to let Malcolm have his head. Malcolm decided what way we would play, what formation we would use, and would talk to Ted about selection. Ted would have the final say but Malcolm would have a big influence. I got injured and missed the start of one season. George Wright took my place but when I was fit and ready Malcolm said to me, "Don't worry," and he went to see Ted. I was back in the team in a week. Malcolm's views were the ones that mattered.'

John Cartwright contends, 'Ted was really nothing in comparison to Malcolm. Ted used to turn up for training and then go off. It was Malcolm and the senior players who were inspired by him – like John Bond and Noel Cantwell – who had the influence and were looked up to by the youngsters.'

Any disagreements Allison had with Fenton took place in private. 'They wouldn't clash in front of the players,' says Bond. But there was little doubt in the squad's mind who held the power. Terry McDonald recalls complaining to Allison about being selected for the A team for a game at Didcot after he had been led to believe he would be involved with the first team. 'When Mal found out he went in to Ted, came back and tore down the sheets. When he re-pinned them, I was the twelfth man for the first team. We always felt Malcolm ran the club and totally transformed it.'

Jimmy Andrews, however, acknowledges Fenton's contribution, especially the feeling of friendship and camaraderie at Upton Park.

'Ted had a lot to do with that,' he explained. 'Ted would occasionally go on about tactics and you'd see Mal looking at him, as if to say, "Oh, shut up, Ted. For Christ's sake, just get on with it!" But in his own way, Ted was a good influence – just in a totally different way from Malcolm. And between the two of them they did a great job. Ted was clever. He was no fool and he thought, "Fair enough, if it's good for the club and the players, let Malcolm get on with it." But Ted was never far away and he was a very decent man.'

O'Farrell also speaks up for Fenton, arguing that Allison was wrong to undermine him to such an extent. 'He did usurp Ted's authority, which I thought was wrong. He thought Ted knew eff all. I felt Fenton bridged the gap between the old-fashioned manager who ruled with an iron hand and the newer generation of manager-coaches who thought hard about the game. Ted wasn't going to come in and say, "This is where you will play." He had team meetings and players would discuss the things they would try to implement. Malcolm thought he did that so he could learn from us! Not everything was perfect, but Ted shouldn't be rubbished.

'Malcolm might claim it was all him and, of course, he did make a great contribution to football and I liked him a lot. But he needed a manager to be that way orientated. Mal railroaded people and it may have looked sometimes like he was the manager. He did argue once or twice with Ted at meetings, but I don't think it is a player's place to question the authority of the manager. He shouldn't try to prove he knows more than the manager – and sometimes Mal would want to do that. His role was to play as a player to the best of his ability.'

O'Farrell confesses, however, that Allison's criticism of Fenton made the players 'more self-sufficient and turned us into managers', adding, 'If we'd have had a strong manager we wouldn't have blossomed the way we did. That's why so many of us succeeded.'

Fenton and Allison could hardly have been more different. Allison's quiff and brooding good looks created an air of James Dean, while the slicked-back hair, tweed jacket, pipe and pointed features of Fenton hinted at Basil Rathbone playing Sherlock Holmes. Fenton was without the charisma and strong disciplinary principles of his predecessor Charlie Paynter. And he lacked natural leadership qualities, which was why Allison was so easily able to commandeer the loyalty of so many players.

While Allison claimed to have 'blanked out the board, the manager – everybody who might get in the way' and said that he 'wasn't sure what Fenton was doing', the manager took his refuge in the club's infrastructure, initiating a youth scouting system, looking after the needs of the staff and manoeuvring in the transfer market.

The dynamic between Allison and Fenton was at the centre of – and is perhaps the most fascinating aspect of – life at West Ham in the '50s. In some ways it was an unintentional prototype of the modern phenomenon of director of football working alongside a coach, or in this case an unofficial player-coach. Yet, tellingly, Fenton made no reference to it in his 1960 book, *At Home with the Hammers*. Even though his publication purported to give an inside look at the club during the decade, the only mention of Allison in the entire 160 pages is a somewhat dismissive six paragraphs, half of which concentrated on the circumstances that led to his early retirement as a player. There is no acknowledgement or discussion of his tactical input; not a word about the group of players who shaped the club from their table at Cassettari's; no reference to Allison in the chapter entitled 'Styling The Hammers'.

In their *Essential History of West Ham*, authors Kirk Blows and Tony Hogg describe Allison as a 'visionary who in six short years would revolutionise the club's archaic regime and transform training, coaching techniques and tactics to secure promotion'. Yet the only nod Fenton is willing to give towards any influence Allison might have had is in the following comment. 'Apart from being a good player, Malcolm was fantastically keen and enthusiastic. He was a fitness fanatic and inspired the others. Because of that I made him club skipper.'

There are conflicting tales about how much influence Allison had over cosmetic matters like West Ham's playing kit. The Hammers were among the first English teams to swap heavy, buttoned shirts for streamlined, tight-fitting, short-sleeved V-necks and to adopt Continental-style short shorts. Noel Cantwell's landlady was given the task of cutting down West Ham's baggy breeches, although, when necessity dictated, Allison would grab a pair of scissors and do it himself before training, administering the same treatment to shirt sleeves. Bond remembers, 'The shorts were so short that we looked like a load of women running around the place.'

Allison quickly abandoned one idea that O'Farrell believes shows how 'sometimes he could be lacking in prudence and judgement and be guilty of not looking ahead'. He explains, 'One day Mal decided that shin pads were a waste of time and just put extra weight on your legs. He told us that we should get rid of them and chose to prove his point by not wearing them. Unfortunately he was up against a Birmingham centre-forward called Cyril Trigg who didn't shirk any tackles. He ended up getting a bloody gash right down his shin. That showed the reckless side of his nature.'

Meanwhile, Allison had been impressed with a pair of lightweight boots that a friend on the Arsenal team had brought back from a tour of Brazil, although he claimed that Fenton had said, 'England's footballers will never wear these slippers.' According to Allison, Fenton had turned away overtures from manufacturers of such footwear. 'It was this fixed stonewall attitude that made me very bitter,' he said.

Eddie Lewis remembers, 'Malcolm would take our old-fashioned boots and get a pair of scissors and cut off the top part.' Fenton, meanwhile, recalls in his book that it was he who contacted the Hungarian football authorities to find out the origin of their boots, after which he acquired two dozen pairs from the manufacturer. He likened the arrival of the boots to discovering that his team had been 'playing the piano in boxing gloves'. He also claimed to have introduced the Hungarian-style aerodynamic kit.

One thing is for certain. West Ham's modernist approach impressed the hell out of other teams. O'Farrell recalls, 'After I was transferred to Preston, one of their players, Bobby Foster, said they had come to see us in a Cup tie at Blackpool. They couldn't believe it when all these Cockney boys ran out in biscuit-coloured tracksuits 20 minutes before kick-off. Nobody came out for warm-ups in those days – you warmed up in the dressing-room. Things like that impressed other professionals.' Lewis also remembers going to see West Ham play before he signed for them. 'I was knocked out. They came out early and had short shorts and looked fit and fantastic.'

Another area where there is variance in testimony about the extent of Allison's influence is the weight training that became a standard part of West Ham's working week. Fenton explains in his book how he introduced it, while Allison claimed, 'I brought in weight-training, heavy weight-training. Ted Fenton didn't want to do it. But I found that our jumping became better. We became stronger and quicker.'

O'Farrell offers this version of events. 'We had a young lad called Alfie Noakes – a likeable cheeky Cockney – who came up with the idea in a team meeting that we should do weight training. Nobody else had come up with that idea. Malcolm said, "Weight training? What do you know? We are not weightlifters or wrestlers." But Alfie fought his corner, which was quite something for a young player. Weight training became part of our routine and subsequently Malcolm became one of the greatest converts. He went a bundle on it.'

Cantwell recalled the importance of the Hammers' aesthetic and athletic upgrades. 'We would go in the gym at quarter past two and have a fairly good work-out and come back and then get prepared. The weight training gave you tremendous confidence. You felt stronger and you felt good. How one looks and how one appears is always very important. I think it helped when we got away from the old baggy shorts and had good gear.'

The playing style of the West Ham team owed much to Allison's interpretation of the Hungarian methods. His main contention was that the ball should be played out from the back, rather than being hoofed downfield in the finest tradition of blood-and-thunder English football. His own instinct as a defender was to look to play an intelligent pass. 'He used the ball quite well for a centre-half,' says O'Farrell, although Bond adds, 'He wanted to play sometimes when he shouldn't. He used to try all sorts of silly things and let himself down at times.'

Eddie Lewis adds, 'West Ham liked to knock the ball around, keep it to feet. And we worked a lot of set pieces. Johnny Bond was one of the best kickers of the ball I have ever seen and there would be a lot of practice on players making decoy runs, allowing Noel to come in at the back to score.'

According to goalkeeper Ernie Gregory, 'In our day we'd play in threes and play the angles. I'd give the ball to Bondy and he'd give it to Andy Malcolm.' But such a patient style of play was not immediately appreciated by the Hammers fans. West Ham historian Brian Belton wrote that it appeared as though West Ham were 'trying to goad the opposition and annoy the supporters'. He added, 'The East End had grown used to solid, hard-working footballers. This group of players looked to play with finesse.'

John Cartwright remembers, 'Malcolm was very interested in people being individual and making up their own mind about things. He liked players who were comfortable with the ball and imaginative. He liked brave kids. I don't mean just physically brave, but in the sense that they would try things.'

Meanwhile, Fenton allowed the Allison-influenced style of play to continue, although some suggested he simply had the good sense to stay out of it because he had no clue what was going on. Whatever the truth of Fenton's feeling towards Allison and his standing in the eyes of his club captain, fate was to bring their complex relationship to an abrupt end.

3

HAMMER HORROR

'You have tuberculosis. We will have to remove one lung'
– doctor at the London Hospital giving Malcolm Allison
the news that ended his playing career

For all the talk of revolution, West Ham's performances during the Malcolm Allison–Ted Fenton era were more indicative of a slow-burning evolution. For several years after Fenton's promotion to manager in 1950, mid-table finishes in the Second Division and early exits in the FA Cup were what Hammers fans came to expect.

The biggest problem was money. While Fenton could identify and doggedly pursue a bargain, he was rarely given the opportunity to be lavish in the transfer market. The purchase of Allison had been financed by the sale a year earlier of winger Eric Parsons to Chelsea for £22,500. Before the opening game of the 1953–54 season, club chairman Reg Pratt noted, 'The buying of high-priced stars is a privilege confined to a few of the present day clubs. Frankly we are not a rich club and our future commitments mean we must budget accordingly.'

Pratt was forced to go into print again in 1956 to explain that the transfer of another popular winger, Harry Hooper, to Wolves for £25,000, had allowed the club to meet a £17,000 bill for building work on a new entrance at Upton Park. 'The directors of this club have for a long time had to face some very hard and disagreeable facts,' he commented. 'We have never been well off. In fact, we have had an uphill struggle all the way.'

Hooper recalled, 'I explained to Ted Fenton that I didn't want to go, but he said there was nothing he could do – the club needed the money because the school in Castle Street wanted back their land, which was then serving as the main entrance to the ground on Green Street.'

Allison's debut for West Ham had been in March 1951 in a victory over Chesterfield. The first of his 10 goals for the club came in a 3–2 home win over Nottingham Forest in October 1952 – a game he finished with concussion and about which he could remember very little. His contribution as a player, although solid, could not compare to his impact around the training ground. Recognising his limitations, Allison strove to improve himself through sheer bloody hard work. Goalkeeper Ernie Gregory says, 'I remember a time when he knocked himself out in training in the week, pushed himself so hard that when we played in the mud at Southampton he collapsed with exhaustion. There were times when I looked at Malcolm and he'd done so much hard work in the week that he was white in the face.'

Frank O'Farrell adds, 'Malcolm enjoyed a good social life but it never affected his football. He always trained very hard. Probably, because he did not have a very high degree of skill, he worked at his game.' And John Bond recalls, 'He could have a night out and come in and train as if he had been in bed all night. There were no excuses.'

On the occasions when a bus would pick up the players to transport them to Chadwell Heath for the starting point of their cross-country run, Allison and a couple of willing companions would get the bus driver to drop them off a mile short of their destination. 'Those buggers would still catch us up,' says Eddie Lewis.

John Cartwright, then a youth-team player, recalls Allison's work ethic setting an example to the club's junior players. 'I was in the first team dressing-room towards the end of the season; the groundsman had said we could train on the pitch. We worked out there all morning, went back in and showered and all of a sudden Malcolm walked into the dressing-room. In those days the kit was a bit baggy and ragged, but Malcolm opened the door wearing a skin-tight T-shirt, very short and tight athletics shorts, a pair of white ankle socks and his football boots. Underneath his arm he had what was, at the time, one of the new white footballs. He walked through the door and he didn't really look at us. He just said, "I am going out on the pitch and I am going to practise because I want to be a great player." He turned round and walked out the door. We all looked at each other and even though we had all just got out the shower, we put our dirty kit back on and went out and joined him for the rest of the afternoon. That was the sort of guy he was – very inspirational.'

Terry McDonald adds, 'Our job on the ground staff was to clean the terraces and the stands. While we were doing that in the afternoons, Malcolm would be back with three or four players and they would practise for two hours. He was so intense about the game. Some people might think that his social life overtook him, but his dedication to football was total.'

One of Allison's favoured drills was to hang up a football and practise headers. Jimmy Andrews recalled that he would 'start foaming from the mouth from the effort he gave out', adding, 'He'd overdo it – you could see it in his face. He lived in another world. He meant to be a great player but he could never be that. But one of the major things in football is that if you think you can do something, you can get further than you would otherwise. He had incredible determination and when he made his mind up about something he'd keep working at it.'

Lack of pace was Allison's biggest handicap, as O'Farrell explains. 'He was tall, a good tackler and was always good in the air. But he was not quick on the recovery.' Dave Sexton, meanwhile, describes him as 'a very impressive figure' and says, 'He wasn't the sort of centre-half you saw in those days. He was more athletic and took over things with his strong personality.' And Bond ventures, 'Malcolm was a useful player, but thought he was better than he was. He was big, with strong legs and a good body, and was as fit as a butcher's dog.'

Allison acknowledged the weakness that prevented him reaching greater heights as a player. 'If I had been quicker I'd have probably got a cap,' he suggested. 'I was a good positional player and I was strong, but I was always more interested in coaching.'

Eddie Lewis agrees with Allison's assessment. 'He had good ability and good vision. If he'd had pace I think he would have played for England. He had a big chip on his shoulder about Derek Ufton at Charlton.' Ufton had been capped by England but Lewis argues that 'Malcolm was a better player'.

Allison was known to take out his frustration on teammates. The late George Fenn said, 'I remember Malcolm doing Harry Hooper in a training match – he envied Harry's talent. So when Andy Malcolm, who was Harry's best mate at the club, saw what happened, he came running over, got hold of Allison and warned him never to go near Harry again.'

The 1955–56 season began with the Hammers fancied by many to challenge for promotion. But they saved their best performances for the FA Cup, knocking out First Division teams Preston, Cardiff and Blackburn to set up Allison's biggest game in a West Ham shirt, a quarter-final tie against Tottenham. It was an occasion that illustrated the insecurities that Allison, for all his growing confidence in his knowledge of the game, still felt as a player.

Entering the field and looking around at the packed White Hart Lane stands, Allison's composure and feeling of keen anticipation gave way to panic. For a moment he was the scared kid at Charlton fretting about having to face Cliff Bastin. 'I felt the strength drain away from me,' he said. 'It took great effort to put one foot in front of the other. My legs felt rubbery. I wondered if I was going to faint.' It took the referee summoning him, as captain, to go to the centre-circle to restore control. The simple procedure of the coin toss appeared to refocus a relieved Allison.

Leading 3–2 at half-time, Allison took command of the half-time dressing-room, instructing full-back John Bond to stick close to Spurs winger George Robb instead of joining the attack. Noel Cantwell explained, 'Bondy had gone up, got offside and went missing. They came down and got one back and Malcolm slaughtered him.'

Allison barked at Bond, 'Make it simple, keep tight on Robb and just play early balls up to the front players.' Yet when Bond tried to carry the ball forward, Robb was free to break down the wing. With the defence stretched, Allison attempted to cover for the full-back and when Cantwell collided with Spurs striker Bobby Smith it left Len Duquemin as a spare man to score the equaliser. 'He knows I'll never forgive him,' Allison wrote of Bond's faux pas two decades later. A 2–1 defeat in the replay cost West Ham a place in the semi-finals and the promise of a four-day jolly to Brighton.

By 1957–58, West Ham were at last poised to claim their place in the First Division. Malcolm Musgrove explained, 'With Allison's coaching, the players we had, and what we had learned in Cassettari's, you felt we were ready.'

A penalty by Allison rescued a disappointing opening-day point at home to Lincoln, setting the tone for a slow start to the season in which 12 points were gained in the first 12 games. It was the signing of goalscorer Vic Keeble for £10,000 from Newcastle that sparked a run up the table and set the Hammers on course for the Second Division title. They clinched the championship with a 3–1 win at Middlesbrough, after which thousands of fans waited to greet them at King's Cross station, carrying Cantwell around on their shoulders. It should have been Allison's moment, yet by that time his career lay in tatters.

Bond explains, 'There had been little signs that something was wrong. We went on a cross-country run and Malcolm finished second, but he was foaming at the mouth and could hardly breathe.' A week later, in mid-September, Allison struggled during a 2–1 defeat at Sheffield United. He simply couldn't keep up with the pace of the game. Opponents were beating him and leaving him in their wake. He put both incidents down to a recent bout of Asian flu and tiptoed his way through the game.

Allison sat in the Bramall Lane dressing-room, his body racked by coughing, and found himself walking around Sheffield 'in a daze' later that evening. Having settled down for the night in his hotel room, his constant coughing kept roommate Cantwell awake, prompting the Irishman to report Allison's deteriorating condition to Fenton the next morning. 'I had long suspected that all was not well with him without being aware how serious it was,' Fenton said. 'For one thing, he showed signs of tiring, a weakness unknown when I first bought him.'

Allison endured a trying return journey on the train, spluttering and bringing up phlegm. On arrival in London, he was sent – despite his protestations – to the London Hospital for chest X-rays. The following day, he was summoned to Fenton's office to hear the specialist announce results that were way beyond the worst he could have feared. 'Mr Allison, I think you have to forget about playing football,' he was told. 'You have tuberculosis. We will have to remove one lung.' Allison's reaction was disbelief. 'I simply didn't accept what he was saying.'

Teammates saw Allison emerge from his meeting in tears. A young Bobby Moore, visiting the ground to pick up his ground-staff wages, spotted Allison crying alone at the back of the stand until his great friend, Cantwell, placed a consoling arm around him. Malcolm Musgrove said, 'It was the first time I saw a grown man cry, really cry.'

The extent of Allison's problem was not immediately made public. More than a week later, the *Ilford Recorder*, having conjectured that his absence from the club meant an impending transfer, was now noting that Allison was at the London Hospital 'under observation' after a recent bout of flu. The fact that one-sixth of the Ilford school population was at home suffering from Asian flu helped to disguise the real truth.

Allison was, in fact, at the aforementioned hospital for surgery. Eddie Lewis was among the post-operation visitors. 'I almost fainted when I saw him; he had so many tubes coming out of him. I heard that he'd chosen to have an operation where there was a higher percentage chance of him being able to play again, but also a higher chance of dying. I admired him greatly for his courage.'

His lung taken away, Allison began a nine-month rehabilitation at the King Edward VII Sanatorium in Midhurst, West Sussex. Teammates, in particular Cantwell and Bond, made regular trips to see their friend and Bond recalls 'having a laugh in his room'. But the high spirits with which Malcolm greeted his colleagues were merely a disguise for his deep depression.

Built in 1907 specifically to house tuberculosis sufferers, Allison's temporary home retained a gloomily early-century feel, despite its palatial architecture and wooded hillside location. The tall chimney from the incinerator block and the midday hooter that sounded lunch added an air of the workhouse and Malcolm struggled to share the enjoyment his fellow patients derived from their daily walks and light gardening chores. Instead, he felt himself becoming increasingly remote from his West Ham colleagues and their achievements. He endured 'long and very lonely nights' and was even driven to visit the facility's chapel – an indication of despair rather than of religious devotion. He asked God what he had done to deserve such a fate, an act he admitted was without regard to the positives in his life. No one, he felt, could understand what it meant for a professional athlete to have lost a lung. Inevitably, there came a time when Allison sought escape, sneaking out to the local pub, where he sipped his drink anxiously with one eye on the door for fear of being caught breaking sanatorium rules.

The moment that hauled Allison back from the precipice of desperation was the simple act of being given the job of distributing the daily newspapers. Forced into regular contact with fellow patients for the first time, his eyes were opened to the problems of others. Their willingness to share their troubles helped him put his own issues into perspective. He was jolted further out of his own misery by the death of a patient only days after he had spent time chatting with him.

As his crisis passed, Allison looked at himself, this time with more objectivity and less self-pity. 'I saw a lot of impatience, arrogance, and perhaps a touch of ruthlessness. I felt some regret for the impatience and anger I had shown to older men.' Allison was not about to shed those personality traits, but he did resolve to quit feeling sorry for himself and prepare for a return to football as a player. As Cantwell drove him away from Midhurst, Allison travelled with a new determination, even though it was tempered by the fear of what lay ahead if he failed in his mission.

He derived additional motivation from what he felt was West Ham's insensitivity towards him in their moment of Second Division triumph. 'When I should have been collecting my first medal in football, I was inhabiting a vast, grey void,' he said. He attended the club's celebration banquet at the Café Royal, but walked out in disgust when he learned that he was not to receive a medal – even though he had played as many games as some of those being rewarded. No one had done more than Allison over the previous few years to propel the club towards their success, yet no recognition was forthcoming. That cut him as deeply as the fears over his footballing future.

It was impossible for Allison to avoid the feeling that he was being punished by the club's management for the confrontations he had instigated over the years. He had fought annual battles over his wages and had even come within minutes of leading the team out on strike before a game against Nottingham Forest. That incident had stemmed from his mistrust of Fenton, who, he once said, 'would cheat you out of anything'. After a game against an England amateur team, which attracted a crowd of 22,000 to Upton Park, the Hammers players were given £5 each – which the club said comprised a basic £3, plus a £2 win bonus. Allison knew, however, that the FA paid a £5 basic per player for such games. As he and his colleagues got changed for their next match, Allison instructed them, 'Don't get stripped, don't get changed. We're not playing unless we get that two quid, the twenty-six quid [Fenton] owes us.'

Fenton had not yet appeared in the dressing-room, and trainer Billy Moore sent the urgent message, 'You'd better come down, they're not getting stripped.'

Allison greeted Fenton with, 'You done us out of twenty-six quid.' Fenton scurried off to get the money and the game went ahead.

Another time, Allison ignored a director's praise in the changing-room after a victory at Huddersfield and received the kind of reminder about manners that one might give to a surly teenager. And he upset chairman Reg Pratt when Cliff Lloyd, preparing the ground for the Professional Footballers' Association's battle against the £20 maximum wage, asked players to detail any illegal payments they had received. PFA secretary Lloyd's argument was that the system – as well as being restrictive on the players – was being abused by the clubs. Pratt summoned Allison and told him that he assumed the players would not be participating. Allison took great delight in informing Pratt to the contrary.

Such battles, he wrote, would help him in his later career, having taught him how to argue a coherent case. 'I had lost any reticence about disputing points,' he said. Allison also explained that he fought club officials 'only when I felt they had treated the players with a particular lack of respect'. In the end, however, their snub to Allison showed that they had found a way to exact some form of revenge.

There was to be one further dispute as West Ham prepared for their first season back in football's top flight and Allison fought to prove that there was room in the team for a one-lunged player. At the start of 1958–59 season, he was offered £17 per week. Allison countered by demanding the maximum of £20 if he gained a first-team place, backdated to the start of the season. The board, wanting evidence of his fitness, suggested £20 a week once he had played ten games in the first team and told Allison that if he refused those terms he would be given a free transfer. The message was clear: the club would rather release him than allow him to dictate to them. One week later, however, a compromise was reached when they agreed that if Allison reached the ten-game mark his £20 would be backdated to 1 August. He felt he had won a point of principle, not an inconsiderable feat in the dark days where the clubs held all the contractual aces and players were treated as little more than serfs. Now he could concentrate on winning back his place in the side.

While West Ham were making an encouraging start to their First Division campaign, Allison was toiling in the reserves, desperate to prove himself up to the rigours of the sport. By the second week in September, after three wins in their first five games, West Ham were facing an injury crisis, with three half-backs – Bill Lansdowne, Andy Nelson and, finally, Malcolm Pyke – ruled out of a Monday night home game against Manchester United. Ted Fenton was left facing a straightforward choice at left-half between the convalescing Allison and 17-year-old Bobby Moore, once described by Malcolm Musgrove as 'Malcolm's pet player'.

It is ironic that it turned out to be one of the youngsters Allison had helped nurture who threatened his ambition of a First Division return. His sessions with the club's junior players had quickly given him confidence in his ability for talent-spotting. He enthused to Ted Fenton about Moore, even though his natural talent fell short of that of striker George Fenn, who had once scored nine goals in a game for England Schoolboys. While Allison reported that Fenn wasn't committed enough, his verdict on Moore was, 'Everything about his approach was right. He was ready to listen. You could see that already he was seeking perfection.'

Moore would tell his friend and biographer Jeff Powell of the debt he owed Allison for teaching him the self-assuredness that became his hallmark. Allison's mantra was, 'Be in control of yourself. Take control of everything around you. Look big. Think big. Be big.' And when Allison told Moore to copy the great Alfredo Di Stefano and think about the next pass before receiving the ball, it was a revelation that Moore likened to 'suddenly looking into the sunshine'.

Powell recalls, 'Malcolm had a big effect on Bobby in terms of understanding the game, reading the play, being aware of what is going on around you, looking up and anticipating, knowing where the ball is going before you get it. He influenced all of those things that Bobby became renowned for.' Moore was unashamed in recalling his admiration for Allison. 'He took a liking to me when I don't think anyone else at West Ham saw anything special in me. Just for that I would have done anything for him. Every house needs a foundation and Malcolm gave me mine. He was the be-all and end-all for me. It's not too strong to say I loved him.'

The future England captain was not alone in his appreciation of Allison, whose impact on the youngsters at the club was as significant as the changes he instigated in and around the senior team. Cartwright remembers the education he received from Allison extending beyond the training ground. 'A few of us, including Bobby, used to go out at night with Malcolm. He introduced us to the West End, where I had never been before. There was nothing riotous about it, we just enjoyed his company and he was showing us that there was another part of the world. But he was saying to us, "There are things that can actually stop you from being top-class players if you let them get on top of you." He was trying to show us, "Beware. This is what is available to you, but if you are not careful it can bring you down." Yet at the same time he was enjoying that kind of life himself.'

Back on the training ground, winger Terry McDonald recalls the conflict between Allison and youth-team boss Bill Robinson, a former Charlton teammate, whose methods included little that could be described as coaching. 'It was so boring – all running, running, running, Malcolm made the game more interesting and you wanted to play. Bill could never laugh or joke about anything, which Malcolm could do with ease. He got you working but you were still relaxed. Malcolm knew your assets and tried to build on them. With me, it was a lot of speed training. He would say, "Your job is to get past your full-back, get your crosses in. Change the game, switch positions, dribble with both feet. If you are playing against a one-footed left-back, drop your shoulder and come inside on his right foot. He'll fall over. Most of all you have got to stay in the game. You can't just stand there at outside-right or outside-left and expect people to give you the ball."

'You had to think about the game with Malcolm. I remember him saying, "It should become clockwork football." He felt everybody should be able to play in two or three positions comfortably. You weren't just a centre-half or centre-forward. He used to change the team around during the game. His ideas were so far advanced.'

Fenn, a member of the West Ham team that lost over two legs in the FA Youth Cup final of 1957, never fulfilled the great promise of his teenage years but his admiration of Allison was so strong that he named his daughter after him. Speaking to *Ex* magazine, he said, 'Malcolm completely changed training for us younger lads. He showed us how to sprint properly, which was unheard of in those days. His ideas and knowledge were 10 years ahead of anybody else's. The stylish football West Ham became famous for was all started by Malcolm – he loved the game so much. I think he loved football more than life itself. We went on a tour of Belgium and Germany and when we got back, Ted Fenton said which boys he thought would make it and those he thought wouldn't. He told Bobby Moore he had no chance; that he wasn't up to it. He said the same to Harry Cripps, who was in tears. But I think Bill Robinson didn't recognise talent, he didn't seem to have a clue and ruined too many young boys, which is why Allison took over the club coaching. In fact, Allison took over the club. Malcolm kept Bobby Moore at the club. He believed in him more than anybody else at that time.'

McDonald adds, 'If Moore had been in our year he might not have gone through – they might have ousted him. But Malcolm saw the potential in him.'

Moore himself recalled the early days of the 1958–59 season before his first-team debut. 'It's not like Malcolm to give up. By the start of the '58 season we were battling away together in the reserves, Malcolm proving he could still play, me proving I might be able to play one day.' Moore was torn emotionally by the fact that selection for the United game came down to a straight choice between the two men. 'I'd been a professional for two and a half months and Malcolm had taught me everything I knew. For all the money in the world I want to play. For all the money in the world I want Malcolm to play because he's worked like a bastard for this one game in the First Division. It would have meant the world to him.'

Ted Fenton was no less anguished, turning for advice to Noel Cantwell, who recalled that 'there was no question in Malcolm's mind that he was going to play again'. Cantwell thought for a while before telling Fenton, 'I'd pick Bobby.' He explained, 'Malcolm was bitterly disappointed when the sheet went up and I didn't like myself for doing it, but we won 3–2. How he got to know I don't know, but he came in the bath at the end and slaughtered me. That upset both of us for a while and Malcolm never played for the first team again, but he eventually realised I did it in the interests of the team and we stayed friends.'

On hearing that he was to play, Moore had walked into the dressing-room – and straight into Allison. While Moore fought the urge to hand his shirt to his mentor, Allison said, 'Well done, I hope you do well.'

Jeff Powell continues, 'The two had become very close. Malcolm was always very emotional behind that front and often cried a bit. He filled up and Bobby said to him, "Don't worry, you'll be back," knowing that he probably wouldn't be.'

Almost two decades after that night, Powell wrote:

Through solitary hours spent counting shadows on bedroom ceilings, Moore still nurses the guilt that his own precocious arrival on the central stage of English soccer denied Allison the fulfilment of his own playing career. In the moment of Moore's accession to the number six shirt, Allison lost his forlorn chance of playing just once in the First Division for West Ham United. Allison, the man who taught Moore all he knew. Allison, his idol. Allison, friend . . . The immaculate Bobby Moore was conceived out of Allison's most grievous disappointment.

Powell adds, 'Malcolm felt a huge sadness at the effective end of his own career and great delight for Bobby, who he recognised as a great player at the beginning of his career. Malcolm did say later, "Well, if I was going to be replaced by anybody, I am glad it was by a guy who became the greatest defender in the world."'

Allison spent the next few months wondering how things could have worked out if he had played against United. He believed that West Ham's superiority on the night would have enabled him to 'cruise through the game', perhaps re-establishing himself in the side. Instead, he realised that there was nowhere left for him to go as a professional footballer. More than a month passed as he faced up to the inevitable. On 22 October, he dropped a letter onto Fenton's desk.

With great regret I feel that I cannot regain the high standard of fitness to do justice to my status as a professional footballer and so the dreaded day has come when I feel I must hang up my boots. I would like to thank you for all the fine treatment I have received in my stay at West Ham and I hope that in the 300 games I have played for the first team I gave you something in return for the transfer fee and good treatment I received.

The club immediately announced that a benefit game would be staged in November and a crowd of 21,600 turned up to see a West Ham team beat an All-Star side 7–6. Jimmy Hill, Frank O'Farrell and Danny Blanchflower acted as match officials and Bobby Charlton, Brian Clough, Jimmy Scoular and Don Howe were among those who played in a match that earned Allison £3,000 – enough for him to buy the club house in Barkingside in which he lived. Despite having been pleasantly surprised at West Ham's gesture, Allison could not avoid heading into the next phase of his life with the feeling that he had been short-changed by fate in general and the club in particular. He would write, 'A terraced house in an unfashionable suburb had never been the sort of goal I had pursued in those nine years at West Ham.

I had given everything I had to the club and I knew that I had done a lot to re-shape it, to prepare it for a new age of football.'

That Allison was not to continue to play an important role at West Ham was a surprise to some. John Cartwright recalls, 'We all thought that when Malcolm had recovered from his TB he would come back into the club as coach. He was the instigator in changing the club's footballing beliefs. The business about the West Ham Academy was basically Malcolm. We assumed that he would come back as a coach, but unfortunately the directors were opposed to that and he never returned.'

Eddie Lewis adds, 'I don't think the directors liked Malcolm. His social life tended to come into that, and he was too over the top with his passion for the game. He upset too many people.'

By the time Allison would be back in First Division football, in 1966, West Ham had won the FA Cup, conquered the Continent in the European Cup-Winners' Cup and seen three of their own – Moore, Geoff Hurst and Martin Peters – lead England to triumph in the World Cup. Few doubt that such achievements would have been impossible without the drive and vision of Allison. According to Cartwright, 'They should have a statue to Malcolm at West Ham. He laid the foundation for the success of the club by what he gave to other people.'

4

RUNNING WILD

'I don't care what a man is as long as he treats me right. He can be a gambler, a hustler, someone everybody else thinks is obnoxious. I don't care so long as he's straight and his dealings with me are fair'

– New York Jets quarterback
'Broadway Joe' Namath

For almost two years, Malcolm Allison turned away from football, stumbling around in a wilderness in which his travelling companions could have stepped out of a Damon Runyan story. Footballers were replaced in his life by gamblers, bookies, showbiz stars and criminals; the invigorating air and healthy banter of the training ground supplanted by the choking tension of the race track and the smoke-filled ambience of London's nightclubs.

Allison admitted to feeling 'numb' for 12 months after his retirement, battling unsuccessfully against the gnawing feeling that 'life has cheated you out of the one thing that seemed to make it worth living'. Tuberculosis had done more than take away one of his lungs. It had robbed him of purpose. 'One day life was touching perfection, a rhythm of physical action and great fitness,' he said. 'The next I was broken, washed up into a situation which resembled a strange and hostile shore.' One of the hardest aspects of his new existence was dealing with the changed attitude of people around him. Used to being surrounded by those who were willing to be led by the force of his personality and the promise of what his creative thought could do for them in a football environment, he was shocked to find a new world of people who were 'hardened' towards him.

Allison turned down opportunities to jump straight into a new football career. Tottenham manager Bill Nicholson approached him about a position on his coaching staff, while Ajax – on the recommendation of Chelsea manager Ted Drake, another of Allison's Lilleshall acquaintances – offered him £34 a week to join them in Amsterdam. After a four-day visit to the Dutch capital, he declined, explaining that money was not enough to persuade him to leave his family. He agreed to help out with a few coaching sessions at Isthmian League team Sutton United, but his depth of disillusionment over the end of his playing career made it hard to view any job in the game with enthusiasm. He'd simply had enough. It was football that had led to his current miserable state of mind and the desire now was to break free of its clutches.

Gambling had always been one of Allison's favourite pastimes and he and his Hammers teammates had become familiar figures at the tracks of Hackney Wick and West Ham. Andy Nelson remembers, 'We all loved going to the dogs and it wasn't unusual for about a dozen of us to go along to West Ham greyhound track on a Friday night. Malcolm was well connected in the racing game and there were some big money bets going on at times. The lads used to be well in with a Brighton bookie called George Gunn but we didn't always win. In fact, there were times when bookies would come to the ground looking for their money on losing bets, and one or two of the players would sneak out of the back door to avoid paying them after the game!'

One former teammate said that Malcolm and his pals would 'bet on two flies going up the wall', and Allison would on occasions stake more than he had in his pocket, at which point the football field became his escape from the debt collectors. There was even a time when Ted Fenton, the Hammers manager, had gone knocking on Allison's door looking for the year's rent he owed on his club house in Barkingside. The problem was solved when Malcolm won £360 that night at West Ham dogs.

After his retirement, Allison continued taking his old pals racing, happily treating them if the dogs had run well. George Fenn, whose career never advanced much beyond teenage stardom, admitted later that he was one who fell under the Allison spell. 'Some of us were a little bit weak and saw Malcolm as a god. I thought he was. I idolised him. But little did I know that by staying out drinking, I was destroying myself. Of course I regret it now.'

In Brian Belton's book, *Days of Iron*, former Hammer Mick Newman says of Allison, 'He had the bearing and looks and he lived a life that impressed most of us. He was having breakfast at the Ritz while most of us were turning over in bed. I don't know where he got the money but he managed it somehow.'

Frank O'Farrell, who had seen Allison let cash slip through his fingers like sand, says, 'The way he looked at it was, "Money is only money." He would go to the dogs and come back skint. His lifestyle wasn't mine because I was one of those people who thought money should be spent on things that were more important, like family. But he was very generous and didn't look on money as a god.'

As much as he loved the feel of cash on his hip, Allison's attitude to it had long been established as 'easy come, easy go'. He even recalled being kicked in the chest in a game at Sheffield Wednesday and going into a panic as he fought to catch his breath. His biggest fear of dying was having left £200 unspent in his jacket pocket. As ex-West Ham striker Vic Keeble said, 'He was a bit of a playboy but he would give you his last ha'penny.'

Allison's only ambition as far as money was concerned was to put it to use as soon as possible, sometimes not even waiting until he had left Upton Park after picking up his wages. Terry McDonald explains, 'On Friday morning we would all get paid and four or five of them, including Malcolm, would be straight off down the boiler house playing cards. Then he would be off to Hackney Wick dogs.'

The greyhound racing would often be followed by a trip into the West End and there was always a spare seat at the bar for anyone who wanted to tag along. 'Malcolm helped me bed down in London,' says Eddie Lewis. 'I had come from Preston and was a bit of a yokel. I'd not had a lot of experience outside the game.'

McDonald continues, 'He took a lot of us younger players with him when he went out. He would take us to clubs and then go off on his own. He liked to show you life. It was all about living it to the full, and he did it.'

Allison admitted as much, eventually writing, 'I do not recall the wildness, the great extravagances with pride. It may be that some people would regard my private life as a disaster area. All I can say is that I have tried to live it to the full.'

Such an attitude was to underpin, some would say undermine, everything he was to go on to achieve in his working life. His triumphs would be followed, with an air of grim inevitability, by what others – although not Allison himself – would perceive as a fall. Never did he enjoy the financial stability that his achievements should have afforded him, even in the days before the cash-rich world of the Premier League. Instead of capitalising upon his greatest period of professional achievement, at Manchester City in the second half of the 1960s, he was more often than not broke. His response to discovering that the money had run out, however, would be to order another bottle of champagne.

For several months while coaching a City team that was the most exciting and successful in the country, Allison would be taking the bus to work, a finance company having repossessed his car. His money at that time was being drained by a restaurant called Napoleon's, which he owned with scrap metal merchant Freddie Pye and businessman Jimmy Walsh. 'A lavish enterprise' that was 'doomed' was how Allison would describe that venture, reckoning that it lost about £20,000 in two years before being sold to a character called Frank 'Foo Foo' Lamar.

Allison would bounce cheques with alarming regularity and on one occasion City manager Joe Mercer handed him £134 in cash out of his own pocket after Malcolm had admitted, 'Joe, I'm in a bit of trouble.' He would at least have the honesty to own up to his failings without looking for excuses. When he made comments like, 'It becomes a bit of a problem when you send people cheques and then they send you them right back again,' there would rarely be a 'but' to follow. No stories of distant relatives needing money for life-saving operations.

Eventually, however, the pattern of spending more than he was earning – established early in his working career – became something he couldn't just dismiss with a wisecrack and he would find himself in court in the early '90s for failing to meet his maintenance payments.

His football career snatched away from him, Allison set his mind to replacing the money he had been earning at West Ham. Not that such deliberations would have kept him awake for long. He had always found ways of supplementing his football wages – so much so that teammates used to joke that he was working as a gigolo on the side. The truth for a while had been a good deal less exotic as Allison filled the summer months by working as a car salesman in Warren Street. His powers of persuasion saw him taking home more than was to be found in his West Ham pay packet, even though his lack of enthusiasm led him to admit, 'I came to consider it an achievement to report in.' And one former colleague remembers his anger when Allison failed to deliver the car he had promised him shortly after his arrival at Upton Park.

Such mundane activity, however, was never going to be considered by Allison as a viable replacement for life as a professional footballer. Allison, the competitor, the gambler, was drawn inexorably to the track.

Initial success on the horses had come Allison's way courtesy of the jockey Jeff Lewis, who had provided a few profitable tips. At Epsom racecourse, Allison ran into the former Arsenal player Arthur Shaw, an old friend who had established himself as a professional gambler. Shaw suggested that his own contacts and information on the horses, combined with Allison's network at the dog track, could make for a lucrative partnership. A new career had been launched.

Allison would prowl the trackside bookies, placing bets and picking up tittle-tattle that could be worked into profit. On their first night together at West Ham dogs, Allison earned £150 and the next day Shaw's knowledge of the horses raised the winnings to £800. 'It was the opening flurry to a year in which I never knew what it was not to have a huge roll of notes in my pocket,' said Allison, who reckoned he won £80,000 in his first year at the tracks. Of course, he spent just as much, splashing out on new cars and expensive suits.

Sometimes, he didn't even get the cash away from the racecourse

– like the time after a big win at Royal Ascot when he was to be found buying champagne all round. Such extravagance was not, according to Allison, born of a desire to be the 'big man'. It was, he said, a simple desire to share his happiness – 'an expression of the mood that came to me when my luck was running smoothly'. Perhaps it was more than that. He had been evicted by illness from the life he knew, one in which his place was secure. It is likely, then, that there was a need for acceptance – a search for a new role and a new sphere of influence. He had established that at West Ham with his personality, knowledge and dedication. On the racetrack, it appeared that all it required was a winning ticket and a crate of bubbly.

Describing his new life as 'pure escapism', Allison watched very few games of football and his only contact with the sport was the evenings he spent entertaining his West Ham buddies. Yet Allison quickly became dissatisfied with winning money on what boiled down to chance. Having been such a strategist, tactician and planner in his former life, having taken such firm control of his own destiny – and of those around him – no amount of money could make up for the empty feeling of having your fate out of your own hands. The rush of seeing a horse charge up on the rails proved shallow and transient compared with the deep-rooted satisfaction of a goal worked out in advance on the training ground.

The long treks to remote courses to place a single bet on a horse began to lose their appeal and there were times when Allison wondered what the hell he was doing. Those days began to overshadow the glamour of Epsom on Derby day or weekends in Deauville, France, where he dined with a female member of the Rothschild family and helped an American millionaire lose £10,000 in 20 minutes in a casino. Allison described that weekend as the highlight of his gambling career – 'a time when, briefly, it did seem to me that there was no other way to live'.

Once the inevitable bad run descended upon him, Allison sensed the hopelessness of his profession. He had come to see it as 'a terrible, desperate business'. It no longer seemed like a job for life and a day of losses in the rain at Kempton Park offered one torn-up betting ticket too many. Before he turned away completely Allison had one last fling, losing £1,500 that he didn't have. He was warned off the tracks for failing to pay his debts to the bookmakers. It was some years before the ban was lifted.

Leaving behind the life of a professional gambler, Allison needed something else to fill his time and provide him with an income. Football had still not re-established itself sufficiently in his bloodstream for him to consider it as a career option. But it was an old contact within the game, Queens Park Rangers chairman Jim Gregory, whom he had got to know through his connections to the motor trade, who loaned Allison £2,000 to launch his next venture. Allison bought himself a club in Soho, the Artists and Repertoire, on Charing Cross Road.

His clientele was an eclectic group – including show-business people such as Harry Secombe and the singer Dorothy Squires, and professional footballers. Players from many of the London teams, including his old colleagues at West Ham, would find their way to the A & R on their return to the capital after away games. Allison also widened his contacts within the criminal world, having mixed regularly in such circles during his time at the track.

One such acquaintance, with a gambler called Joe Lowery, had led to him spending four hours being questioned by police at Doncaster. Lowery got to know Allison and his West Ham teammates after watching them losing their weekly wages at Hackney dogs. He approached them to place bets for him instead, a task for which they were well rewarded. Allison confessed to his suspicions about the legitimacy of Lowery's operations and was not altogether surprised when his new pal was warned off greyhound racing for suspected doping. Lowery turned his attention to the horses and after the favourite came a cropper in the St Leger, police became suspicious about Allison's long trackside conversation with Lowery. It took several hours, and the intervention of Joe Shaw, for Allison to persuade the constabulary that they had been discussing nothing more sinister than old times at the dogs.

Allison's non-judgemental loyalty to his friend was such, however, that when Lowery began a subsequent five-year jail sentence, he sent him some equipment for the prison team. And when Lowery was released shortly before the 1969 FA Cup final, Allison loaned him £200 and secured him an invitation to Manchester City's post-game banquet. 'Joe came from a murky corner of my past, but I wasn't about to disown him,' he explained.

There were other memorable encounters. Allison recalled being challenged to a fight with axes by a character called Albert 'Italian' Dimes over the £300 Malcolm believed he was owed, and he got to know the Great Train Robber Buster Edwards. For a while he even thought he was going to be called to give evidence on his behalf at the Old Bailey.

Some years later, the Manchester City players would see the evidence of an acquaintance Allison had established with the notorious Kray twins, Ronnie and Reggie. Staying in London after a game, the team had gone to the club where Britain's most infamous siblings happened to be drinking. One of the players established winking contact with a girl who was sitting at a table with another man and when the player visited the gents, the girl's companion followed him in to warn him that he would lose his kneecaps if he persisted in his flirting. The shaken player reported the encounter to Allison, who went straight to the Krays' table and conveyed the events to them. A word from Mal was enough to send the twins immediately over to the potential aggressor, who was seen moments later hurrying nervously out of the club.

Allison admitted getting to know a group of men who had been involved in a gold bullion robbery, although he stressed, 'It was not a world I wanted to get too closely involved with. What I could do was appreciate their sense of humour and an intelligence that, if channelled into legitimate business, would have made many of them rich men.'

The circles in which he moved, coupled with the fact that most people knew that he was skint more often than not, made him an obvious candidate to be approached with the odd dodgy proposition. On one occasion, an American pornographer sought out Allison in his club to explain his network of wealthy clients around London, before asking him to collect money and letters for him from a post office box. Even with his unstable finances, Allison was not tempted to go down that road. Being friends with criminals was one thing; becoming one of them was an entirely different proposition.

Meanwhile, Allison's chances of becoming rich through his own legitimate methods, his nightclub business, were doomed from the start. Even though trade was healthy, his head was never made for business. His attention was too easily diverted from the profit-and-loss column by the promise of another drink with one of his new, glamorous pals. Mal drank away the profits, becoming more miserable as he did so, slipping into a life of all-night boozing and all-day hangovers. He found that he was starting to mirror some of the customers, seeing himself reflected in the way they depended on drink to get them through their lives. 'They could make "set them up, barman" the most miserable words in the language,' he commented. And recalling the time he helped a wealthy, drunken, customer out of the club, he added, 'He had no control over himself. He had become a clown. I have never forgotten the thought that came into my head: "So this is being a playboy?"'

While the Conservative government's policies of reduced taxation and economic expansion in the late 1950s saw televisions, washing machines and refrigerators flying out of the High Street stores, Allison's murky, twilight existence appeared more closely aligned to a Chicago speakeasy during the prohibition days than Britain's new age of prosperity and consumerism. But now he was ready to step back into the sunshine and during long stints behind the bar his thoughts had gradually been turning back towards football.

He had turned out a few times in charity games for the TV All-Stars but, realising that he needed a greater escape from the increasingly claustrophobic walls of his club, he went to see Jack Chisholm, manager of Southern League team Romford. His health and fitness, he felt, were up to playing a few games for a semi-professional team. He was not doing it for the money, which was just as well as Romford, despite being in the top flight of the Southern League, were virtually broke. Allison told Chisholm, 'Jack, I am spending my days and nights in a smoky nightclub in London. It's not my scene. I want to get the feel of football again.'

Romford took over Allison's playing registration – still held by West Ham – in August 1960 and he turned out in three pre-season trial games. Described by the *Romford Recorder* after the last of those matches as 'a player to be reckoned with', he made his debut for the club at centre-half in a 6–2 Eastern Counties League Cup victory against Sudbury. The local reporter stated, 'At the end of the 90 minutes we were left with the comforting knowledge that Allison has forgotten very little of his skill. His coolly enthusiastic but intelligent performance completely booted out the Sudbury spearhead.'

The majority of the 22 League games Allison played for Romford in 1960–61 came in the second half of the season, meaning he missed out on the club's run to the second round of the FA Cup, where they lost at home to Northampton. He was a valuable contributor, however, to the team's fight to stave off relegation, something they eventually achieved when they won 2–0 at Folkestone. There, Allison was praised for his 'incessant promptings' and was the 'mastermind of the victory and star of the defence'.

He missed the last couple of games of the campaign after a sending-off at King's Lynn, but entered the summer months buoyed by the confidence he had regained in his physical well-being. He had proved that he could last a competitive 90-minute match and make a contribution to his team. He went as far as saying that he had 'saved himself' by stepping back into football. 'It put into perspective the flashy, big-time Charlie days on the racecourse and in the nightclub,' he said.

Further realisation of how much he had missed the sport was provided by Chelsea and England forward Jimmy Greaves, who sat in Allison's bar in April 1961 waiting for news of an exciting, life-changing transfer to AC Milan. Greaves was set to become one of a group of British international strikers – along with Denis Law of Manchester City, Hibernian's Joe Baker and Aston Villa's Gerry Hitchens – who were escaping the feudal world of the £20-a-week maximum wage in favour of the riches on offer in Italian football. Within months, their departures would have given decisive momentum to the crusade of the Professional Footballers' Association, led by chairman Jimmy Hill, to rid the game of such an outdated and punitive system. The exiles would return, mostly disillusioned by their Italian experience, to reap the benefits of the new order of English football. For now, however, Allison looked at Greaves and saw the excitement and the great possibilities that stretched out in front of a young man with the world at his feet. 'His hope and optimism had taken me out of myself,' he remarked.

Unknown to Allison, certain wheels were turning at that time that could have taken him back into football full-time – at Upton Park, of all places. After dispensing with the services of Ted Fenton, the West Ham directors had appointed Ron Greenwood, formerly coach of Arsenal, as their manager. Greenwood knew the history of the Cassettari clan and could still sense Allison's influence at the club. To him, the idea of having Allison return as youth-team coach was as obvious as it had been to the young players who had expected their mentor to be given that role immediately after his retirement as a player. In his book, *Sincerely Yours*, Greenwood would explain:

> I inherited fertile ground and Allison was one of the men responsible. He is a natural coach, a man with real insight into the game, and he proved his ability with youngsters right from his early days at West Ham.
>
> I thought he would be ideal but when I put the proposal to the board their reaction surprised me. They listened attentively, but then said, firmly, that they did not think Allison should come back to the club. They told me one or two things had happened which would not make it a good idea and they were clearly not going to change their minds. I had to accept their decision. I had not mentioned anything to Malcolm so it was just a bright idea which never got off the ground.
>
> It would have been his first full coaching post and it is of course impossible to say how things would have worked out. I still believe he would have been perfect for the job for a while. Sooner or later he would have been on his way. It is impossible to keep outstanding lieutenants.

Allison was at the stage in his life where he would probably have relished the chance to return to the game on a daily basis. In the meantime, he signed up for a second season at Romford, under new player-manager Ted Ditchburn, the former Tottenham and England goalkeeper. Named club captain, Allison's commitment to the cause is evidenced by the fact he was booked four times in the early weeks of the season, some feat in the days when only the most extreme misconduct would prompt most referees into such action. 'It's time manager Ted

Ditchburn had a long strong talk with skipper Malcolm Allison,' wrote *Romford Recorder* reporter Johnny Morris after the third caution had resulted from an argument with the referee in the first qualifying round of the FA Cup. This time around, Allison was to be the key figure in Romford's return to the second round proper, a run that began with a 6–2 home win against Wembley. The same Morris was obviously not a man who was easily pleased, describing the Romford performance as 'a disgraceful exhibition' and adding that it was 'utterly amazing that so little effort should have brought such great reward'. ITV had filmed the game for future broadcast but it was Morris's fervent hope that the recording would never see the light of day.

Further home wins followed against Leytonstone and Dagenham, in a replay. Yet some of the club's fans were proving as hard to please as Morris in the press box, taking exception to Allison's unrelenting high-decibel cajoling of those around him. Reporter Paul Paris noted, 'I hope all those sniping supporters took note that when Allison eased up the shouting, Romford eased up their play.'

In the fourth qualifying round, drawn at home again, Romford trailed to Cambridge United when they were awarded an indirect free-kick in the 55th minute. Cambridge put 11 men in front of goal and Allison simply blasted the ball at the lot of them. It ended up in the back of the net, with Cambridge convinced it had found its way there without touching anyone. Photographers behind the goal tended to support their view but the referee ruled otherwise. 'Well, er, I was watching the ball as I kicked it and when I looked up it was bulging the rigging,' said Allison later with the air of a schoolboy having been caught scrumping apples. Seven minutes later, Romford were given a penalty for a harsh-looking handball and Allison, who had earlier been forced to leave the field to have his studs filed, slammed it past the keeper's right hand. 'The plaudits really belonged to the brilliant Allison, whose stentorian shouts sounded over the roars of the 5,323 Cup-happy soccer fans,' raved the *Recorder*.

The first round did not reward Romford with Football League opposition. Instead, it was Walthamstow Avenue who arrived at Brooklands. It is the game that lives most in the memory of anyone who watched Romford during Allison's two years at the club. The local paper's match report began like this:

Magnificent match-winning Malcolm Allison, cool, calm and cultured hero of Romford's incredibly exciting FA Cup run, shot Walthamstow Avenue out of the competition last Saturday in a last-minute incident that left Boro fans white with fear. Boro's cocksure clown conjured up victory with as cute a piece of gamesmanship as you could wish to see.

Romford forward Barry Cappi, who scored one of the goals that had left the game tied at 2–2, was fouled in the box in the closing seconds and Allison stepped up to strike the penalty beyond the reach of goalkeeper Gary McGuire. Referee S.S. Mundy, however, ruled that a home player had encroached into the area and ordered Allison to take it again. This time Allison added to the dramatic effect by indicating to McGuire that he intended to beat him to his right-hand side once again. As McGuire stood motionless, trying to figure out whether this was bluff or double bluff, Allison placed it to the other side to win the game. Relating the incident recently on the club's internet site, one Romford fan adds, 'They say Malcolm was grinning as he placed the ball again, pointed to the same corner, and calmly knocked it past the keeper. Cue pandemonium and Romford were through to a home match against Watford.'

Things did not go so well for Allison in the second-round tie. With Romford having performed creditably and holding Watford after 64 minutes, he gave away a penalty with a late tackle. The kick was converted by Tommy Harmer and Watford were on their way to a 3–1 victory. The remainder of the season became another battle against relegation and once safety had been achieved around Easter, it became evident that Romford, under new manager Harry Clarke, and an increasingly injury-prone Allison would be going separate ways.

But far from marking an ending, Allison's departure from Romford enabled him to take a further step back into the sport he once thought he had left behind – this time in the role for which he had evidently been born, coaching. The surroundings, though, were not those that a working-class south London boy like Malcolm would ever have envisaged for himself. Steeling himself for a journey into the unknown, Allison accepted an offer to coach the undergraduates of the Cambridge University Football Club, a move that, he said, 'completed my recovery'.

Allison drove into Cambridge on the kind of sunny late summer's day that showed the historic buildings of the city in their best light. Football was not exactly the most prominent of the extra-curricular activities at the university. Cambridge had established itself as the home of the satire movement that was transforming British comedy. Future Monty Python members John Cleese, Graham Chapman and Eric Idle were treading the boards of the Footlights Club, while in the week that the final trials for the football team took place, the university newspaper was pondering the likely success in America of the touring *Beyond the Fringe* squad of Peter Cook, Dudley Moore, Alan Bennett and Jonathan Miller.

Allison had been wary of accepting the job offer, wondering whether someone whose life's classrooms had been the barracks, football field, racetrack and nightclub would be accepted into the world of academia. Yet he was put instantly at ease when met by team captain Howard Moxon, who greeted him with, 'We're all very thrilled that you're coming to work with us. We've heard a lot about you and we're ready to start when you are.'

Concerned about his ability to communicate with his players, Allison was relieved to discover that the students were keen to soak up the knowledge he was able to impart and were well used to processing such information. 'Whatever training routines I laid down were followed slavishly. I would travel back to London knowing my instructions would be followed.'

On completion of the trials for the team, *Varsity*, the university newspaper, reported confidently, 'Under the guidance of Malcolm Allison a powerful side will doubtless emerge.' The overriding goal for any Cambridge team was, of course, to beat Oxford in the Varsity Match early in December. In preparation for their big game at Wembley, Allison supplemented the usual schedule of games against the likes of the Royal Navy and FA representative sides with matches against strong Tottenham, Arsenal and West Ham teams. It meant that the Light Blues suffered a run of defeats in the build-up to the Oxford game, but come the big day Cambridge were favoured to repeat their victory of the previous season.

Facing Allison in his first coaching appointment at Wembley was a former teammate, Malcolm Musgrove. The ex-West Ham winger was considered to have produced a team that was more deliberate in its approach to play than Cambridge, who had been well schooled in the art of turning defence swiftly into attack. Allison gave his team a final tune-up at White Hart Lane on the day before the game, and was rewarded by seeing them race into a two-goal lead inside six minutes. The coach's Continental influence was obvious in the way he employed his number 9, Keith Sanderson, in a deep, scheming role and it was he who put two passes through for left-winger Clayton to fire in right-footed shots. Oxford pulled a goal back before the interval but a burst of three goals between the 70th and 80th minutes set up a final scoreline of 5–2.

Yet, greater than the joy of victory at Wembley, Allison's most valuable gift from Cambridge was the calming atmosphere of the colleges, the respect for fellow human beings that he felt and witnessed and the eagerness of his students. All had combined to further rekindle his love for football. He now knew that coaching and management was the path he wanted his working life to take. His nightclub was being forgotten – 'neglect born of boredom and something approaching distaste' – and would soon have to do without him completely. Football was beckoning him more strongly than ever, and this time Allison was ready to give in completely to its call.

5

PART-TIME LOVE

'It's a novel experience to see genuine football thinking being put into practice at lowly Bath'

— *Bath Weekly Chronicle*, September 1963

Set among the genteel countryside of Somerset, the city of Bath, with its Roman history and Georgian crescents, had never been what anyone would describe as a hotbed of football, the game of the working-class, industrial masses. It was the local rugby team that held sway when it came to grabbing the attention of local sports followers, even in the days before professionalism and any kind of national competition. By the time the 1962–63 season approached, however, Bath City Football Club could at least count themselves among the premier non-League teams in the country.

The Southern League, of which Bath had been members since 1921, was acknowledged to represent, along with its Northern Premier League counterpart, the highest level of football outside the full-time professional ranks. Having won the title in 1960 and recently finished runners-up behind Oxford United, Bath could rightly claim to be among the elite in their field. These were the days when the Football League was still a closed shop, with the club finishing in 92nd place forced to apply to their peers for re-election – going up against the best of the non-Leaguers in a ballot to determine their status in football's hierarchy. League clubs were rarely reckless enough in their thinking to ignore the fact that they could find themselves in a similar position in future years, so they tended to look after each other. When Oxford were given the key to the locked door of the Football League it was because the bankrupt Accrington Stanley had tendered their own resignation.

Bath looked forward to the new season with optimism, the ascent of Oxford having left them as de facto favourites for the Southern League championship. It was, therefore, a disappointment to the Twerton Park fans to have to wait until the fifth game of the season for their first victory. Injuries to key players didn't help and as the end of 1962 approached, and the first gnawing of a harsh winter began to bite, the club found itself closer to the foot of the table than the top.

At the end of November, manager Arthur Coles resigned – an action that, if nothing else, drew the sting of disgruntled fans. Representatives of the supporters' club had been due to meet the board on that same day, although they went ahead and told the press what they would have said had the showdown taken place. The directors and management, they claimed, were taking the club in the wrong direction. They argued that the fans' attempt to buy 500 shares at £1 each had been rebuffed, while the supporters' donations of £36,000 over the previous six years had been squandered.

As is often the case, the change of manager – even though there was no permanent replacement – brought improved results, with six unbeaten games straddling a six-week period of inactivity caused by one of the iciest British winters on record. Naturally, speculation had grown during the barren weeks about the identity of the new man in charge. Former Bath goalkeeper Ian Black, who had left the club for Canterbury the previous summer, was reported to be the favourite.

Meanwhile, Malcolm Allison's experience with Romford and Cambridge University had served to convince him that a full-time job in football was what he craved. His job search was aided by *Daily Express* writer Bob Pennington, who questioned in his newspaper why one of the country's three best coaches, as he put it, was not employed in the Football League.

Allison, who had played no further games for Romford after the end of the 1961–62 season, had been contacted by Bristol Rovers with a view to joining the coaching staff when Bath City approached him with an offer to become manager. In years gone by, Allison had seen non-League football as a 'wasteland' inhabited by has-beens and those who never-would-be. But Romford had been an enjoyable experience, broadening his mind to the opportunities the semi-professional game could offer. Allison was late for his meeting with club president Arthur Mortimer after misjudging the time it would take to drive from London, but he got there in time to be impressed by the local businessman's ambition for Bath City, which included taking on the big clubs in FA Cup ties. He eagerly accepted the position.

Arriving in his office in the middle of March, Allison learned a quick lesson about the life of a non-League manager. 'I came in that morning and opened three letters. As the players were all part-time I couldn't do much training until the evening so in the afternoon I went to the pictures and saw *On The Waterfront*, thinking that if this is management then it's a doddle.'

Bath winger Ron Walker had played against Allison for Doncaster Rovers during Malcolm's West Ham days. He recalls that his first thought upon meeting his new boss was, 'He is too good for Bath,' adding that 'it was obvious he was a chap who wanted to get on'.

Allison's first game in charge brought a 2–1 victory at league-leading Cambridge City, and a couple of three-goal wins against Clacton and Rugby lifted Bath into the top half of the table. The club's unbeaten run, now standing at nine games, came to a shuddering 4–1 halt at Romford. In a move typical of Allison's belief that a team that looked and felt right on the field would produce improved performances, the players had arrived in the visitors' dressing-room to find a modern new kit laid out for them. The fact that it didn't work on this occasion did little to alter Allison's thinking.

The season finished with the team in 10th place, and the club reported a £1,551 profit on the season, due largely to the supporters' donation of £14,000. As he planned for his first full season in charge, Allison was determined that the players should benefit from the healthy bank balance and had their pay increased from £13 to £15 a week. They would have to earn it, though. They had already felt the hard edge of the new manager when he ordered them in for Sunday training after dropping a point against champions-elect Cambridge and now he would be demanding extra practice sessions. The part-time nature of his squad, which had at first forced him to seek out the company of Marlon Brando at the local cinema, was something that Allison could capitalise upon. Often he would have only small groups to work with but far from being a hindrance, he found it helped him spend time on specialised skills and tactics and offered additional opportunities for individual tuition.

Allison turned out for the club in a friendly in Holland and even hinted that he might play some games at centre-half once the season began. There were, however, plenty of new faces for him to select from. Ex-Portsmouth and England wing-half Len Phillips joined the club on a free transfer from Chelmsford at the age of 41 and other new arrivals included goalkeeper Ray Drinkwater from QPR, defender Tony Gough, who returned to the club that had released him as a 16 year old, and forward John Cartwright, one of Allison's former West Ham pupils, who had just left Crystal Palace. Cartwright comments, 'When Malcolm left West Ham I got lost – from being, at one stage, the biggest young signing at the club, my career went backwards – for various reasons. Malcolm had got me interested in coaching and I had got my certificates and started coaching at various schools. I had just left Crystal Palace when Malcolm called me and said, "Come and play for me down at Bath." He said I could train in London and arranged for me to work a couple of nights a week with the youngsters at West Ham. I wouldn't have gone down there other than to play for Malcolm.'

Despite his new signings, the pivotal player in Allison's plans was one he inherited, club captain Tony Book. One of Allison's first engagements as Bath manager had been to visit the building site where his skipper was working as a bricklayer. A formal introduction took place and Book recalls that, 'Malcolm just looked at me as if to say, "What are you doing?"' Book, meanwhile, was equally unsure of the man in front of him, noting his expensive jacket and thinking him a 'flash sod'. His first impression was that 'this fish was definitely too big for our pond'.

Allison's affection for Book quickly grew when he saw the pace and professionalism of the slight, angular-looking defender. 'I was simply astonished by his quality the first time I saw him play. He was one of the best and quickest defenders I had seen in any class of football. There was a timing, poise and a tremendous recovery rate. I knew too that he looked after himself. I reckoned there was ten years of professional playing life in him.'

For his part, Book was won over by the professional approach Allison took towards the new campaign, which included taking the team to Weston-super-Mare for a training camp. 'We used to train on Tuesday and Thursday, but Malcolm came in and changed it to four nights a week. It didn't go down too well at first and I think people were a little suspicious of him. He had that West Ham swagger about him. You could see it when he came out training. He had these great big legs, shorts pulled up high and showing off all the muscles in his thighs. But once he got into the football you respected what he said. All he was doing was trying to improve results and looking for new things. The players accepted it when they saw it was producing results.'

Impressive form in the club's pre-season friendlies had fans talking excitedly about the versatility of the systems Allison was trying out and had the players appreciating the value of the new training regime. Book continues, 'A few times after sessions he'd pull players to one side and tell them he wanted to do an extra 20 minutes one-on-one, if he felt there was something he could improve. He showed an interest in me and undoubtedly made me a better player. The whole place lit up in a short space of time and only Malcolm could have had that effect.'

Ron Walker explains further, 'He clearly knew what he was doing. He didn't change things too much but he got the players wanting to play. He thought a lot about the game and he used to take the trouble to find out about the opposition and play to their weaknesses. He would get us together whenever he could and we would do extra training for special matches.'

When the competitive season kicked off at Wellington, Bath included six summer signings, although it was veteran Charlie Fleming whose hat-trick led them to a 5–2 win. The *Bath Weekly Chronicle* recorded that 'the influence of new manager, FA qualified coach, Malcolm Allison, was clear enough' – although when Yeovil were beaten only 1–0 two days later the paper accused Bath of 'returning inexplicably to the "rush and bother" methods of last season', describing the team as an enigma. In general, however, the *Chronicle* was clearly impressed by Allison's credentials and appeared to be feeling a touch of awe at the great force within its midst. The publication was at pains to explain Allison's methods when, after drawing with champions Cambridge City in their third game, he made several changes for a Southern League Cup first-leg tie at Poole and lost 2–1:

> When City's new manager Malcolm Allison, a man wedded to the ideas of modern coaching and enlightened management, made a few surprising changes in the City XI in midweek, he wasn't just picking names out of the hat.
>
> At first sight the changes in the side that met Poole from that which played with such spirit against champions Cambridge City were surprising . . . it was to be the new 4-4-2 line-up common on the Continent but out-favoured in Britain by the much-vaunted 4-2-4 formation.
>
> The fact that City lost may set that wise old man on the terraces shaking his head in sad dismissal of the side's Southern League chances. Less experienced but more hopeful fans might give a new manager the benefit of the doubt. After all, Allison has concrete evidence that he knows full well what he is doing. He is a qualified Football Association coach and you don't earn that honour just for doing physical jerks.
>
> His unusual choice for the Poole game was all part of the kind of realistic attitude towards matches that characterises so much competitive football in the Sixties . . . it's a novel experience to see genuine football thinking being put into practice at lowly Bath.

Such thinking, Cartwright recalls, included the nurturing of a style of play that was advanced even for professional teams, let alone a group of part-time players. 'You can only do so much with the players you have got, but Malcolm was moving towards the Dutch idea of Total Football,' he explains. 'He got people from the full-back positions getting forward; front players dropping out; and players going on beyond them from midfield. Some of the stuff we were doing was quite innovative.'

A 2–0 victory at Hinckley meant seven points from four games and a brief spell on top of the Southern League table although, once their unbeaten start to the season had ended, Allison's team settled into a long stint tucked in just behind the leaders. It was the FA Cup that provided the club, and the town, with its real excitement. Drawn at home against Falmouth in the fourth qualifying round, they gained revenge for defeat by the South Western League team a season earlier with a 2–0 victory in front of more than 4,000 fans at Twerton Park.

Allison and Bath City officials gathered in the offices of the *Bath Chronicle* to see the ticker tape from the news agencies reveal that a trip to Athenian League Maidenhead United awaited them in the first round proper. An unconvincing display produced a two-goal victory against a team that had little ambition beyond earning the financial boost of a replay. Cartwright broke the deadlock with an individual goal after 64 minutes, setting up a second-round tie against more non-League opposition, FA Amateur Cup holders Wimbledon.

The game at Plough Lane, where the Dons were unbeaten for two years, attracted a crowd of 8,000 – approximately 3,000 of whom had travelled from Bath. Allison was clearly achieving success in diverting the town's attention towards his team, as Walker remembers. 'Bath was a rugby town, but when Malcolm was down here football certainly got more attention and more supporters. There were two train-loads travelling to the Cup games.'

Those fans saw a 30-yard effort from Cartwright give Bath a 2–1 lead in the second half, only for a late header to save the home team. A crowd of 5,627 saw the replay three days later, by which time the draw for the third round had identified a home game against First Division Bolton Wanderers as the reward for the winners. Keith Sanderson, whom Allison had signed after coaching him at Cambridge University, followed up a rebound to put Bath ahead after 24 minutes. A good move late in the half saw the ball move through three players before Fleming cut in from the left to score the second goal. Ken Owens and Cartwright added second-half goals for a 4–0 victory that left Allison saying, 'It was the professionals against the amateurs. I played on the weakness of their centre-half.'

Allison, who by now had taken to wearing a Russian fur hat to games – early echoes of the 'lucky' fedora he would sport at Crystal Palace more than a decade later – relished the prospect of testing himself against a team from the highest level of English football. Typically, he stated, 'I wanted to play a good team and I'm quite happy about this draw. We could pull off the shock win of the Cup.' He also took great pride in having realised Arthur Mortimer's long-standing ambition of bringing First Division opposition to Twerton Park. Mortimer greeted his manager after the Wimbledon victory with the words, 'That's it. I don't care what happens now.'

Cartwright credits much of Bath's success that season to the positive environment Allison created for his players. 'We had some big players down there but Mal was such a big personality that they responded to him. He created the right atmosphere and team spirit. Everybody liked him and enjoyed playing for him. He had this ability to set people at ease. He was a real good friend to players, although he was a hard person if necessary. No one wanted to get on the wrong side of him, though, because they all enjoyed what he stood for. He wanted to play the game the right way.'

Allison missed his team's loss at Cambridge – their first league defeat for almost three months – to watch Bolton draw against West Bromwich Albion, but he was at pains to keep the build-up to the big game as near normal as possible. There was no disguising the temporary stand that was erected at the Bristol end of the ground, nor the special all-ticket arrangements put in place, but Allison stressed that he would not be getting the players together for a special pre-game meal. 'It creates an atmosphere,' he said. 'I want the players to arrive at Twerton Park as relaxed as they would be if we were facing a Southern League team.'

Although his players needed no additional motivation for the biggest game of their lives, Allison felt that his club had a point to make to Bolton manager Bill Ridding, who had angered him with derisory comments about his club's ticket allocation arriving in a biscuit tin. 'Bath was a little club without pretension,' said Allison. 'And it was filled with people who loved it for its own sake.'

In front of 12,779 packed into all corners of the ground, Bath had the better of a game in which Bolton never performed near their top-flight capabilities. Book, whose participation had been in doubt until that morning because of injury, marshalled the defence calmly with Gough, while Bolton needed England keeper Eddie Hopkinson in top form to keep out the home team. With 17 minutes left, Phillips played in Owens, whose dummy freed Fleming. He rounded the keeper and squared for Owens to finish the move from close range. But with an unlikely victory in their grasp, Bath sat back and Bolton at last roused themselves. Ironically it was their young, blond forward, Francis Lee, so important to Allison's future success, who denied him on this occasion. Within six minutes of Bath scoring, the game was level after Lee was brought down in sight of goal by a desperate Ian MacFarlane. Lee converted the penalty himself, although he admitted later, 'I have never wanted to take a penalty less. Picture the scene with the crowd close in around the goal, standing right beside the post. All I could see were anxious faces. In addition was the fact that the pitch was heavy and lumpy, the ball like a sphere of lead and there was a slope slanting across the goalmouth.'

As Lee celebrated, he had time to notice Allison's anguish, spotting his future manager throwing his hat in the air and then stamping on it. Even Bolton boss Ridding felt some sympathy for the non-League team, heading to the dressing-room after the game to tell them how unlucky they had been. 'We should have won, but we gave away that stupid penalty,' says Walker, as if the game were four days ago, not more than four decades.

The great adventure ended with a 3–0 defeat in the replay at Burnden Park later that week. Playing in front of more people than any Bath team had ever experienced – almost 27,000 – the non-Leaguers were, according to the *Chronicle*, 'majestic in defeat. They carried on where they left off at Twerton Park on Saturday, producing a blend of footballing craft that Bolton never reached.' That might have been a slightly one-eyed view but Bath did again stifle Bolton's forwards in a tight first half and even finished the opening 45 minutes with the upper hand. According to Walker, 'We played well enough, but they got the breaks and we didn't.'

Bolton began to convert their possession into chances after the break. Teenaged winger Gordon Taylor cut in from the left and caught out Ray Drinkwater from a narrow angle. A penalty decision against Drinkwater for a foul on Peter Deakin allowed Lee to score another penalty, and a third goal arrived via Welsh centre-forward Wyn Davies three minutes from time.

Bath's handsome consolation for their efforts was a £4,482 share of the gate receipts, and while the directors counted the cash, Allison pointed his team back in the direction of the Southern League title. He saw his side gain momentum with a 2–1 win at leaders Romford when Walker scored twice to turn around a deficit. In the next game Cartwright scored a hat-trick in a 6–2 win against Cambridge, a feat he repeated a couple of games later when Rugby were beaten by the same score, Fleming also scoring three times. That result left them one point behind Romford with three games in hand, and they hit the top two games later when a late penalty salvaged a point against Guildford.

Easter, however, saw the wind taken out of Bath's championship sails and, not for the last time in his career, Allison's team selection at a crucial stage in the season was questioned. Facing a home game on Good Friday against Nuneaton, Allison opted to rest four first-team regulars, saving them instead for the next day's game at fourth-placed Chelmsford. A second-string forward line wasted chance after chance in a frustrating 2–1 loss. A day later, the full strength team was unable to regain momentum in a 3–1 defeat. An Easter Monday victory at Nuneaton left them in third place behind Yeovil, but the tide had turned against Allison's team. Only three of their final eight games were won. The last match was memorable as a statistical footnote, with Allison pressed into service because of absentees and helping Bath to a 6–3 win. The *Bath Chronicle* said of Allison, 'Although not match fit he prompted the City attack with a stream of man-finding passes.' The result saw Bath close the season in third place, six points behind champions Yeovil, but having achieved enough throughout the campaign to send the fans into their summer holidays with hopes of good things to come. Allison, however, would not be around to deliver them.

6

PILGRIM'S PROGRESS

'Malcolm taught us things we had only seen on the TV'
— Former Plymouth Argyle striker Mike Trebilcock

The road from Bath to Plymouth runs at a little under 150 miles. Even in a standard 1964 saloon, which would have set its owner back about £650 if he'd answered the advert for the new Vauxhall Victor in the *Western Morning News*, it was not much more than three hours given a decent run. Malcolm Allison's life, however, rarely ran in straight lines. For him, the journey began in a London hotel on FA Cup final day, lasted more than two months and included a couple of return trips across the Atlantic Ocean.

The Cup final that year was approached by Allison with far greater anticipation than he ever could have imagined during his soul-sapping nights behind the bar of his nightclub. At that time, the thought of former West Ham colleagues like John Bond, Ken Brown and Bobby Moore lining up at Wembley would have brought remorse, regret and self-pity crashing down on him like waves. But now he was excited at the possibility of taking another big step in his football career by becoming a Football League manager. Plymouth Argyle, struggling in the Second Division, were looking for a new man to take over from Andy Beattie, moving on after a long stint as caretaker manager following the early-season resignation of previous full-time boss Ellis Stuttard. Allison, having come to their attention through the achievements of Bath City, had been summoned to meet the Argyle directors at the Savoy Hotel, after which he would watch his old pals take on Preston North End at Wembley.

The Savoy summit went well, with Allison outlining his vision of the way a club should be run. Other candidates, he was informed, were still scheduled to be interviewed, and reports in the succeeding days would name former Exeter boss Frank Broome and ex-Aston Villa manager Eric Houghton as the subjects of those interrogations. But Allison was able to watch West Ham's 3–2 victory with a feeling of confidence in his gut.

As his former protégé, Bobby Moore, lifted the trophy, Allison left the stadium for his final engagement of a hectic day. An aeroplane seat awaited him, bearing him to a summer adventure in Canada.

The bulk of Toronto's population had cast scarcely an uninterested glance in the direction of the Eastern Canada Professional League – even with three of the organisation's five teams situated within the city boundaries. There was, however, a hard core of support from the city's ethnic factions and part of Allison's job after being approached to spend a six-week spell coaching Toronto City was to tap into, and play up, the rivalry between the British-supported City and their Italian rivals at Toronto Italia and Toronto Inter-Roma. The selling of the sport in one of football's frontier lands fascinated Allison, and the role of showman, naturally, was well suited to his personality. He had eagerly asked Bath City's permission to take the position when it was offered by millionaire team owner Steve Stavro.

In accordance with Stavro's wishes, it didn't take long before Allison had his team well-practised at winding up the opposition. In one game against Italia his team ignored the pre-game convention of waving to all sides of the stadium by pointedly ignoring the area where the rival fans were congregated. They finally indulged in an orchestrated salute of that section once they had taken the lead. Allison admitted it was a 'crude ploy' but knew that the tribal atmosphere it stirred up was exactly what was demanded of him.

Yet, to a fierce competitor like Allison – especially one who had arrived in Canada feeling that he was 'on a winning streak' – pumping up the crowd was only part of the job description. City had finished fifth and last in the competition in 1963 and Allison's determination to bring about a dramatic improvement took some by surprise.

In his team were several Football League veterans, including former England and Crystal Palace forward Johnny Brooks, the South African ex-Sunderland striker Ted Purdon and former Aston Villa goalkeeper Nigel Sims. 'When I left Villa and agreed to go out to Toronto I had no idea Mal was going to be the coach,' Sims recalls. 'It turned out to be one of the best periods I had in all my time in football.'

Sims admits that most players had been expecting an easy ride. 'The players, including me, thought, "Let's have a summer holiday." But on his first day Malcolm said, "Come on, we'll get fit and we'll bloody enjoy it." We did – and I became the fittest I had ever been. Mal approached the job in a very serious way. That is how he was when he was around football. Everything was business. He was completely in charge and everything was left to him. He ran it the way he would have run a Football League team. He was the best coach I ever had – he was so positive in the way we approached training and went through our routines. We had a really great time and hardly lost a game. I enjoyed it so much I went back the next couple of years.'

Also flying out to join the team a couple of weeks after Allison's arrival was Bath captain Tony Book, beginning a pattern of loyalty to Malcolm that would extend over the next couple of decades. 'I think Mal made up his mind out there that I might be able to do it at a higher level. He was seeing me as a full-time professional for the first time. I had never trained during the day before.'

It was in Canada that Book was given another early insight into Allison's willingness to employ innovative, unorthodox methods in an effort to keep the players interested. 'Malcolm took it very seriously but would always come up with something different. I remember after I had been there a couple of weeks he took us up into the mountains for a couple of days, just to break the routine. We lived in log cabins and did a bit of fishing.'

While Toronto were setting out on a season that would see them finish top of the league with only four defeats in 24 games and win the championship play-offs, Allison journeyed back to Plymouth to enable the Argyle directors to confirm his appointment. It had not been an entirely done deal, however, having come down to a choice between him and Eric Houghton. Significantly, club chairman Ron Blindell voted against Allison's appointment and made no comment to the press when the Pilgrims' new manager was introduced. It was left to fellow director Doug Fletcher to act as spokesman, noting diplomatically, 'We were very impressed with both candidates.'

Allison told reporters, 'This club has great possibilities. There is much potential here and I'm very ambitious. I'm delighted to get the post. It will be a big battle for the first two or three months while I'm straightening things out. I'm always fair with my players but I expect them to work hard for me.'

He admitted later that only his professional ambition had wrenched him away from Bath, where he loved club president Arthur Mortimer. 'It would be a long time before I worked for a man as straightforward and appreciative.' Allison had admired the way Mortimer would dig into his own pocket to make sure the team had what they needed and had enjoyed the experience of working without the backdrop of petty bickering that he would soon be witnessing from close range. He described Bath as 'the perfect place to gather up again the pieces of my career as a professional football man'.

But now he was manager of Plymouth, with a two-year contract worth £2,500 per season, plus bonuses, and a club house and car thrown in. Having quickly agreed those terms with Argyle's board, he headed back across the water to complete what he would describe as a 'marvellously exhilarating summer'.

Unlike some of the fledgling teams that would, in future years, join the burgeoning North American Soccer League, Toronto City were never short of money. The bankroll of Stavro, who would go on to own ice hockey's Toronto Maple Leafs and basketball's Toronto Raptors, made sure of that. In the team's first season, in 1961, he had paid to put Danny Blanchflower, Stanley Matthews and Johnny Haynes in City shirts and he was happy to reward his team if they produced results.

Under Allison, the results kept coming and Sims's memory of 'going across the road from the stadium to the Park Royal after games for a couple of drinks' barely hints at the high life Allison enjoyed. By his own admission he was 'able to live extravagantly' in his lakeside apartment, supplementing his income with a few winners at the racetrack. He even had enough cash in his pocket to outbid Richard Burton and Elizabeth Taylor for the attention of a waiter at the renowned Swiss Bear nightclub – a victory he celebrated by sending six bottles of champagne to the band and six more to the singer to get them to perform songs of his choice.

Yet it couldn't last for ever. Nor would Allison have wished it to. Putting aside any end-of-vacation blues and secure in the knowledge that City were heading to the title, Allison left the lakes of Ontario and headed excitedly towards the life of a Football League manager among the cliffs and beaches of Devon.

The fact that Plymouth Argyle had needed goal average to survive relegation to the Third Division at the end of the 1963–64 season did not bother Allison one bit. He saw it as a positive situation, far less pressurised than taking over from an established and successful regime. Besides, his confidence in his ability was soaring. He had achieved encouraging results with the university students of Cambridge, the part-timers of Bath and the summer-season professionals of Toronto. He knew that he could teach, motivate and plan tactically. He was ready for the real thing.

The local constabulary were also prepared when Allison arrived in Plymouth on 6 July 1964. His first day at work very nearly ended in jail.

Walking into his office with his Canadian-produced tan and home-grown strut, Allison found two officers waiting to arrest him for £94 worth of unpaid parking tickets. Clueless about how much money he had in his account, he nervously wrote a cheque as bewildered office staff looked on. The incident might explain the somewhat disinterested look on the face of club chairman Ron Blindell and Allison's own preoccupied expression in the picture that appeared in the next day's *Western Morning News*, purporting to show the new manager being taken on a tour of the premises. To Allison's relief, his bank cleared the funds and he was free to set about the task of rebuilding Argyle. 'At that moment I think it dawned on Plymouth that their new manager was a bit of a lad,' he said. 'I think some of the board were a little perturbed that they might have introduced some sort of tearaway to the town.'

The impact was no less dramatic when Allison was introduced to the players. Mike Trebilcock, a promising 19-year-old striker from Cornwall, remembers being star-struck. 'I wasn't aware of Malcolm Allison before he came to Plymouth. He was just there one day. But I loved the man from the start. He was fantastic. The way he stood, the way he dressed, the size of the man – he was unbelievable. I was very impressionable and he was everything you'd want to be. Previously as manager, I'd had a cigarette-smoking Yorkshireman with wide lapels who just went, "Come on, lads. Let's get stuck in." And then came this classy guy. I adored him.'

Allison explained to reporters his plan to play a series of pre-season games in Holland and refused to be drawn on the question of new players. 'In these pre-season games I will weigh up the players, assess their abilities and see if I need to buy,' he said.

Instead, following the pattern that would become a trademark, Allison's first priority was to bring his existing players to an increased level of fitness – by using methods that would engage, rather than browbeat, them. The coastal landscape offered a natural training ground and Allison identified Plymouth Hoe and the local seafront as perfect sites, forcing his men to clamber down cliffs with their training gear to gain access to the beach. Training was followed by lunch on the sand and then afternoon swimming sessions. But Graham Little, who would become Argyle club secretary the following year, recalls, 'Plymouth Hoe was hallowed ground, with its war memorial, so when they started kicking the ball around someone sent for the park superintendent. Malcolm told him where to go and it was all over the local paper.'

Club captain John Newman remembers the favourable impression created by Allison's methods. 'I knew a couple of the Bath players, who always spoke highly of Malcolm as a coach. He was the sort of man who, when he walked in the room, your head went back and you paid attention. He earned respect immediately. After the pre-season we had with him at Plymouth, it was pretty obvious he knew what he was doing. He modernised things, presented new ideas and it made it very interesting. We'd been used to doing a lot of heavy running, but he had a way of getting us fit without a lot of that being done. He introduced weight training, which we hadn't done before, and had us running on the beaches, which wasn't easy. He revolutionised the whole thing. His training sessions were condensed. Whereas before you would go for three hours, he would keep it to an hour and a half. He believed in having a break and a bit of lunch and then another session in the afternoon. It wasn't a soft touch, believe me, but it was a modern idea of getting people fitter. Then, when we had a session working on tactical or technical things, it could go on for two hours or more. It was not heavy, physical stuff, but you had to work at it.'

Allison brought a thoroughness to his preparation that was uncommon for English teams of that time, especially those outside the top flight. Once the weather began to turn in the late autumn, he would ensure that training remained as productive as possible by introducing indoor sessions at a local naval gymnasium. He explained, 'I'm sure this skill practice indoors will improve many players in the winter months. There is nothing more demoralising than having to train on a wet, heavy pitch when it's cold and raining, so I think we can keep the lads in good spirit.'

As the summer wore on, Allison turned his attention more closely to the need he had now identified to strengthen his squad. A popular game among the local press was to speculate about which of his old colleagues would find their way to Home Park. Former West Ham teammate Jimmy Andrews, coaching at Queens Park Rangers, was said to be poised to join Allison's staff, while his great friend Noel Cantwell was suggested to be on his way from Manchester United. Another member of the Cassettari clan, winger Malcolm Musgrove, then at Orient, was touted as a possible player-coach.

On the field Allison turned to Tony Book, a man with no Football League experience but whose defensive versatility, he felt, could offer him valuable options in the tough world of the Second Division. After more than 400 games for Bath, Book was given the opportunity to play professionally when his old boss offered a transfer fee of £1,500. Bath's first reaction was to turn it down but after Book pleaded with the directors not to deny him his dream, a deal was struck and Allison noted the disbelief in the eyes of the Bath director who gratefully accepted Plymouth's cheque.

Book's belated entry to professional football was, he says, down to 'somebody recognising that I wanted to be a player'. He continues, 'I had been striving all my life to be a full-time pro. I had been knocked back and all of a sudden this fellow takes an interest. Through that interest he made me want it again because I thought it was all over at nearly 30. I don't think anyone else would have taken a chance, but he had seen something there. He knew I could cope with the fitness.'

One small detail remained to be taken care of before Book's transfer went through. In order to get the Argyle board to sanction the transfer, Allison asked him to alter his birth certificate to take two years off his real age of 29. 'He was a bit concerned about the age I was, 30 the next month. He said, "I don't think they will stand for that." So I rubbed the year out in the crease where it was folded, so it looked like 1936 instead of 1934.'

There was another raid on his former Bath City team on the eve of the new season, a move that gave further evidence of Allison's willingness to remain loyal to those players in whom he had faith. Inside-forward Keith Sanderson had played for Allison at Cambridge University and Bath and his move to Argyle less than 48 hours before the new campaign kicked off upset Bath manager Ivor Powell, who had already named Sanderson in his team for the opening game. Allison, who cared little for such niceties, then invested £6,500 on another of his former charges, ex-Bristol Rovers centre-half Norman Sykes, who had played in Toronto as a rehabilitation exercise after being told his career was in jeopardy because of an arthritic hip.

Plymouth approached their opening game in high spirits, particularly Trebilcock, whose nine goals in four pre-season matches included hat-tricks against Exeter and Torquay and owed much to Allison's tuition. 'He taught us things that we had only seen on the TV and had wondered how it was done. Suddenly we could do it. Before he came, I remember [former manager] Ellis Stuttard walking out on the pitch with a cigarette in the corner of his mouth and his hands in his pockets. If you hit the ball at him he would chest it off this nice white shirt of his and say, "That's how you do it, lad." That was all he said to you. Then Malcolm came and explained exactly how things were done. He changed everything – even down to the way we looked and the tracksuits we wore.'

Trebilcock credits Allison with giving him knowledge that would not only benefit Plymouth, but would be crucial when, as an Everton player, he scored twice to help his team come from two goals behind to beat Sheffield Wednesday in the 1966 FA Cup final. 'I marvelled at him and he made me a better player, without a doubt. As a striker the first thing he taught me, which I had never heard before, was that when you are in the box you have more time than you think. I had never thought about that before. Looking back there were times when I snatched at shots when I could have taken another second and set myself. Everton won the FA Cup because of the things Malcolm taught me. For the first goal, when the ball dropped in front of me I remembered what he said. I just took my time. I didn't overreach and I put it in. The second one was also down to Malcolm. He always used to say to me, "Trebs, when you go in the box, go as quick as you can because if someone touches you and you go down, even if it is not a penalty it looks like one." So, for the second goal, I went into the box as quickly as I could and the ball dropped right in front of me. Nobody else was moving. I'd had the advantage of getting in there quick and early – that is how I got the chance for the second goal. So both goals were due to Malcolm's contribution.

'I hung on to every word he said because I admired the man that much. When I got to Wembley there was a telegram from Mal saying, "Trebs, it's just another game." He believed that if you have the fundamental skills they come back at the time you need them and for me, twice they came back when I needed them on that day and that was because of Malcolm.'

As a man who was to become a symbol of football's new television age, it was appropriate that Allison's first game as a Football League manager should be on the day that the BBC launched *Match of the Day*, the show that was to hasten football's development into a branch of the showbiz and entertainment industry. Until the BBC brought highlights of one of the day's most compelling games into the living room every Saturday evening, the public had relied upon the spoken and written word of radio and newspapers to provide their mental pictures of most professional footballers.

Television coverage had been reserved for Cup finals and major internationals, but the BBC's weekly offering – placed initially on

BBC2 and replicated a few years later by the ITV network's regional Sunday afternoon programmes – would turn even journeyman players into familiar faces. Glossy youth-orientated magazines like *Goal* and *Shoot!* and collections of *Soccer Stars* stickers helped take the game colourfully into the playgrounds. As the media appetite for football increased, so did the need for big personalities to fill the space that the sport now commanded in all sections of the newspapers. Allison would prove more than equal to the task.

All that was still some way off, however, when Allison's Football League career got off to an inauspicious start with a 2–0 defeat at Coventry, where his team worked hard but lacked inspiration. There followed a goalless home draw against Huddersfield, after which the *Western Morning News* reporter, Tamar, wrote, 'There is still a long way to go but manager Malcolm Allison can hardly be happy.' Going into the third game against Cardiff, Allison promised, 'We want goals and I'm going to work on this problem until I've got it right.' It took Frank Lord, a physical centre-forward, only 45 seconds to put Argyle on the way to a 3–1 victory. Victory by the same score at Preston saw Tamar showing his support for the new regime by writing, 'Clearly manager Allison has created a roaring enthusiasm in the dressing-room that has to be seen to be believed.'

Two more new arrivals showed up at Home Park. Wales winger Barrie Jones was secured for a club record £45,000 – although there had been talk of an alternative bid for Bolton's Francis Lee when the deal seemed to be stalling. And old friend Derek Ufton, who played with Allison at Charlton and had since invited him to be best man at his wedding, accepted the job of coach, having just reached the end of his first-class cricket career with Kent. That prompted the departure of Stuttard, who had retained that position since stepping down from the top job.

Results in the first few weeks of the season were mixed, yet Allison insisted on sticking to a controlled passing game, building patiently from the back – the methods he had attempted to instil in his West Ham colleagues several years earlier. Referred to by reporters unused to seeing such methods as a 'Continental approach', Argyle's style offered an easy target when things didn't quite go right. After a 2–1 defeat at Crystal Palace, Tamar questioned whether Allison had the players to suit the system. But his comment was mild compared with the attack the Palace match programme – obviously accustomed to seeing the ball hoofed downfield at any opportunity – made on Allison's team in its next issue.

> Argyle's tactics were tortuous. They played the ball square, or frequently backwards, in defence, dallying in possession until the way was open for an incisive thrust . . . it is a strategy we have seen many Continental teams employ in televised matches. The difference is that the better Continental teams strike with far more deadly intent than Plymouth showed on this occasion.

No one criticised an Allison team without risking a backlash. 'If Palace want to play defensive football on their own ground then their supporters will have to suffer,' he hit back. 'It reduces soccer to a farce. The crowd don't come to see eight players standing along the 18-yard box for most of the game.'

Allison got even more radical early in October. Having seen his team pick up a moderate 12 points from 11 games, he announced that he would be using Book as a sweeper behind the back four in away matches. He was perfect for the position with his speed on the ground and quickness of thought. 'We are going to play it tighter away from home,' said Allison. 'These are the most important games to me. Tony can adapt. I played him in this role in Canada and he was very successful.'

Argyle winger Norman Piper, who would soon be making his professional debut under Allison, explains, 'Malcolm was a real technician of coaching. He kept changing the system depending on the situation and the opposition – like playing five at the back, which was never heard of before. He would change the system to fit in with a particular plan.'

Book describes the instructions he was given by Allison. 'He basically wanted me to sit in there and as long as the centre-halves had their men marked, I had enough experience at that level to read the situations. That was one of my assets. He knew I would fill in if we were caught out and he always gave me credit for having the pace and the nous to sort things out.'

Allison's experimentation, which he had instigated at Bath City, was notable for being so uncommon in English football at the time. Despite the influence of the Hungarians more than ten years earlier, teams were still only gradually freeing themselves of the straitjacket of the old 'WM' formation. The revolution had gone little further than the tentative notions of a wing-half dropping back to play alongside the centre-back and one of the inside-forwards playing a withdrawn role to create English football's standard 4-2-4 formation.

Future Manchester City and England midfielder Colin Bell recalls coming up against Argyle's innovative methods while playing for Bury. 'They came to Gigg Lane twice in the space of eight days and played the sweeper system. They won both games [without conceding a goal] because we hadn't got a clue how to break them down. We weren't as adept at tactical thinking at Bury as they were at Plymouth. Malcolm was ahead of his time.'

Ufton, who remembers Allison's ability to 'make players feel ten times better than they were', believes that the strength of his tactical experimentation was never forgetting the abilities of the players at his disposal – a quality he would be accused of misplacing in the later, less successful, phase of his career. 'It wasn't until later that he became more theoretical in his outlook. The trouble with footballers is that if they are down a couple of divisions from what you are used to they are not always going to be good enough to do what you want.'

Allison saw his sweeper system as being well within the scope of the likes of Book and viewed it as more than just a way of bolstering his defence. He would later write:

> It is a stimulating position to play. Certainly this reduces the number of forwards, but the full-backs, and to a lesser extent the half-backs, have been freed from much of their territorial restriction. Full-backs particularly can commit themselves more to attack.

The tactical reappraisal had been prompted partly by a 6–1 loss at Bolton, a game Trebilcock remembers for the rollicking he received from his manager after scoring a meaningless consolation goal. 'Malcolm wasn't a great shouter, but he did shout at me that day. We were getting beat 6–0 and I scored at the end and just walked away as if to say, "Well, that's no big deal." I remember Mal getting cross and saying, "Don't ever do that again. When you score a goal, you celebrate it." Even though we were 6–1 down!'

Allison put the Bolton result down as 'just one of those games', but Newman recalls the manager's typical response to a poor performance. 'He didn't go around shouting and bawling, but you knew when he was upset because he went quiet on people. I can remember him coming in after games where we hadn't performed and he would just sit at the end of the dressing-room and look at you. The last thing you wanted to do was look him in the eye. He would sit there for a few minutes and you could hear a pin drop. Then he would walk out and would have more to say about it on Monday morning. His reaction earned him a lot of respect. He would tell you when it wasn't right, but he very rarely bawled people out. He would leave you out of the team – and that was the worst thing. It hurt.'

Piper explains that quiet analysis of individual mistakes was more important than throwing tea cups around the dressing-room. 'Malcolm was the kind of coach who knew that if you made a mistake it was how you reacted afterwards that was important. You are all going to make mistakes and he would say, "You are a good player right now, but if you do this and this you will be an even better player." He had a positive way of talking to the players and wouldn't tell people they were terrible.'

Improvement in results – the Bolton loss was followed by seven wins in nine games – meant that Plymouth were genuine promotion contenders by the time Manchester City visited Home Park late in November. A 3–2 victory saw them draw level with Newcastle in second place in the table, but Newman had shown little evidence of pressure when, with the scores level at two goals apiece, he stepped up to the penalty spot. Instead of shooting for goal he rolled the ball forward for Trebilcock to run in and thrash home, while City's defenders remained obediently motionless on the edge of the penalty area. A move that Arsenal's Thierry Henry and Robert Pires would mess up four decades later against the same opposition hardly seemed designed for such a crucial moment.

After the game, Allison played down the danger, saying, 'It was common practice for Raich Carter and Peter Doherty to take penalties this way in charity games. Psychologically, it eases the tension and doesn't throw the onus on just one player.'

However, Newman admits, 'It was a tight game and if it hadn't gone in there would have been ructions and that would have been the end of me. I learned it from watching the great Peter Doherty in a testimonial game and I never thought I would have the nerve to do it. But I had done it previously against Aston Villa a couple of years earlier.'

The penalty offered City striker Neil Young an introduction to the personality of the man for whom he would score some vital goals in years to come. 'That was the signal for Malcolm to leap from his seat, turn to face the crowd with his arms stretched in the air like some great warrior acclaiming his flock and then bow low towards the directors' box. What a showman.'

Four days after the City game, Plymouth were due to entertain Northampton in the quarter-finals of the League Cup, a competition in which they had been playing consistent football. Two goals by Lord produced victory over Sheffield United in the second round and after disposing of Bury, First Division Stoke City were brushed aside in a replay. Only a late scrambled goal had saved Stoke on their own ground, but a hat-trick by Lord reflected Plymouth's superiority in a 3–1 win at Home Park. The local paper reported that Argyle 'toyed with their opponents, keeping possession of the ball in Real Madrid fashion'. Stoke manager Tony Waddington was the latest to complain that Plymouth were negative, but Allison put the complaints down to the fact that few teams had ever given much thought to the problem of beating the extra defender.

The good form continued against a Northampton team that was unbeaten in 18 games and heading for promotion to the First Division. Newman scored the only goal when he ran onto a neat chip by Duncan Neale after ten minutes, setting up a two-legged semi-final against First Division Leicester. Even in the days when the elite of the First Division teams ignored the competition it was an achievement that put Allison and Plymouth on the country's football map.

Newman recalled Allison's desire to improve players' individual performances: 'Through that period we played some good stuff, tactically he was sharp and he could address the team in the way he wanted them to play. He knew that you had to lay out a system and tactics, but he knew that the most important thing was getting the players performing to the best of their ability within that system. He wanted us to be better technically – that was the biggest advance. He was very good at one-on-one talks. There was a lot of that and there was encouragement to use your ability. He made things simple to grasp, but he expected you to carry it out.'

Allison chose the first leg of the League Cup semi-final at Leicester's Filbert Street ground to hand a first-team debut to Glyn Nicholas. It was the third consecutive game in which he had given a teenager his first taste of professional football, having played 16-year-old forward Richard Reynolds in an FA Cup tie against Derby and introduced 17-year-old Norman Piper for the Division Two game at Ipswich.

The decision to blood Piper was in part due to the youngster's dedication to his prescribed programme of weight training and the physical progress he had achieved. Allison would frequently become exasperated in future years at players' reluctance to build on their strength and fitness. 'It is a frustrating thought that thousands of players are not giving their best because they lack one quality which is well within their grasp,' he wrote.

Meanwhile, Piper recalls Allison's fearless attitude towards playing his young charges. 'He evaluated players tremendously well. When I made my debut at Ipswich I had been down as twelfth man but Nicky Jennings got sick the night before the game. Malcolm said to me on Saturday morning, "Norman, you are playing – at left-back." I had never played there before, but he knew I could do it. He knew I had a soccer brain and could play anywhere and he showed that he had confidence in me. Malcolm taught me a lot. He used to say, "Norman, you don't have to tackle to be successful." He taught me to always be aware of where you were when you received the ball. That is what I did. I used to be able to give up the ball as soon as I got it, play one-twos. He taught me that. His attitude on Saturday was to just go out there and play – what you have been taught will come through. He knew the game was all about doing simple things quickly.'

Newman remembers, 'Malcolm liked technically strong players and he liked players with a lot of character. He always used to talk about winning headers, which I think is one of the biggest disciplines in the game – you have got to be brave to go and win headers. He was always on about being brave and hard against the opposition. Although he was brought up at West Ham, who were always a technically good side, he still knew that the physical side of the game was very important.'

It was the young players like Piper and Trebilcock upon whom Allison concentrated his individual coaching efforts. 'We used to come in and train in the afternoons as well,' says Piper. 'It was fun coming to the training ground. If we ran we did it with a ball and at that time Malcolm was into weights. We used to do it twice a week to make the young players stronger, but when you got to 18 he cut it down because he didn't want us to become too bulky.'

Book adds, 'Malcolm loved finding young players – that was his forte. If a youngster showed something he would always give them a chance.'

At Leicester, Allison was unafraid of having all three rookie teenagers in the line-up for one of the biggest games in the club's history and was rewarded by a heroic performance. Johnny Williams put Argyle ahead after 35 minutes with a 25-yard shot but Leicester levelled with an own goal by Williams shortly before the hour. Trebilcock restored the lead when he pounced after a header had been blocked – another goal that he credits to Allison. 'He improved me 100 per cent and I saw the game in a different light. He taught me how to bend the ball and against Leicester the ball bounced right in front of me on the 12-yard spot. Gordon Banks was in goal, larger than life, so I just bent it up into the top left-hand corner. Gordon went up as far as he could and the ball went into the corner of the net. Malcolm taught me that.'

Leicester's Bobby Roberts equalised almost immediately and with four minutes left, Dave Gibson scored the home team's winner after referee Dick Windle allowed play to continue having appeared ready to blow for handball against Leicester. Newman recalls, 'The League Cup run was great fun and we had some super games. We were a couple of minutes away against Leicester and should have won up there. We were the better team for a long while but couldn't quite hold on. I can remember Malcolm getting on the coach and he was sick about the result because of how well the team had played.'

Having lost again at Leicester 5–0 in the FA Cup, Plymouth were unable to overturn the one-goal deficit in the second leg of their League Cup tie. The First Division side's methodical defence was too strong and their first-half goal was the only one of the game. 'I'm bitterly disappointed,' said Allison. 'We lacked experience but Leicester played well defensively.'

From defeat against Leicester, Argyle's season proceeded to fizzle out. Their League form had already been dipping and a 3–1 win at Middlesbrough was their first victory in nine games. The broken leg suffered by top scorer Lord just before the New Year hit them hard after he had scored 16 goals in 28 games. 'We just didn't have quite enough player-wise to finish it off,' says Newman. 'We didn't have the finance. You get yourself to a position where you think, "If we could just get a couple of players in now it would make a difference." Mal tried his hardest but it didn't quite come off.'

7

WHINES AND WOMEN

'John Bond has blackened my name with his insinuations about the private lives of football managers. Both my wives are upset'

– Malcolm Allison

Malcolm Allison had brought more excitement to Home Park than Plymouth Argyle fans had known for a number of years. But when his departure from the club was announced, it had become a sadly inevitable conclusion to a messy final few weeks of the season. As the team slipped towards their eventual position of 15th in Division Two, a series of confrontations with the club's directors – including the chairman's public criticism of team selection – appeared to make his position untenable. Less than a week after the final game of the campaign the club issued a statement that Allison had resigned. A decade later, Allison would write that he had been dismissed. Given the circumstances, it appears probable that he was given little choice but to go quietly.

I wasn't shocked – or really surprised. I had given my support to the chairman, and he was involved in constant, bickering battles with his boardroom colleagues. I became an issue. Some felt my style was too aggressive, too flamboyant for Plymouth. My arrogance offended some of them and I had started to get into trouble with the FA over my onslaught against referees. There was also the fact that I didn't exactly lead a monkish life.

Unknown to him at the time of his appointment, Allison had walked into the middle of a battle for power in the boardroom. The day after his memorable arrival at Home Park, a group of three directors – vice-chairman and majority shareholder Robert Daniel, supported by Douglas Fletcher and Stafford Williams – declared their intention to make £100,000 available to the team if they were left in control and if Ron Blindell, the man who had opposed Allison, stood down. The money was needed badly after a reported loss of almost £28,000 the previous season. Within a week, Blindell had ended his seven years in office and the new men in charge announced, 'When the manager wishes to buy there will be made available up to £100,000. He must build his team as he believes to be right and we in turn assure him of every support.'

This state of happy families lasted only a few weeks, until Fletcher and Williams resigned amid claims that Daniel had gone against their agreement by using a casting vote to elect himself as the new club chairman. Meanwhile, the Home Park Shareholders Association called for an independent board to be appointed and there were even the stirrings of a 'Bring Back Blindell' campaign.

Some sort of compromise was reached and it was all change again in January when Daniel handed over the chairmanship to Williams, a 57-year-old restaurant owner. Allison, who had developed a rapport with Daniel, threatened to resign when he heard of the change, although he subsequently withdrew the warning, saying, 'The board meeting and the arguments that followed are over and done with.'

By this time, however, the Argyle directors were getting frequent reminders of the personality they had installed in the manager's dugout, and it was Allison's actions in that particular location that were causing concern. In the home game against Manchester City in November, play had been stopped so that the referee could order Allison to desist in his coaching of his players from the sideline – an activity outlawed in those distant times before the manager's 'technical area'.

A few days later, the Football Association issued a reminder that coaching from the sideline was banned, adding that managers should sit in the stand if a seat was available. Allison's response was typically robust. 'If you have 20,000 people shouting and someone else shouts a bit louder what difference does it make? If I sat in the stand I would inconvenience other people. I sit in the trainers' box and inconvenience no one. I don't coach from the touchline. I can't coach unless I am ten yards from a player and that doesn't often happen in a match. I'm just an enthusiastic supporter.'

And the postscript that would land him in hot water was, 'I'm afraid that these amateurs who run professional football are way out with their ideas.'

It didn't take long for an FA letter to drop on Allison's doormat asking him to verify the accuracy of the comments attributed to him in the newspapers. He delighted in doing so. That produced a warning from the authorities about his future behaviour and a demand for a written undertaking not to repeat such misconduct. In the meantime, he continued to sit on the touchline, saying, 'I'm no troublemaker, but nobody tells me where to sit in my own ground. If the FA eventually rule that we must not be on the line I will have a special box built just back from it.'

The FA subsequently clarified their previous statement as having been a 'recommendation' as opposed to a 'directive' and Allison, given clearance to remain on the touchline, continued to make the most of it. Referee Rex Spittle reported Allison for an ungentlemanly remark after a game at Charlton, and in both legs of the League Cup semi-final against Leicester Malcolm had to be ordered to stop issuing instructions to his players.

It was clearly all becoming something of an embarrassment to the new chairman, for whom the final straw was Allison's ever-changing selection policy over the final few weeks of the season. Hampered by injuries, Allison chopped and changed the side. He confessed later that his 'first big tactical mistake' in football had been to try to reorganise the Argyle team to compensate for striker Frank Lord's absence instead of replacing him from the reserve team and maintaining continuity of playing style.

With the final week of the season approaching, Allison – much to his disgust – was ordered to explain his team selections to the board the day after a 3–0 defeat at Swansea. Particularly in question was his decision to persist with goalkeeper Noel Dwyer, bought from Swansea for £8,000 early in January. Allison announced eight team changes for a midweek game against Northampton, including the dropping of Dwyer. The match was won 5–2, but when Allison stated his intention to reinstate Dwyer for the last game against Bury, chairman Williams made public his criticism.

Williams claimed that Allison's constant team changes were driving away the crowds from Home Park. 'The fans won't buy programmes these days because they have to make too many alterations,' was his bizarre argument. 'Some questions are going to be asked at next Tuesday's board meeting. The directors are fed up with the manager's controversial team choices.' Williams pronounced himself baffled by the decision to drop goalkeeper John Leiper and happily boasted that it had been the directors' pressure that had led to him playing in the previous game. He also criticised the inclusion of Mike Trebilcock for the season finale. 'One thing is certain,' he concluded, 'the directors have not agreed with many of the manager's team selections, but we made a pledge to the public at the start of the season that we would not interfere. Now questions have to be asked.'

At the subsequent board meeting, the club's five directors spent two hours in discussion before summoning their manager. If they had expected him to stand meekly before them tugging his forelock, they knew even less about Allison than he felt they did about football. Dressed in his best suit and pulling on the biggest cigar he could find, he strode confidently into the kangaroo court to defend his methods. Although he retained the support of former chairman Daniel, it is impossible to imagine someone as self-assured as Allison looking with tolerance upon his inquisitors. 'I laughed at them,' he said later. It was no surprise, therefore, when Argyle fans read of their manager's 'resignation' on the front page of the local paper.

Once safely away from Plymouth, Allison would revise his public statement to declare unequivocally that he had been sacked by Argyle. But for now – presumably to safeguard any pay-off – he stuck to the agreed formula for his departure, although he didn't feel obliged to hold back in his criticism of the club. 'I must stick to my principles,' he said. 'If I am manager I want to manage. I am not prepared to be a yes-man for anyone. I have resigned. I have done my best. I tried to create something at Home Park.'

Williams merely added, 'We are not worried what the public think; they must draw their own conclusions.' The obvious conclusion being that having a more desirable character than Allison at the helm of their quiet seaside club was of greater importance to the directors than the possible success he could bring them.

Added to the football-related issues identified by the board, the question of Allison's lifestyle was never too far in the background. 'Some were scandalised that I wasn't always home by 10 o'clock,' Malcolm said of his employers. 'I was being dismissed for my independence, my indiscretions and my lifestyle.'

Plymouth players fondly recall Allison's determination to enjoy life to the full away from the training ground, but don't believe it ever undermined the professionalism of the team. 'Next day it was, "Right, I am the coach",' says Trebilcock. 'I remember once being out with him and we said, "How long have we got?" He answered, "Be at training at 10 o'clock in the morning."'

Norman Piper adds, 'Malcolm was flamboyant on and off the field but he knew that the players knew what to do before a game. He treated them like adults, like professionals. You respected a guy like that. He was flexible and that is why he was successful. If you looked after Malcolm, he looked after you and you wanted to play for someone like that.'

John Newman concludes, 'He was a socialiser, no doubt about that – nobody can deny that. He probably socialised with the players more than some managers would, but I didn't see that as a big fault.'

It was a surprise to his team, then, when the arguments with the board escalated into Allison's departure from Home Park. Newman concludes, 'We were obviously upset about it, we didn't have enough time with him. It needed three or four seasons with Malcolm to establish a pattern and build up a side, but there were always rumblings and I know his attitude and approach weren't always what the board wanted. I remember occasions when the players would say to me, because I was captain, "Go down and see the chairman because we think Malcolm is in trouble again." I remember telling Stafford Williams that the players were behind Malcolm. I said, "Whatever you are thinking about doing, keep him at the club." You can see how much influence I had. The feeling was that he could make you a better player. There were an awful lot of young players coming through in that team who became very good players because of Malcolm.'

One of those players, Trebilcock, admits, 'I can't imagine that I have admired any man more than Malcolm. He was father, teacher – everything to me. This guy came in and took us to another level of football that we had never seen before. It wasn't until Malcolm came along that we were taught how to play. I was 18 then and if I had been coached by him when I was 15, I could have played for England.'

Allison never made any attempt to disguise the importance that women held in his life. He was certainly convinced that they played a part in his departure from Plymouth, having, he admitted, been a regular feature of the social escapades to which the Argyle directors took exception. 'I found the women of Plymouth very aware of the opposite sex,' he said. 'Perhaps it was because of the town's naval background, but whatever the reason it was sometimes a hard job to keep from being entangled with some woman or another.'

Tall and broad-shouldered with a rough charm matched only by his love of the extravagant gesture, Malcolm was a magnetic figure. More than one reporter likened him to a Hollywood character in the mould of Dick Tracey or Sam Spade. Even the men could appreciate why women gravitated towards him. Tony Book recalls, 'He always had this swagger about him. He was a big, strong, good-looking fellow. In those days we had free-standing weights and once you had done your exercise he would just lift the weight off your shoulder and hand it to the next man. Easy as anything.'

Derek Ufton concurs with those comments, 'When I was playing cricket at Canterbury, Malcolm used to come down at the weekends and on warm summer days he would walk along the beach at Whitstable, looking like Tarzan in his leopard-skin trunks. He liked the thought that people noticed him.'

Trebilcock states, 'He was a playboy. He was a James Bond of our time. We just admired the man because he could do things that other people couldn't do. He could go out and mix with anyone.'

Journalist James Lawton, who would become a close friend and confidant of Malcolm's, adds, 'He was such a terrifically handsome man; the women just made a beeline for him. You were always aware of his charisma, particularly as it affected the opposite sex.'

And as Allison's features became as well known as they were striking, there would even be demand for him among the photographers of the day. Terry O'Neill, the renowned celebrity photographer, took Malcolm into the studio several times in the early '70s, snapping him in the latest lines of clothing or making the most of his physique by putting him in shirts open to the waist, fancy medallions to the fore.

He might not always have kept his shirt buttoned up while in Plymouth, but Malcolm did abstain from any serious alliances, largely because he was still getting over the break-up of an affair with a girl called Suzy. He had met her in his West End club and she had helped integrate him into the Mayfair set. Allison claimed that he had never been involved with a woman outside of his marriage until after his illness, and that it was Suzy who was the first. The truth of that statement probably depends on liberal interpretation of the world 'involved'. It was his refusal to take Suzy out to Canada with him that had caused the relationship to fade, although Malcolm confessed, 'It had been something new in my life and I was reluctant to let it go. It was a long time before I could forget her.'

In Plymouth, therefore, he had not sought a replacement, describing his year there as 'a period of evasive tactics' while hinting, 'Sometimes, after a few drinks, I might not be so evasive.'

However, it was by the Devon coast – shortly after his arrival – that he met a 16-year-old girl called Serena Williams. He casually asked her for a date as she walked past him at a dinner dance in the hotel in which he was staying and he ended up taking her out several times. Allison told her she was too bright and intelligent for such a town. She eventually moved to London to take a job as a bunny girl at the Playboy Club, which seems like a typical piece of career advice from Malcolm. The two would maintain casual contact and in 1972, she became the woman in his life.

Allison had married while at West Ham, at the age of 26 – four years earlier than the time frame he had originally set for himself. He would argue that it was his illness, and the restlessness that it introduced to his life, that prevented him leading a 'conventional married life' with his wife, Beth, whom he had met in a Bexleyheath dance hall.

The phrase 'long suffering' could have been conceived for Beth. Early in their marriage, it was football that was Malcolm's mistress. Later, according to one of Allison's former players, she was forced to 'turn a blind eye' to Malcolm's escapades, while an ex-West Ham colleague said, 'He was a womaniser. He had a beautiful wife, beautiful kids, but he still fancied the birds. That was his biggest downfall.'

Former Hammers teammate Eddie Lewis says, 'He had a lovely wife. Beth was a gorgeous-looking girl but I think he treated her badly. I felt he didn't give her a fair crack of the whip.'

It is a view expressed by other West Ham wives of that era in Brian Belton's book, *Days of Iron*. Jimmy Andrews's wife, Dot, said that 'he treated Beth like dirt', while the wife of Bert Hawkins, Katherine, said, '[Malcolm] was an awful man. He didn't get his wife a bit of clothing. He was out with all these women and she didn't have two ha'pennies to bless herself with.'

One of Malcolm's Bath City players, Ron Walker, recalls, 'Malcolm loved to socialise and I had one or two nights out drinking with him. Without going into it, you could say he was a ladies' man. When Malcolm got going us married people left him to it.' It was obviously easy for Allison to forget that he was supposed to have been one of 'us married people'.

The Allisons' marriage hardly got off to the most auspicious of starts. On the eve of the wedding, Malcolm gambled away £80 – all the money he had. He turned up at church with two shillings in his pocket and had to force Derek Ufton to pay up the £26 he owed him. He also managed to make an impact on the beginning of Bobby Moore's married life in 1962. Moore's bride, Tina, heard through her mother that Allison and his pal Noel Cantwell were due to be in Majorca at the same time as the Moores' honeymoon. Tina dreaded their arrival because she knew how easily they could lead her new husband astray. A week into their honeymoon, the duo arrived and promptly got Moore horribly drunk. He threw up and spent the night in Cantwell's room while a tearful Tina sought refuge with Noel's wife, Maggie.

Malcolm and Beth had four children – two boys, David and Mark, and two girls, Dawn and Michelle. Allison would admit that the eventual, inevitable, break-up of their marriage 'has everything to do with my nature, which is a bit wild'. His failure to be the conventional father figure was something with which he struggled, although when his children grew he felt confident that they understood that not all people are programmed for the same mode of behaviour. He wrote:

> I believe, for instance, that a man will ultimately do what is right for him. He will live in the best way he can. That may be selfish, but it is realistic. Perhaps all I can really say is that I have never lost my respect for a woman who has borne me fine children and proved an excellent wife.

While Malcolm chose his own lifestyle and rarely looked to excuse his wayward nature, it would be unfair to assume that he had an emotional shallowness that numbed him to the pain it could cause. Through working with him on numerous newspaper columns and on his 1975 autobiography, *Colours of My Life*, James Lawton was offered as much insight as anyone into Allison's emotional disarray. 'He felt badly about things with Beth, but it didn't work because they were different animals. Beth wanted a normal orthodox life. Malcolm loved his wife and he loved his family but he was drawn to a different kind of life. He used to convey to me the pain that you acquire if you get into these situations. I think he felt a bit guilty about not seeing so much of his children. But I remember once that Bill Friar, a reporter of the old school, was assigned with me to a piece about Malcolm. He and Bill were on different planets. Bill was chipping in with questions and he said, "Now, Malcolm, it is fair to say you are a family man." Malcolm looked at him with glazed eyes and said, "No, Bill, I love my family, but I don't think you could fairly describe me as a family man."'

Life on the racetracks and in the post-twilight world of the West End had offered Malcolm plenty of opportunity to indulge his weakness for women – a pattern that would continue wherever his career took him. Some of Allison's conquests were far from anonymous strangers passing in the night. The singer Dorothy Squires, the former wife of actor Roger Moore, was someone with whom Allison spent several nights, and in future years there were the inevitable beauty queens.

Having moved to Manchester, Malcolm embarked on an affair with a model called Jeanette. The relationship had been sparked by her initial rejection of his advances, which he admitted was 'a real challenge' and 'rather turned me on'. When he eventually got her to invite him back to her flat for coffee he discovered that she had not yet got round to buying a bed. Allison made his intentions known the next day by calling a furniture store and asking them to deliver, as a matter of urgency, the biggest one they had. They shared good times, mostly based around Allison's timetable, and Malcolm would leave tickets for her at Maine Road under the name of 'Lady B'.

A year later, Allison was approached at a party by Jennifer Lowe, a contestant in the forthcoming Miss United Kingdom contest, and asked if he would give her some fitness training. 'It was an offer that was difficult to refuse,' is Allison's wry explanation of his acceptance of the invitation. The two would spend long Thursday afternoons locked in the City gymnasium. While players nudged each other about what was going on behind the bolted doors, other members of the staff strained to peer through a fanlight opening. Allison ordered them away, telling them they were distracting him from what he described as 'a small, pleasant affair'.

He was soon embarking on a different kind of relationship with a Miss United Kingdom winner, Jennifer Gurley, with whom he admitted to nearly falling in love. The physical aspect that dominated most of Malcolm's relationships with women was missing, by mutual choice. Instead, she would visit the flat he had moved into after he and Beth decided to separate, and acted as housekeeper, tidying and cooking. Allison even suggested that if he had taken the job offered to him by Juventus in the summer of 1969 he would have asked her to live in Italy with him. His son, Mark, relates, 'I asked him once why he turned down the Juventus job and he said it was because he had a girlfriend back home, which was more important to him.'

Perhaps, the most notorious of Allison's lovers was Christine

Keeler, a former call girl who had made national headlines in 1963 by admitting having an affair with Defence Secretary John Profumo at the same time as she was sharing a bed with a Soviet military attaché – an act that, at the height of the Cold War, caused the kind of ripples Rebecca Loos would set in motion when claiming to have bedded David Beckham four decades later, by which time celebrity gossip had taken the place of political espionage in the public's imagination. Even without the reality TV circuit to sustain her public profile, Keeler was, according to Malcolm, 'a bit of a challenge to my ego'. He confessed that it was her notoriety that made her so attractive when she walked into the club in which he was drinking. When he took her to a restaurant on their first date, a waiter dropped a plate upon seeing her. 'I recall that we made love,' is Allison's understated description of the denouement of their liaison.

Other partners over the years included, according to Malcolm, the wife of a club director who doggedly wore him down with her advances and then boasted of it on the telephone to her husband while Allison was listening. Claiming to be no expert on women – finding their 'moods and thoughts elusive' – Malcolm was openly addicted to them, the more so as he got older, he confessed. At the same time, though, he strove to ensure that such exploits did not define him and that his image as a womaniser was kept in some sort of check. 'The impression may be of a Casanova-like series of bedroom romps,' he conceded. 'But it is a false one. I could never claim to be monkish, but the deceits, the elaborate, sneaky planning involved in a series of affairs has always struck me as absurd.'

Allison's year in Plymouth, then, appears to have been no more charged with sexual activity than any other of his ports of call – possibly even less so. Promiscuity was part of Malcolm's well-established lifestyle and always would be. The delicate souls of Home Park would not be the last ones to take umbrage at Allison's antics, but their sensitivity was about to propel him towards the most professionally successful period of his life.

8

MADE IN MANCHESTER

'Your father's got a 20-year start, but I'll pass him in three'
— Malcolm Allison speaking to the son
of Manchester United manager Matt Busby

By the spring of 1965, Manchester City, relegated from the First Division two years earlier, had apparently decided there was no tearing hurry for them to force their way back. Their fans, however, felt compelled by a greater sense of urgency, to the point where some were prepared to throw house bricks through windows. Others had simply accepted the situation and turned their backs on the club. Three days after a third-round FA Cup defeat at Division Three Shrewsbury, City's lowest-ever crowd for a home League match had been recorded when 8,015 rattled around Maine Road for the visit of Swindon.

Mike Summerbee, a man who would become accustomed to hearing 40,000 voices bouncing his name around the same ground, ran out on that occasion in the visitors' colours. 'I could not believe it when I gazed around at those empty terraces,' he recalled. 'The entire scoreboard end of the ground was deserted.'

The game, in which Summerbee contributed a goal towards Swindon's 2–1 victory, prompted demonstrations among those who had bothered to drag themselves along. Nine years earlier, City fans had been celebrating FA Cup victory; now they were hurling missiles at the windows of the club offices. The fact that Manchester neighbours United, with a boy wonder called George Best, were on their way to winning the League title while City were stumbling towards an 11th-place finish in the Second Division only made things more unbearable.

Why was it, City fans pondered gloomily, that they were condemned to live in the shadow cast by Old Trafford? Even when they enjoyed that Wembley victory in 1956, United had gone one better by winning the League. Far from turning the tables when United won the FA Cup in 1963, City's response had been to get themselves relegated. Now, while United were dreaming of Madrid and Milan in the European Cup, City couldn't even look forward to being beaten again at Northampton Town. The Cobblers had passed them on their way up to the First Division.

Into such an environment stepped a new manager, Joe Mercer – a man who only a year earlier had been forced to quit football after becoming ill under the strain of trying to turn around another sleeping giant, Aston Villa. The City job, which became vacant when George Poyser was sacked at the end of the season, was hardly what the doctor ordered. It was certainly against the wishes of Mercer's wife, Norah.

Mercer's playing career had straddled the war, bringing him five England caps at wing-half. After playing in the powerful Everton team of the 1930s, a knee injury threatened to force him out of the game. But Arsenal gambled £7,000 that there were still a few miles left in his famously crooked 31-year-old legs and were rewarded by seeing him lead them to a pair of League Championships and an FA Cup victory.

Finally forced to retire in 1954 after suffering a broken leg, Mercer attended coaching courses at Lilleshall. In August 1955 he accepted his first managerial position, taking over at Sheffield United following the death of incumbent Reg Freeman. An unhappy first season, during which he suffered interference from the club's 15-man board, saw the team finish bottom of the First Division. In a statement that would have significance later in his career and with which Malcolm Allison would heartily agree, he said, 'Divided boards are no good to any club. It spells ruin in the long run.'

Linked to Arsenal's vacant managerial position in the summer of 1958, Mercer stayed at Bramall Lane – only to move months later to

Aston Villa when they sacked manager Eric Houghton after a poor start to the season. Although Mercer led Villa to the semi-finals of the FA Cup, they were condemned to relegation on the final day of the season.

Mercer guided Villa back into the First Division at the first attempt, reaching another semi-final along the way. His young team, tagged 'Mercer's Minors' by the media, finished ninth in their first season back in Division One and lifted the inaugural League Cup, beating Rotherham over two legs in the final. Progress halted, however, and in 1962–63 it needed a late rally to avoid another relegation. It was Villa's victory over Manchester City that sent down the Maine Road team.

The struggles at Villa Park had started affecting Mercer's health. In December 1963, with the club in the midst of another disappointing season, his five-year contract expired and, Villa having won only eight of 25 League games, there was speculation that Mercer would not be offered a new deal. Almost immediately, Villa were knocked out of the FA Cup by Fourth Division Aldershot. Abuse from fans grew to the point where he had rubbish thrown at him during games.

In May 1964, Mercer, whose workload had increased when he agreed to help with the England Under-23s, suffered pins and needles in his legs while draining water from his car radiator. The symptoms were diagnosed as a minor stroke: a result of stress and exhaustion. Doctors told his wife not to let him come downstairs, as the mere effort of it could kill him. But after a few weeks away from work he returned to the club, still a long way from full health. His welcome-back present from the board was the sack, the directors having decided during his illness that he was not the man they wanted in charge. He said later, 'I felt like a farmer who has ploughed his field, sown his crop, kept it free from weeds, watched it develop and then, when just about to harvest, is evicted to find another farm.'

Mercer's achievements with Villa were remembered, however, when Manchester City chairman Albert Alexander and his board went looking for a new manager a year later. Having thought that the game had written him off because of his illness, Mercer found the offer irresistible, saying, 'Life was a void without the company of players.' Yet the memory of being struck down was still vivid enough for him to approach his interview with an air of realism. 'I could no longer afford to be a loner,' he said. 'I needed to be fit and I wanted a lieutenant.'

Meanwhile, Malcolm Allison had been 'less than shattered' by his sacking from Plymouth. He was confident that his achievements were being noticed and his methods proving effective. Shortly after his departure from Home Park, Amsterdam club Blauw Wit made 'a generous offer' for him to take charge of their team, while Raich Carter, manager of Middlesbrough, enquired about Allison becoming his coach at Ayresome Park.

Allison, who had impressed Carter during coaching courses at Lilleshall, recalled having made the arrangements to travel to Middlesbrough when he phoned Mercer to congratulate him on his appointment at Manchester City – at which point Mercer suggested that Malcolm stop in on his way to Teesside. Mercer remembered it slightly differently, saying that it took him two days to track down the man he had earmarked as his number two. Either way, Allison admitted, 'I sensed I would never complete my journey to Middlesbrough.'

Mercer and Allison had also first met at Lilleshall, more than a decade earlier. Finding Allison attempting to learn to curve the ball, Mercer told him, 'You want to try kicking it straight first!' At their latest meeting, Allison told Mercer that he would happily accompany him to Maine Road. Not only was he keen to work with the cheerful character the football world would come to know as 'Uncle Joe', but he was excited about joining a club with which he had felt empathy since an early age. Mercer, for his part, knew that Allison was an 'extrovert, ebullient character', but was happy to live with the moods and outbursts of the younger man as his own form of health insurance.

There remained the formality of an interview with the club directors, at which Allison was struck by the advanced age of most of the board members. When it came to discussing a contract, Allison cut through the negotiating and posturing by announcing, 'Look, gentlemen, you don't know me and I don't know you. I'll work for you until Christmas for £30 a week, then we will have another talk,' – a discussion that subsequently earned him an extra £10. The pieces for a remarkable period of football history were in place and seven days after the appointment of their new manager, City introduced Allison as first-team coach.

As much as he'd had fun out in the sticks of Bath and Plymouth, Allison was made for big city life. If he couldn't be indulging in the excesses of the '60s in his favourite West End nightclubs, then Manchester was a good place to be. London, with its beautiful people posing for the tourists in Carnaby Street, might have provided the heartbeat of England's swinging decade, but the north-west cities of Liverpool and Manchester were the lungs of the nation. While the Beatles presented Liverpool to the world and a whole musical movement followed in their wake, Granada Television offered a slice of Manchester verité to the rest of the country with the birth of *Coronation Street*. As a counterpoint to the gritty reality of Len Fairclough and Elsie Tanner there was the glamour of George Best, while a thriving theatre and arts scene established the cultural credentials of the city. And as Mal was quick to discover, the nightlife wasn't bad either.

At Maine Road, City's historic home in the densely populated Moss Side district in south Manchester, Mercer and Allison inherited a first-team squad of 21 players, many of them young and untried. In the subsequent first edition of the *Manchester City Football Book*, Allison recorded the steps he took to impress himself upon his new charges.

There were players on the staff who possessed lots of qualities and skills that had not been brought out; there were others, just one or two, who were well past their best. I was a new face to them. A complete stranger with a bit of a reputation. So naturally some of them were slightly suspicious of the newcomer. But I pulled the first trick. Before my first day's training, I obtained pictures of all the players and memorised them so that the following day I would know each one individually.

It was a bit of a shock to some who were trying to hide away when I called them out by name and they were all soon made to toe the line. They thought it ridiculous I should know them so personally at such an early stage, but previously they had had no one who had been so direct with them.

Given the lack of experience in the squad, it was to the accompaniment of raised eyebrows that former England centre-forward Derek Kevan, the previous season's top scorer but now recovering from a knee injury, was shipped off to Crystal Palace. Allison, however, had devised training routines specifically designed to probe Kevan's willingness to make testing runs and pointed out to Mercer his apparent unwillingness to do so. It was an early sign of the influence that Allison would wield within the partnership when it came to personnel and tactics. Mercer was clearly happy to let such responsibility rest with his assistant, viewing his own priority as the creation of an environment in which the talents of those around him had the best opportunity to blend and flourish.

He freely admitted that 'Malcolm is in touch with the players and is closer to them than I am', adding, 'It's not that the game passes you by as much as it becomes more of an effort to keep in touch with it.' He would explain, 'I saw my role of manager as making things easy for Malcolm, smoothing the way for him and helping him along.' Whenever Allison went to his boss with a new idea for the training ground, Mercer would smile like an indulgent parent and say, 'Yeah, OK, Malcolm. You do it.'

Sometimes Allison's theories and ideas – formations, training exercises and personnel moves – would come to him as thick and fast as flies buzzing in front of his face. He'd briefly swat at one and then move on to the next, while many were simply forgotten or ignored completely. One of his more bizarre notions crops up several times during players' recollections of his tactical experimentations over the years: the wheel. That revolved, literally, around the notion of keeping possession of the ball within a ten-man circle of players that gradually rotated its way towards goal before the circle broke and someone took a shot. Allison appears to have toyed with that one for several years without ever working out a way of converting theory into practice.

Journalist Jeff Powell even remembers it being the topic of conversation during a night out at Tramps nightclub with Bobby Moore and George Best, by which time Malcolm was calling it the 'O system'. 'He had this system where all the midfield players, and even the guys from the front, would join in and would circulate and leave this hole in the middle of midfield. Bobby said, "Yes, but if the opposition puts a guy in the middle of that hole then he can run the game." Malcolm tried it in a game a few weeks later and got slaughtered so when Bobby saw him again he couldn't resist asking, "Are we going to see it again?"'

City's squad members had never experienced a coach with such direction and drive, but Allison's early impression was that their confidence had been completely eroded. Wing-half Alan Oakes, for example, was one of the best of a group of players developed at the club, but would break into a nervous sweat before games. It meant that some bullying and pushing was required. For the quieter players – men like Glyn Pardoe – it took some time to get used to a physically imposing coach, dressed to impress in a bright red tracksuit, bellowing and barking at them. Allison's strength, though, was his ability to persuade them that, however flash and fancy they might think him, he had a genuine interest in them as individuals. He sensed the growth of their belief in him and themselves.

As a player whose career had been snatched away from him, he was able to transmit his passion to his players, as Summerbee testifies. 'In a sense, his life had been cut short and his ambition to be the best was channelled through us. His enthusiasm spread throughout the team and we loved him. He had a belief in himself, in what he was doing, and he got the response he wanted. The only people who didn't like him were the players' wives. They felt like we were having an affair with him, we thought so much of him.'

Midfield player Mike Doyle, another player who had grown up at Maine Road, immediately sensed a new purpose about the place, a belief that the club was about to take off. In his book, *Manchester City: My Team*, he explained:

Malcolm was the man who did most to create this impression, for he worked and almost lived with the players and he introduced new ideas into our training sessions – in fact, for the first time in my experience, I really began to know what good coaching was all about, and what a difference it could make to a team and their game. From the moment we walked through the doors on the Monday morning we were planning how to beat the opposition the following Saturday. Big Mal had ideas which revitalised our training routines and he was very definitely the man in charge of things out on the park. The only time we saw Joe, basically, was when he came in to give us our team talk before a game.

Protective of Mercer's memory, Colin Bell, a first-season signing by Mercer and Allison, recalls the manager's contribution a little differently. 'We would see Joe at the start of every day and if there was one person Malcolm would listen to it was Joe. He let him do his own thing most of the time but if Malcolm went off the straight and narrow, Joe was there. It was a father–son combination. Joe would get up and say a few words before matches then Malcolm would take over on the tactics and formation.'

On occasions, though, those talks from Mercer could be a source of some amusement. Typically, his pre-season introduction would be little more than a wistful look at the lush grass and a reminder to the players what a 'lucky load of bastards' they were. Before games, his notes would often be scribbled on a newspaper and there was one occasion when he spent Friday lunchtime warning of the dangers of Leicester's forwards, forgetting that the next day's opponents were Wolves. But Summerbee points out, 'The boss was always there and he was the figurehead. He was one of the icons of the game at that time, like Matt Busby and Bill Nicholson, and when we got off the team bus at away games it was always Joe that fans wanted to see first.'

Allison recalled Mercer coming to the ground 'after playing golf' and running through a check-list of things that he felt Allison should have done. The answer to virtually every question was positive. 'But then he would come up with a little thing and I'd say, "No, I haven't done that." Those tiny things make a good team.'

The first new face added to the City squad by the managerial team was Rangers forward Ralph Brand, signed for £25,000. Those fans who had been suspicious of Kevan's departure, gained little reassurance from Brand, who would score only two goals in two years and who Allison felt gave the ball away too much. The second player brought in by the new management team, however, proved far more influential. Mike Summerbee had first attracted Mercer's attention at Villa and with his Swindon team having been relegated to Division Three, he called the new City manager to express his interest in joining him. Packing in his summer job as a deckchair attendant, he signed in time for the season kick-off for a £35,000 fee – an acquisition Allison later called 'a master stroke'.

Summerbee explains, 'I had a bit of a rude awakening. I signed on the Thursday before the season and thought I was very fit. I was slim and I had done a full pre-season at Swindon. Malcolm took me out to the pitch and had me working for 45 minutes. It was an eye-opener compared to what I was used to doing at Swindon, where we did old-fashioned laps. I realised I wasn't as fit as I thought, but it was great fun working with Malcolm.'

As well as preparing City for the Second Division campaign, Allison had been quickly developing a chip on his shoulder about the status enjoyed by their neighbours at Old Trafford. 'One of the biggest fallacies in football suggests that Manchester United are an attacking team,' he argued. 'They never have been, or at least not for the last ten years. United rarely have more than two or three forwards up.'

Proving that strong anti-United resentment is not just a product of the Premier League age, he admitted that he 'loathed the bumptious, patronising tones of some of their players, their hangers-on and many of their supporters'. Allison saw United as a self-satisfied club with an over-inflated sense of importance, and hated seeing more boys in red shirts than blue kicking balls around in the local parks and streets.

Ian Niven, a lifelong City fan who, in the early 1970s, would begin a 30-year stint on the board of his beloved club, recalls, 'Out of 200 people in the office where I worked, I could only find half a dozen City supporters. It shows how we had lost out to the club across the road.'

Allison remarked years later, 'One problem [in Manchester] was David and my other kids. They would say that if we didn't beat United in the derby matches they wouldn't go to school. Their education was in good hands – in seven years we only lost twice to them!'

Only a few days after arriving in town, Allison was invited to United's League Championship celebration dinner, where playing the gracious guest proved beyond him. Matt Busby recognised him during his speech, saying, 'We welcome an outstanding young coach to town because we think he will give us some strong competition.' Instead of smiling politely, Allison responded, 'You can bet on that, Matt baby,' and then told anyone who would listen, including Busby's son Sandy, that their club's days of dominance were numbered. In later years he would endear himself to Old Trafford fans by strolling in front of the Stretford End fans before the game, holding up five fingers to indicate his predicted scoreline and making gestures as if brushing United aside like pieces of dirt.

It had not taken Allison long to demonstrate that he was going to be 'good copy' for the city's journalists, although James Lawton, then a young reporter on the Manchester edition of the *Daily Express*, remembers that Malcolm's trust had to be earned. 'He was pretty user friendly and he liked the publicity, but he had his favourites. He had a particular respect for Ron Crowther of the *Daily Mail*. I always used to get a bit restive if Ron was at a press conference because he was a good old-style reporter who would ask pretty good questions and Malcolm respected him. It stuck in my mind that Malcolm was not just there to cultivate anybody who would write any crap.'

Allison was also very clearly of the old school of football personality who, in the days before tabloid muck-raking became more prevalent, would socialise comfortably alongside members of the media. Lawton continues, 'It was obvious that Malcolm had a very sharp intelligence and was lively company. Stockport County used to be run by a guy called Victor Bernard and their Friday night games were a bit of a social occasion. People such as Pat Phoenix of *Coronation Street* used to go there and it was a bit of an institution in football terms in Manchester. Paul Doherty of Granada TV was there with Malcolm one night and they were obviously going out on the town, but Bernard was telling them how Stockport were going to get promoted, how they would get into the Second Division, then the First, and do it in a certain way. He was going on a bit and Malcolm turned to Paul and said, "I think we'd better fuck off before he wins the European Cup."'

City's first League game of the new season was at Middlesbrough and it was on the way to Ayresome Park that Mercer made a comment that would later be the cause of great friction between the two men.

As they sat side by side on the team coach, Mercer said to Allison, 'Son, if you do well with City there will be great rewards. Two years will do me.'

It was with those words ringing in his ears and the promise they held pulsing through his veins that Allison delivered his final pre-game reminders. While City would become known as a swaggering, swashbuckling team under his guidance, the romantic was still at this stage balanced by the pragmatist. Allison knew he had to produce a team that was tough to beat and he handed a man-marking role to midfielder David Connor, whose toughness and stamina had impressed him in training. His effectiveness in shutting down Ian Gibson, Middlesbrough's primary source of creation, played a large part in City forcing a 1–1 draw.

The game, and its aftermath, offered Summerbee a clear view of the excitement that could lie ahead under Allison. 'Although I was outside-right at Swindon, I almost played like a wing-back. I played deep because we were struggling. That first game at Middlesbrough was nerve-racking because City was a massive club even though they were in the Second Division. I played in my normal position, very deep, and I didn't do badly. I went down the line and crossed in for us to score and Malcolm said, "Well done," as I came off. I felt pleased, but on the bus to go home he came and sat next to me. He said, "Listen. If I had wanted a full-back I would have signed one. You attack people all the time. Don't come back and defend."'

Allison urged Summerbee, as he did all his wingers, to push the ball a good ten yards past the full-back, giving himself the opportunity to reach top speed before having to check to play the ball again. 'In our first home game against Portsmouth I was up against Ron Tindall, who was an ex-centre-forward but was playing left-back and had good positional sense. At half-time Malcolm said, "All I want you to do is push the ball past him and run." I kept doing that. Sometimes he'd take the ball off me, sometimes I would win a corner. With five minutes left I went straight past him, crossed and we scored. Malcolm said, "That is the best game of football you'll play. That's all I need you to do."'

City proceeded to remain unbeaten in eight games, a significant step in ridding the club of the stench of failure that made Allison recoil upon his arrival. He had described Maine Road – built in the 1920s as the second-largest stadium in the country – as a 'mausoleum'. Such had been the depression around the place that, before their first few home games, either Allison or Mercer would walk down the tunnel prior to kick-off to check how many had bothered to take their place in the stands. Yet it took only until the sixth home game, against Norwich, for the attendance to reach 34,000, allowing Allison to collect on a £10 bet he'd made with United player Pat Crerand, who had claimed that City would never attract 30,000. What made it even more meaningful was that it was a bigger crowd than at United's most recent home game against Fulham. The jokes that had been circulating about Stockport County being Manchester's second team were being laid to rest.

Such achievements were quickly winning over those who had been somewhat sceptical upon initial sightings of Allison prowling the Maine Road touchline. Ian Niven says, 'I remember the first time I saw Malcolm. I was in the stand and there was this tall fellow on the touchline in a Cossack hat. He always had to have something a little bit different – either a hat or a long scarf twice the length of what it should have been. I thought, "Christ, we have got another maniac here. Who is this fellow?" In those days coaches and trainers sat in the dugout and rarely ventured out.'

In the dressing-room, Allison had found the ideal conduit for his enthusiasm and passion in the Northern Ireland inside-forward Johnny Crossan, bought the previous season from Sunderland and now appointed captain. The line-up was further bolstered by the signing of George Heslop from Everton, a £25,000 solution to the long-standing problem at centre-half, and midfielder Stan Horne, who had played under Mercer at Villa.

Meanwhile, Pardoe, a former youth-teamer, was defying Allison's first thought of him as 'a bit of a dumpling' and Neil Young was getting over a 'timid approach' to emerge as a skilful striker. Allison himself was instigating some thoughtful changes to the team's shape, moving Young inside from his position on the wing and recognising that Doyle's ability in the air and Pardoe's versatility made them ideal candidates to interchange their respective positions of right-half and centre-forward. By the end of October, City were leading the

Second Division and on the first day of 1966 a crowd of 47,000 saw them play a top-of-the-table battle against Huddersfield. Crossan's disputed penalty and a second-half goal by Doyle settled a bad-tempered game in which the famous snout of Summerbee was broken in two places.

Such success meant that Mercer's role as a diplomat was regularly called upon to temper the boasting of Allison. As soon as he had arrived at City, Allison had been telling the media that City would win the Division Two title. 'I used to say things like that off the top of my head, but I was always a confident person.' It was hard for anyone to be unimpressed, though, when City beat Leicester – twice finalists in the four previous seasons – in the fifth round of the FA Cup. After almost 57,000 had seen City fight back from two down to draw at Maine Road, Young scored the only goal of the replay. Allison felt sure that his team would make their mark in the city's newspapers with this result, but it was his luck that the same night would see the birth of a football phenomenon. Facing a difficult second leg in Portugal in the quarter-finals of the European Cup, United were inspired to a magnificent 5–1 victory over Benfica by the stunning individual performance of Best. 'El Beatle' was born and George became 'Georgie' – the first football star to truly cross over to everyday celebrity status. City were relegated to the inside pages. Once more, and not for the last time, fate had conspired to deny Allison and his team the full recognition of their achievement.

Eventual Cup winners Everton ended City's run in the quarter-finals before a Maine Road crowd of more than 63,000 and Mercer and Allison were left to concentrate on getting across the line in the promotion race. In search of new players to provide some late-season impetus, they cast their eye on Wyn Davies, Bolton's Welsh centre-forward, and Colin Bell, a strong and talented midfielder at Bury. Their different approach to such matters reflected their partnership as a whole, with Mercer looking cautiously at the quoted price and Allison urging a buy-at-any-cost strategy if it meant getting the right player.

Mercer and the City directors fretted anxiously about whether to stump up the £45,000 being asked by Bury, leaving Allison the task of making sure that First Division clubs were kept at bay. He made it his personal mission to track Bell as much as possible, sitting close to other scouts and managers in the stands and bellowing out how one-footed the youngster was and that he couldn't head the ball. Whether or not it fooled anyone, Bell remained available until City had scraped together the necessary cash, signing him on the eve of the transfer deadline in spite of a rival bid from Blackpool.

Mercer remained unimpressed on first sight of Bell, an unimposing, nervous 20 year old. When Bell scored on his debut against Derby, a lucky deflection, Mercer was still saying out loud in the stand, 'What have I done?' and asking his assistant, 'How did we pay £45,000 for that player? He's hopeless.' Bell, however, played a vital part in the season. According to Allison, it was his energy and drive that pushed them through the latter weeks as elevation to the top flight was clinched with victory at Rotherham and the Second Division title won with a 3–2 victory at Charlton.

Despite achieving promotion within a season of his arrival at Maine Road, it would be wrong to assume that Allison had got along famously with everyone and that the new regime was universally welcomed. For every player introduced to the team, there was, of course, one who had been cast aside. Some inevitably retain feelings of bitterness about their fate, in the same way that those who thrived have few negative memories. In his book, *George Best and 21 Others*, author Colin Shindler spoke to former members of the Manchester City youth team who had been deemed surplus to requirements by Allison.

Phil Burrows, a wing-half who failed to break into the City side, felt that Allison could have shown more interest in the reserves. Instead of dispatching them to play a game in the car park, he believes they should have been nurtured, given at least a small piece of the confidence-boosting attention that Allison happily lavished on his first-teamers. And centre-half Alf Wood believed he had been instantly disregarded by the new coach because he was not part of Allison's social circle.

Meanwhile, Allison's triumph, as so often in his career, had been tempered by disappointment – and the kind of insult he had felt when West Ham went ahead with their Division Two celebrations without granting him a medal. Chairman Albert Alexander informed him that Mercer was receiving a £600 bonus, while Allison and secretary Walter Griffith were to be awarded £400 each. 'Yes, I thought the secretary did very well,' Malcolm sneered. 'He booked us into some nice hotels.' Finding himself, as so often, in financial difficulty, he eventually convinced the directors to pay off his £600 overdraft.

The summer of 1966 belonged to Alf Ramsey's England team. But while the nation rejoiced in victory over West Germany in the World Cup final, Malcolm Allison – who had taken the opportunity to observe the methods of the Portuguese team at their training base in Manchester – would learn to look back on the most famous day in the country's sporting history with mixed feelings. As much as he took pride in the assured manner in which his protégé Bobby Moore led England to victory, he would come to believe that Ramsey's unimaginative tactics became a millstone around the neck of the English game. Allison claimed disdainfully that Ramsey had 'elevated power beyond skill' and was to be a frequent critic of his methods and teams in the later years of his reign as national team manager.

For now, with City preparing for life in the First Division, Allison's concerns were more parochial. He saw the coming season as one of consolidation and his first priority, as 12 months earlier, was to ensure that his team was built on strong foundations. He needed someone who could support the experienced Heslop in marshalling a defence that included the promising trio of Pardoe, Oakes and Doyle.

Allison's search had led him to an inescapable conclusion. He told Mercer, 'I've been to watch four top full-backs and there is a player playing at Plymouth who is better than all of them, Tony Book.' Mercer listened and, without responding, went off to make some calls to his contacts. The following day he pointed out to Allison that Book was 31. It was not much of an argument from a man who had been even older when he began his successful stint as Arsenal captain. Besides, Allison knew Book still had enough pace to beat men ten years his junior – a quality upon which he placed a great premium. Allison, who observed many coaches leaving defensive duties to the slowest members of the team, argued, 'It is a mistake to put all the speed up front and the slowest at the back.' Mercer was persuaded to give Book his chance and settled on a fee of £17,000 with Argyle.

After City drew their opening match at Southampton, First Division football returned to Maine Road with the visit of champions Liverpool, who were beaten 2–1 by goals from Jimmy Murray and Bell. Victory over Sunderland made it a highly satisfactory five points from three games, before a sequence of one point from five matches brought them back to earth. The manner of City's 1–0 loss across town at United disturbed Allison, who sensed that his players had been in awe of their opponents, an emotion of which he had been trying to rid the club ever since his arrival in Manchester. 'That game made me determined from then on that my team would not be afraid of anybody. The players didn't want to go on the pitch before the game. I went mad at them afterwards, calling them "a load of fucking cowards".'

Allison chose to combat the bad results by reprising his old Plymouth ploy of utilising Book as a sweeper. Despite victory over Blackpool, it wasn't quite an overnight success and City's harshest lesson in the realities of Division One was delivered by Tommy Docherty's Chelsea team. 'Docherty's Diamonds' – as they were known according to the prevailing custom of giving any semi-successful team an alliterative nickname in honour of the manager – made light of the problem posed by an extra defender in running out 4–1 winners at Maine Road. BBC commentator Kenneth Wolstenholme struggled a little more with what he described as City's 'rather strange format', continually referring to Book's position as 'sweeper-up' and marvelling that the home team could have the impudence to play Pardoe at right-back when he was wearing the number 9 shirt.

A bad result such as that against Chelsea would leave Allison in a quiet, brooding mood. Despite the outburst in the Old Trafford dressing-room, Bell recalls, 'Malcolm would never say much after a bad game. Maybe one or two things to a couple of people but basically he would leave it. He'd let the dust settle and address it on Monday. Individually, you knew if you'd had a bad game. Everyone gave 100 per cent, but in a team of 11 there could be two or three off the ball. We are individuals, not machines – and you could have flu or family problems.'

Preservation of their newly won First Division status now became City's priority. But as much as Allison recognised the importance of not being soft touches in the First Division, he still had too much of the idealist in him to go as far down the road of physical, aggressive play as Mercer was urging. Allison sensed that Mercer was still snake-bitten by the relegations he had suffered at Sheffield United and Aston Villa and was all for playing a power-based game. He also saw him being influenced too much by the style with which Don Revie had taken Leeds from a lowly position in Division Two to the elite of the top flight, and the manner of England's World Cup victory. Allison reminded his boss of his own instincts for 'good, cultured football' and once again Mercer relented, his confidence in Allison's wisdom growing all the time.

A top-class goalkeeper was considered a priority and when Gordon Banks became available from Leicester, who were keen to push Peter Shilton as their keeper of the future, Allison was all for making a bold move. 'They were letting him go for £50,000. Now, Joe was a bricklayer's son and money was always an important factor to him, whereas to me it meant nothing at all.'

Allison's typically blunt instruction to his boss was, 'Ring up Leicester and tell them we'll buy Gordon Banks for the £50,000.' But when Mercer reported back, Allison was exasperated to hear Joe tell him, 'I've bid £40,000.'

Allison lamented, 'He always wanted to do a deal! He couldn't do anything straight forward, he always wanted to haggle. In the end Banks went to Stoke for the £50,000.'

Good results began to be sprinkled among the traditional travails of a newly promoted team, although a few weeks without a win either side of New Year meant that City were still stuck in 19th position with 25 games played. The FA Cup not only proved a catalyst for an upturn in the team's fortunes but proved Allison's instincts correct and gave a hint of what could be achieved by this City team. Following a 2–1 third-round win against Leicester, City remained unbeaten in their next five League games and would eventually climb to the safety of fifteenth place after losing only four of the last seventeen matches. Cardiff and Ipswich were both removed from the Cup in replays, setting up a quarter-final tie at

Leeds, who were involved in their annual unsuccessful quest for a League and Cup double.

Having achieved a 0–0 draw at Elland Road in the League three weeks earlier, Allison predicted that Leeds manager Don Revie would be expecting his team to stick to the methods that had served them so well – with Book at sweeper and Connor as a midfield marker. Allison knew that few managers prepared their teams as thoroughly as Revie, who would have studied that game, thought deeply about it and probably come up with a trick or two to counter City's tactics. Allison's thought process amounted to, 'Bollocks. Let's go out and attack them.'

City lined up with what Sky's Andy Gray – even though he was still in shorts at the time – could have explained to Kenneth Wolstenholme was a flat back four. 'Leeds were really rocked back on their heels as we hit them with everything we had,' Book recounts. Had Bell been sharper with a couple of good chances that came his way, it could have been City who advanced to the semi-finals. Instead, Leeds scrambled through courtesy of their trademark tactic of having long-legged centre-half Jack Charlton clamber all over goalkeeper Harry Dowd to head in a second-half corner.

By common consent, this was the day that City's golden era was born. With the team's First Division status consolidated, Allison and Mercer had now seen what could be attained if they let the players off the leash. 'City were brilliant that day,' said Mercer. 'We had found ourselves. We were on our way, we started to stretch defences. Fear was scoffed at!'

Allison stuck with the system for the rest of the season, with Book recalling, 'The outcome was that we won many more matches than we lost and hoisted ourselves into a position of respectability. Next season we came out attacking from the start.' The man who would soon be skipper of the team, adds, 'We'd played the sweeper a few times, but with the players we had there I don't think it really suited us. We were better going forward.'

Meanwhile, Allison's reputation as a football intellectual and innovator was growing. His peers were to find out more about his philosophies and methods at Lilleshall, where Allison was regularly asked to be one of the FA's course instructors. Soon to establish a reputation himself as one of the country's finest coaches, former England full-back Don Howe was a regular attendee while on the staff at Arsenal. Howe comments, 'People like Malcolm and Dave Sexton were the ones we looked at most closely on those courses. Every club sent at least one person – even Bill Shankly used to come – and Malcolm showed us what we should be working at. Malcolm loved to be inventive and be the first to try things. He had great football knowledge, could make sessions interesting and had a terrific sense of humour.'

Howe recalled one hot summer's day when Allison suddenly left Allen Wade, the FA's director of coaching, in charge of his group while he disappeared over a fence onto the neighbouring golf course. 'We were working on dead ball kicks or something and wondering where he had gone when he came back – without saying anything. All of a sudden two blokes from the course came walking across our pitch with two trays holding about 20 pints of beer, one for everybody. We were all clapping and drinking our beer when Malcolm turned to Allen and said, "I've got no money – you'll have to pay."'

During one of the courses several years later, the joke would be on Malcolm when he became a victim of the 'fake sheikh' trick – more than three decades before Sven-Göran Eriksson. Howe explains, 'There had been a lot of speculation about Malcolm being offered a job in the Middle East so one day one of the lads on the course dressed up in Arab gear with a big turban and another posed as his wife by completely covering his face. We all knew about it so when they came walking across the pitch and said, "I would like to speak with Mr Allison," we were saying things like, "Malcolm, here are your people from the Middle East." So Malcolm is strutting around looking pleased with himself, but in the end we just had to burst out laughing. Malcolm, for once, didn't quite know what to say.'

Malcolm had plenty to say for himself, however, as he completed work with journalist Gerry Harrison on his book *Soccer For Thinkers*, published that year. The book, offering an intriguing insight into Allison's tactical brain, is a textbook for coaches, instructing them how to get their best out of their players, rather than an instruction manual for the players themselves. Theories, suggested training drills and opinions abound in a publication that still retains a high place in the regard of modern coaches.

Interviewed when appointed Nottingham Forest manager in 2005, Frank Barlow cited Allison's book when asked if any particular publication had helped him during three decades in coaching. 'I had to get it when it was out of print,' he said. 'It's not really a coaching book . . . I'm recommending it as a read. I think he was way ahead of his time.'

No one unfamiliar with English football before the early '70s would believe that *Soccer for Thinkers* had been written by the man they knew as Big Mal. Serious and academic, the book offers no hint of the character they saw filling their television screens and tabloid newspapers. Obviously the two books are very different in nature and polished by different ghost writers but the contrast between 1967's *Soccer for Thinkers* and Allison's 1975 autobiography, *Colours of My Life*, goes beyond mere content. They are products of a different manifestation of Malcolm Allison. The latter is loaded with arrogance and swagger, the other a surprisingly tentative, at times almost apologetic, attempt to instruct and indoctrinate. For all its sound theoretical sense, *Soccer for Thinkers* appears to equate little to the man who would make those theories spring to life on the field, where his methods were reinforced by the power of his personality. The book lacks any real measure of the man himself. The only time you sense you actually hear Allison's voice is when he becomes agitated at those who decry weight training.

One suspects that had he written it five years later, after success at City had transported him into the world of celebrity, even the restrictive medium of the textbook would have struggled to contain him.

9

ANATOMY OF A CHAMPIONSHIP

'Our approach wasn't about keeping a clean sheet and scoring one. Malcolm knew we were a good attacking side who could score more goals than the opposition'
– Former Manchester City midfielder Colin Bell

Derrick Robins picked up the morning newspaper and settled over his breakfast. He was interested to read the latest speculation about the appointment he, as chairman of Coventry City, would soon be making for his club. What he didn't expect to see was the leading candidate for the manager's position announcing to the world that it was already his. Malcolm Allison had just managed to talk himself out of a job.

It was two months into the 1967–68 season when developments in the world of televised sport very nearly changed the course of Allison's career. The success of *Match Of The Day*, which was moved to BBC1 as the corporation looked to cash in on the surge of interest in football after the 1966 World Cup, had not gone unnoticed by the ITV network. A similar-format highlights show formed a large part of the business plan for newly formed regional stations like London Weekend Television, which, in the late summer of 1967 appointed a new head of sport in preparation for its launch a year hence. Jimmy Hill, whose promotional expertise as manager of Coventry had brought him as much recognition as his achievement in leading the Sky Blues to promotion to the First Division, was the man appointed to work on plans for the launch of *The Big Match*.

Allison had established enough of a reputation to be mentioned when such managerial vacancies arose and enjoyed an encouraging discussion with Robins about moving to Highfield Road. Their conversation ended with Allison stating that he would need to get permission from the City directors before accepting any formal offer. But before hearing back from Allison, Robins instead saw him crowing about having secured the position and announcing, 'Who would turn their nose up at £100 a week?'

Robins's response was uncompromising. 'Malcolm Allison will not be coming to Coventry,' he stated. 'I asked Allison to keep the whole thing absolutely quiet and breathe not a word to anyone else. That was about five o'clock on Monday evening. By 10 p.m. I heard that the story was on the streets in print. Today Allison gave the news that he had got the job. But it takes two to make an agreement.' Instead, Robins went for Malcolm's old pal, Noel Cantwell, who, since leaving West Ham, had captained Manchester United to victory in the 1963 FA Cup.

Allison, meanwhile, was left to focus on a City campaign that had begun with a couple of overriding priorities. The feeling that a more attacking approach was the way forward had become well established in his mind, but he still felt that there was a gap or two to fill in the forward line in order to make such methods successful. One addition had been made in the final weeks of the previous season when Allison had again persuaded Joe Mercer to trust his instincts. Left-winger Tony Coleman had arrived at Maine Road via a circuitous route that, on more than one occasion, appeared to have sent his career down a dead end. The problem with Coleman was that he was virtually uncontrollable off the field. Stoke and Preston had both decided he was beyond all hope. Here was a man who had supposedly thrown a bed out of a third-floor window to relieve the boredom of a training course at Lilleshall. He wound up at Bangor City, where his performances had prompted Allison to attempt to talk Mercer into spending £3,000 on him. The image of the flying bed was all Mercer needed to keep his chequebook pocketed. Having moved to Doncaster, Coleman's value had risen to £12,000, but when he struck a referee he proved that he was as much of a gamble as ever. Allison went to work on Mercer again, this time convincing him that he could tame him. If anyone could relate to the personality of a hellraiser, it was Malcolm.

The final component of one of English football's most famed forward lines would have to wait until the new season was several weeks old, however – by which time the execution of Allison's other objective for the season was well under way.

Allison felt that his players had to increase their fitness if they were to compete with the top teams in the First Division. As much as he was acknowledged for encouraging players to work with the ball in training, he had always valued physical preparation at all of his clubs. In the late summer of 1967, his concern was to raise levels of fitness to the point where his men were as fast as sprinters and had the stamina of milers. When he told a journalist friend Bill Fryer of his plan, he was put in touch with former top-class athlete Joe Lancaster – a man the City squad would come to curse every Monday.

Allison charged Lancaster with devising a programme that would ensure City lasted the distance in the league. At first, the players were reluctant to buy into the philosophy that an athlete could devise a strategy to see them through a 90-minute football match. Giggling and smirking, mixed with resentment, greeted Lancaster's introduction to the squad. 'You could almost see the contempt stretch across their smug expressions,' Malcolm recalled.

From now on, the working week would start in Wythenshawe Park, a green swathe of land on the outskirts of Manchester. By the end of the first session, players were sinking to their knees and some were being sick. The vomiting confirmed to Allison that his approach was the correct one. Lancaster was given permission to turn up the intensity of the sessions. Typically, the morning would begin with a long run to get everyone warmed up, followed by a series of bursts over a quarter of a mile, 220 yards and 100 yards, with strict target times in place for all of them. After a short break, the sequence would be reversed. Then would be a session of *fartlek* – a Swedish word meaning, literally, 'speed play' – a sequence of sprints and interval running aimed at replicating the stop–start tempo of the football pitch.

Allison outlined his policy in *Soccer for Thinkers*, where he wrote:

A game is in bursts. Training should be in bursts. One of the biggest failures of English training is that if an hour is laid down on the schedule, then the coach will work the players for an hour. This is a mistake. Work in bursts – three minutes, four, five, six – then stop. Rest for two minutes. Ball juggling, anything. Then off again for five minutes. Players can be stretched this way. Alertness and sharpness can be injected into their game.

Such an environment would prove a culture shock to former Bolton striker Francis Lee when he joined the team early in the season. 'Malcolm's training methods were very scientific but very hard,' he recalls. 'There was no chance to ease up in training. I could see that as far as dedication and purpose were concerned I had moved into another world.'

Lancaster's programme was designed around six weeks of slog followed by three weeks' rest, after which other athletes like Derek Ibbotson, the former world mile record holder, and local sprinters Danny Herman and Barrie Kelly were called in to work with the team. Players like Summerbee, Oakes, Bell, Young and Book found they could beat the sprinters over certain distances up to 60 yards, although the real runners maintained the edge over 100.

Mike Summerbee remembers that it didn't take long for Allison's sceptics to be converted. 'First of all we were all moaning and groaning and thought, "What are we doing this for? Athletes and footballers are not the same." But within about six weeks you realised that this was key to it all. We could play on heavy pitches and we weren't even out of breath. We were superfit.'

Allison's desire to embrace knowledge from outside the boundaries of his own sport was a recurring theme during this stage of his career, when his thinking was at its sharpest and his hunger for success most acute. He would pick the brain of Dr John Books at Salford University to study the performance of the human body under physical stress and work with psychologist John Kane to help infiltrate the mind of the professional sportsman. He would even use professional dancing champion Len Heppell to replicate the balance and footwork programmes he had carried out with Newcastle United forward Bryan Robson, his future son-in-law. Allison was one of the first men in English football to take diet seriously, making sure his players ate chicken, fish and salad before games instead of the traditional red steak.

Don Howe, coach of Arsenal at the time, remembers another of Allison's experiments. 'We were up at City and after coming off the pitch at half-time, all of a sudden I could hear this noise coming from their changing room. I could hear running and shouting and it seemed like they must be having some kind of ding-dong. After the game I asked Malcolm what had happened and he said it was a new idea of his. He'd found that after sitting down and relaxing it was hard to get the system going for the second half, so they were training at half-time!'

Tony Book remembers, 'He was up to a lot of things at that time, talking to the top men at universities about diet, weight and everything else. I can remember him coming to me and saying, "Look, I need you to go to Salford University. There is something there that we are going to try out and I need you to be a guinea pig." It was a treadmill, maybe one of the first. I went down there and they wired me up, but when they started it up I flew off the back of the machine because I didn't know what was going to happen.'

Colin Bell adds, 'Malcolm was into eating the right things on match days, drinking the right drinks. He would bring in anyone or any little thing that improved your performance. At Salford, he would make us run around in a gas mask to make us breathe more economically. You couldn't get the air in quick enough, the gas mask stuck to your face – you wanted more air in than the gas mask would allow. I remember running round Wythenshawe Park during a training session with a box strapped to my back. I looked like Quasimodo because I had this box under my shirt. It was all to do with reading your pulse and heart rate and measuring recovery time. Then he had somebody from the university go to one of our matches to note the distance I ran, walked, sprinted and jogged during the game. He tried to have his finger on the pulse of everything.'

For all the determination to drive his players to the outer limits of their ambition and to squeeze every drop of potential out of City's preparation time, Allison ensured that a relaxed atmosphere prevailed at Maine Road, one in which people would look forward to going to work. According to Lee, there were 'no hard and fast rules' at the club. 'Generally speaking, you decide for yourself what time you go to bed before a match,' he said. 'The view is taken that we are all pros and know what is best for ourselves. It is typical of the club that there are not too many rules; and because the players are treated like adults it helps to build individuality.'

Summerbee adds, 'Training was so enjoyable. We couldn't wait to get started. Most of us got to the ground at nine, even though we didn't start until ten. Then a lot of us would stay behind afterwards to practise different things.'

Allison remembered that inside every professional footballer lived the young boy who had started out kicking a ball around in the park or the street, dreaming of emulating his heroes. Bell explains, 'He said to me towards the end of my career, "As a coach, when you go out, don't just walk out and call everyone together like a schoolteacher. See that they are enjoying themselves. Even though they are grown men, let them shoot in from ten yards, and then after a few minutes call them together." He used to come out to the middle of the park and watch for ten minutes before he said, "Right, let's start."'

Bell also recalls that there was always an air of mystery around the day's training. 'He put a lot of thought into it on a day-to-day basis. It is like any job – if you do the same thing every day for ten months it gets boring. Other than the running on Monday, we never knew what we would be doing. We might come in one day and find a bus there and Malcolm would say we were going to Blackpool for a sauna and lunch.[2] He knew it would take the edge off your game if you got bored in training. At Bury, I knew every day what we would be doing; it was always the same pattern.'

Allison was keen that nothing would take place on the training field that would not have a direct bearing on Saturday's events. Summerbee explains, 'Everything was set in match-type situations. It would be forwards against defenders and we would be working on specific things, like running in or checking out. Nothing was done that was meaningless.'

---

[2] There was also a hint that the frequent trips to the Norbreck Hotel in Blackpool owed something to the fact that the landlady quite fancied Malcolm.

Allison didn't expect his players to change their personalities during training, as Book explains: 'We had a lot of people who wanted to be winners. Even in the five-a-sides on Friday, there were times when we went over the top. But Malcolm knew that if you were a committed player you couldn't just switch it off. If you don't do it in training, I don't think you can do it in games. That is how that team was. I could only train the way I played.'

Bell has vivid memories of those games at the end of the week, when the defence would take on the attack in fierce competition. 'When I think back, I wonder how we managed to get 11 men on the field on Saturday. We used to kick lumps out of each other. Malcolm never told us to take it easy. The forwards wanted to win and the defence wouldn't want to concede a goal for love nor money. Summerbee and Lee would get stuck in, Alan Oakes and Doyley would give people what for.'

Pre-season results, for all their renowned unreliability as portents of the months to come, offered reasons for optimism at Maine Road, with wins on tour in Germany and Belgium being followed by a 4–1 home victory against German team Borussia Dortmund, winners of the European Cup-Winners' Cup little more than a year earlier.

The First Division season kicked off with a 0–0 draw at home to Liverpool, a game marked by ugly scenes among a crowd of almost 50,000 and a penalty miss by Book, named as club captain following the departure of Johnny Crossan to Middlesbrough. After defeat at Southampton, the third game at Stoke was the backdrop for a disagreement between Allison and Mercer about where Summerbee should play. Having missed out the previous season in attempts to sign Wyn Davies from Bolton – before his transfer to Newcastle – and Burnley's Andy Lochhead, Allison felt that the control, speed and toughness of Summerbee could be transferred from the wing to fill the perceived deficiency at the apex of City's attack, where Mike Doyle was being asked to wear the number 9 shirt. Mercer, however, insisted on keeping Summerbee wide and City lost 3–0 to drop to second-bottom in the table.

For the next game, Summerbee played at centre-forward, leading the line with imagination and guile and helping Bell and Neil Young to score two goals each in a 4–2 win against Southampton. 'I could hold the ball up and set things up for other players,' Summerbee explains. 'And I was a bit of a masochist. I enjoyed being kicked, it made me play better.' By early 1968, Summerbee's switch to centre-forward would prove so successful that Sir Alf Ramsey was following Allison's lead and naming him to lead the England forward line.

The next three League games were won without a goal being conceded, after which Leicester were dispatched 4–0 in the League Cup, with two goals by a young forward by the name of Stan Bowles. Then Sheffield United were the victims of a sparkling City display, their 5–2 win putting them level on points with the League leaders. Bowles marked his First Division debut by scoring twice more.

A single-goal defeat followed at Arsenal, but Gunners full-back Bob McNab remembers the esteem in which City were beginning to be held around the League. 'They were a great team. They weren't all the best players but they were coached well. They were doing all kinds of stuff and I knew when I was playing against them that this team was oiled, well organised and well coached.'

Next up was the first Manchester derby of the season, played at Maine Road. Goalkeeper Harry Dowd was missing after breaking a finger in training, meaning a City debut for Ken Mulhearn. Having failed in his attempt to sign World Cup winner Gordon Banks, Allison headed into the biggest game of the season with a man plucked from Third Division Stockport County only two weeks earlier for £25,000. This was one of those occasions when Allison remembered his days at Charlton, the experience of being pitched untested, overawed and intimidated into a big game. He recognised Mulhearn's nerves and took him into the treatment room to give him the opportunity to calm down away from the other players. City lost 2–1 after taking an early lead through Bell's fierce strike, but Mulhearn ended up retaining his place for the rest of the season.

The game was a typically passionate City–United game, with referee Kevin Howley stretched to keep control. Bowles and United striker Brian Kidd had to be pulled apart by police after coming to blows in the second half. The men escaped with a booking each but Mercer insisted on Bowles playing along with the media and posing arm-in-arm with Kidd the next day. Mercer believed in the Corinthian spirit of losing with grace and dignity, while Bowles – in an approach that Allison would have identified with – thought of the ways he could spend the banknotes that the pressmen pushed in his direction in return for participating in the stunt.

In the wake of a defeat that had put City back in their place in the Manchester hierarchy, rumours were growing of an imminent bid for Bolton forward Francis Lee. After eight years at Burnden Park, Lee felt his career had ceased to progress and his unhappiness was well known in football. He had requested a transfer, but knew that his club would not simply hold the door open for his exit. 'Many players will back me up when I say that you almost had to tunnel your way out of town to leave Bolton Wanderers,' he said.

Bolton were persuaded, however, to allow Lee to speak to Allison and Mercer. The next day, 24 hours before City's game at Sunderland, Lee agreed that a move to Maine Road was preferable to the offer he had received from Stoke City. But when the Football League refused to rush through his registration in time for the game at Roker Park, Mercer told a distressed Lee that the deal was off. Finally, the paperwork was completed and three days after a 1–0 loss on Wearside, Lee was a City player for a fee of £60,000.

Lee and Allison had crossed paths before. It was Lee whose goals had ended Bath City's dreams of an FA Cup upset four years earlier, and he'd had his first personal interaction with Allison during a night out at the Empress Club in Bolton, where Malcolm was in the company of Alan Ball, Nobby Stiles and Lee's former teammate Tommy Banks. 'He came over to talk to me,' Lee remembers. 'He'd obviously had a few and he said to me, "If I get my hands on you I will turn you into a top player." I said, "I am a top player." He just laughed.'

Lee came away with the impression that Allison was nothing but a loudmouth – hardly the first time someone had formed that impression. Little did he know that Allison would one day have the chance to add substance to his boast. Stocky, direct and explosive with a barrel chest that seemed to reflect his self-confidence, Lee was, in fact, every inch an Allison player. 'I loved the swagger and aggression in his play,' Allison commented. 'It was so much more than mere cockiness. All I had to do with him was encourage his aggression, remind him of all his natural assets.'

Allison's method of doing that was to deliver the same message he gave to Summerbee when he first signed for City: forget about spending too much time in his own half. Allison wanted him where he could hurt the opposition. Lee explains, 'What he did with the forwards was encourage you to play to your strengths and skills. He used to tell Mike and me to get the ball, take defenders on and beat them. Training was built around that and only when he got that going to its full potential would he work on other things, like closing people down.'

With that kind of encouragement, Lee's direct approach on the right, from where he could cut in with devastating effect, gave Allison his desired balance in attack. Lee's first three games in a City shirt were all won, Lee himself scoring his first goal in a 4–2 win at Fulham. Bell's winner gave City victory against Leeds, a result that moved them into fourth place in the table and emphasised the reality of their improvement in their second season in the top flight. Two weeks later, Young and Lee scored two each in a 6–0 win against Leicester. City were fast establishing themselves as the team to watch, a 3–2 win at West Ham and a 4–2 success against Burnley leaving them one point behind leaders Manchester United going into December.

The seemingly carefree nature of City's victories was the manifestation of Allison's approach to matches, where as little time as possible was spent worrying about the opposition. In fact, it mirrored his approach to life. The old gambler was never far from the surface. However many the opponents scored, Allison believed his team could get one more. 'Ninety per cent of the preparation and team talk was about us,' says Bell. 'If we performed then we could get a result against anyone. In the team talks he would go through a few of their players and some of their set pieces. But just one or two things, he didn't want to baffle you. He wanted you to play your own game. Malcolm wouldn't accept going somewhere to pinch a draw. To him it was about planning about how you could win a game and more often than not, it worked. We would entertain and score goals. I can't remember him ever rapping too many knuckles for conceding goals – maybe the odd bad one here and there – but if we conceded four and scored five, that was the name of the game.'

City's forward line that season rarely failed to deliver. Summerbee and Lee would interchange positions effortlessly; Coleman could be mercurial on the left; Young's free role and powerful left foot provided any number of crucial goals; while Bell's renowned dynamic running, while providing the pulse of the team, often served to overshadow his own qualities as a thoughtful, skilful player. Behind the front five, City fielded a versatile and adaptable group of players who could contribute all over the field. It might not quite have been what the Dutch would develop into 'Total Football', but the influence of Continental teams and coaching on Allison's football philosophy was evident in his team's fluid defensive formation. In the number 4 shirt, Mike Doyle would play as the more attacking wing-half, mostly occupying a midfield position, while Alan Oakes, at 6, filled in alongside centre-back George Heslop. But with Oakes and full-backs Book and Pardoe given rein to get forward whenever possible, Doyle was flexible and aware enough to drop deep to provide cover.

Allison wrote, 'Wing-halves must obviously be more defensively minded [than inside-forwards] with clear cut responsibilities and less freedom. Fluidity, however, is the heart of good attacking football and in a good team these players will interchange cover and run for each other.' No way was he going to slavishly follow what he saw as the safety-first methods that Alf Ramsey had used to win the World Cup and which more coaches were looking to as the way forward. 'We played the system which suited us and did not conform to the "new age",' he would say many years later.

Summerbee asserts, 'The Dutch learned from us. We attacked quickly and could be shooting at goal in three passes. Our forwards were never in the same place, we could switch positions, and we played simple football at a fast pace. Teams were afraid of us. We never passed the ball square; the intention was to get the ball and run at people. We had Doyle and Oakes coming forward and Bell making his 40 yard runs. People ended up talking about Lee, Bell and Summerbee because we were the forwards, but we had good players throughout the team. It was guys like Alan Oakes and Glyn Pardoe who were the mainstay – men who created those situations.

Manchester United might have had better players individually in those days, but collectively no team was as good as us.'

Book continues, 'We went out and passed the ball around and tried to get into wide areas because people like TC, Mike and Franny could deliver quality into the box. We used to get the ball down and pass it as quick as we could and from the two full-backs and centre-half, we used to go forward and play. We just defended when we had to. Because we knew that we could win the games by the odd goal or two by going forward, we would give the odd goal away.'

Bell remembers that 'pass and move' was the instruction drilled into them by their coach. 'It was all one-touch or two-touch. That's what we worked on in training and it all became natural, with people moving players all over the field. The beauty of that side was that we didn't have any individuals. Nobody would keep the ball and do his own thing to be eye-catching. Nobody was better than anyone else.'

The pieces might all have been in place for a successful team, but Allison knew that nothing could be achieved if individuals did not perform to their full potential. Having the pitch watered on the morning of the game to ensure a slick surface for City's passing game could only go so far towards ensuring victory.

Lee explains, 'We realised that we had got the making of a good team and Malcolm recognised that we were a very good attacking side and he worked on it all the time. The players responded – none of them had ever won anything so we were hungry for success. It doesn't matter what coach you are, it is down to the players eventually because it is a spontaneous game to play. When we were on the pitch on Saturday afternoon, players took no notice of Malcolm shouting from the touchline. You played your own game. But one of Malcolm's great attributes was getting players to be ultra-confident in themselves and their game. He would work with them on their own and tell them, "You are a fucking good player. You can do this, you can do that. Let's see it a bit more." He was a great motivator that way.'

To a man, City's players recall that their confidence provided the edge that would make them so successful. For example, Joe Mercer always believed that Young, the slim hotshot who had come through City's youth team, could be even better than all the imported stars if he had more self-belief. Allison made it one of his projects to build him up, constantly pointing out how well he played against established international defenders, urging him to go looking for the ball all over the field and encouraging him to shoot more often. 'Malcolm goads you, persuades you, using any means possible to simply get it through that you are the best player in the Football League,' Young explained. 'His psychology is simple; it gives you confidence.'

When Allison looked at Bell he saw a player he felt could be among the best in the world if he set his sights higher, made the most of his talent and 'freakish strength' and went out to grab greatness. 'Colin Bell was the best player I ever worked with,' said Allison, whose message to him was, 'Every time you walk off the pitch unable to say you were streets ahead of the other 21 players you have failed.' Malcolm also sensed that Bell could fret if he believed he wasn't 100 per cent healthy, so would cajole him through fitness tests with comments like, 'You're flying.'

During a game against Sunderland, Allison charted players' passes and pointed out to Bell that, while the Scotland and former Rangers hero Jim Baxter gave the ball away six times in about forty passes, he had relinquished possession only twice in the same number of attempts. 'At this stage Bell's confidence was low and evidence that he was more reliable than Baxter could hardly be anything but flattering,' said Allison.

Bell, who went on to win the first of his 48 England caps at the end of the season, raves about Allison's man-management abilities, saying, 'As well as motivating as a team, he would treat people as individuals. We had a room at the top of the Maine Road tunnel and he would pull individuals in to chat to you. He'd give you a load of spiel about how you were the best player in the world, but you appreciated it because he knew the game inside out and you took it all in. And you walked out feeling ten feet tall. It is all about reading the player's personality. You don't get anything out of some people if you give them a good talking to. But if you gave Mike Summerbee a bit of stick he would bite at it, and go, "Right, I'll show you." If you said that to somebody else they might go into their shell. Malcolm knew the personalities of the players and how to get the best out of them.'

Summerbee recalls Allison's method of helping him rediscover his lost form. 'I had a very volatile relationship with Malcolm,' he admits. 'He would slag me off and have a right go at me. I remember when we played Leeds in the Charity Shield after we won the FA Cup. I was fit but my way of life had changed. I was married and I was getting regular meals, living in a comfortable heated house. My metabolism changed. I didn't play very well and at half-time Malcolm said to me, "They are carrying you." After the game he said, "You are finished, you can train with the reserves."'

Summerbee's mother, Dulcie, happened to be visiting and she marched to Allison's house the next day to confront him, informing him that he was 'a bugger'. Summerbee barely saw the first-team players in the following week but on Friday was told by Allison that he was getting 'one more chance'. Summerbee went out and gave Sheffield Wednesday the runaround, saying, 'Psychologically, Malcolm had got the best of me. He could belittle me, abuse me, say hurtful things, but he knew it would make me perform.'

Book also recalls an example of Allison resorting to tricks when he thought a player needed to be geed up: 'We were sitting in the communal bath and I'd been struggling a little bit. All of a sudden he said to the reserve-team right-back, "I hear you are playing out of your skin at the moment." He did it to get into my mind; a reminder that if you weren't doing it, someone else could.'

Meanwhile, Lee quickly discovered that the brash figure he'd met in the nightclub was 'very soft-hearted'. Lee recounts that when he experienced a downturn in form for a few weeks during that first season at City, Allison recognised that his striker was feeling troubled and offered to take him for extra training sessions. 'I know everybody thinks he is bombastic but he was like a mother hen, willing me to get over the bad spell. This was the man I had been doubtful about, and when you have had two or three years of the press image of Allison rammed down your throat I suppose it is difficult to change your opinion overnight.'

According to Mike Doyle, '[Malcolm] wanted to prove that if he hadn't been an international star, he could turn other players into world-class material. Certainly more than one of the footballers at Maine Road owed part of their rise to international stature to the tuition and guidance of Malcolm Allison.'

Summerbee is not about to disagree with that comment. 'Malcolm could make the people who had a limited amount of ability play beyond their potential. He made me into a player who could really play, and look at Tony Book: he was playing like a 16-year-old. Malcolm was the best coach in the country and still would be in the modern game.'

10

PARADISE CITY

'Champions aren't made in the gyms. Champions are made from something they have deep inside them – a desire, a dream, a vision'

– heavyweight boxing legend Muhammad Ali

Manchester City might have approached the winter of 1967–68 in a challenging position in the First Division and with Malcolm Allison harbouring thoughts of the championship, but his players were still grounded in realism. Colin Bell admits, 'You never thought about the title until you were three-quarters of the way through. The League was so competitive that you never knew at the beginning of the season whether you were going to be up at the top or fighting relegation. Everybody was a good side at the start and everyone took some beating on their own patch. If you got a point away from home you had done well. Nowadays, most teams are just worried from day one about relegation. In our day you could shuffle the pack and it could be anyone up there.'[3]

The onset of an English winter gave City the opportunity to turn in a performance that, perhaps more than any other, marked them down as serious contenders for Manchester United's crown. It is still remembered as one of the symbols of their season of

---

[3] The facts support Bell's point. Between 1967 and 1973, seven different teams topped the Football League. From 1963 to 1974, the FA Cup ended up in 12 different sets of hands.

glory.[4] When FA Cup holders Tottenham arrived at Maine Road, it appeared they had made a wasted journey. The concrete-hard pitch was white with snow, yet referee David Smith ruled that the surface offered no danger to the players and allowed the game to go ahead.

City fans might have been wishing he'd decided otherwise when Jimmy Greaves scored after six minutes, but they watched in delighted awe as City skated across the surface like sure-footed alpine experts, causing the game to be remembered as the 'Ballet on Ice'. They tore Spurs to shreds. City had already missed several chances before Bell fired home after efforts by Francis Lee and Mike Summerbee were blocked. Summerbee arced a header over Pat Jennings from Neil Young's cross five minutes after half-time and Young himself rattled the bar a couple of minutes later. Tony Coleman cleaned up after Jennings saved a shot by Lee and the fourth goal came when Young was on hand after a save from Bell. With only 20 games of the season played, City's vibrant style had already produced more goals than their entire safety-first campaign of a year earlier. A further source of pride for Allison was that the legendary Everton centre-forward, Dixie Dean, sought him out to inform him, 'That is the most brilliant side I have ever seen.'

Yet City's cavalier approach meant that a setback was never too far away and an unbeaten run of 11 games was ended by a 3–2 defeat at West Bromwich Albion on Boxing Day. There was never any question, though, of Allison compromising his beliefs by going down a more cautious route; he clung instead to his vision of City winning the title with dash and daring. Bell continues, 'We could paralyse teams at home but away from home there was a bit of a question mark. Malcolm knew that if he changed, with the type of team we were, we would have lost even more. It would have backfired because we didn't know another way to play.'

---

[4] Partly, this is because it was the only time all season that the *Match of the Day* cameras went to the home of the subsequent champions. Meanwhile, Second Division QPR, thanks largely to their proximity to BBC headquarters, were visited three times. In total, only three City games featured on the show, while Manchester United were aired on eight occasions.

Four days later, City were beaten 2–0 at home by the same West Brom team – a game that offered an interesting postscript. Driving home, Mike Summerbee's anger had led him to put his foot down too heavily on the accelerator, attracting the attention of the Manchester constabulary. When the police stopped his car the quick-thinking forward informed them, 'Malcolm Allison's just passed me doing 90 and he's pissed.' The patrol car disappeared in pursuit of the potential of a headline-grabbing arrest. Whatever the truth of the story, it does indicate the elevated nature of Allison's profile in the city – and demonstrates what people found easy to believe of him.

Starting 1968 five points behind United, City's year kicked off with a pair of 3–0 wins away from home followed by a resounding 7–0 FA Cup replay triumph at Reading. Francis Lee recalls, 'We'd gone on a run that lifted us near to the top at Christmas and everybody started believing in themselves and that the team could play in the way we were expected to play. We went off the boil a bit around Christmas but about early February we started to play well. We went right through, won some big away matches, built momentum and no one could stop us.'

City were hard on the heels of United and second-placed Leeds by the time Coventry visited Maine Road on the second Saturday in March. The result was a 3–1 victory, but it was not without its drama. Both Summerbee and Bell needed treatment as Coventry attempted to put up a physical barrier against the home team's attacking force. A nasty-looking tackle by full-back Dietmar Bruck on Coleman saw tempers further frayed, before referee Ray Tinkler angered the home team by deeming John Tudor's tackle on Summerbee not worthy of a penalty. Three minutes before half-time, the volatile Coleman – always a candidate to blow up in a game like this – aimed a kick at Bruck and both men were sent off. Players from both teams jostled Tinkler, with Allison eager to join in. Half-time eventually restored some semblance of order before City completed their win.

A week later, they hit the top of the table on goal average after a 5–1 home win against bottom-placed Fulham. Their lead lasted only until the next game, a 2–0 defeat at Leeds. Don Revie's team, whose scowling and scuffling not only overshadowed their technique and skill in the eyes of the public but was anathema to a man like Allison, had just finally won their first major trophy – after several years of near misses – by beating Arsenal in an ugly League Cup final. Leeds skipper Billy Bremner left the field after ten minutes to get a head wound patched up after a clash with Summerbee and second-half goals by Johnny Giles and Jack Charlton settled the game.

The defeat meant there was no room for error four days later when City went to Old Trafford, where a Wednesday-night crowd of more than 63,000 awaited a game that could either terminate or re-ignite City's title challenge. That it was United, the old nemesis, who presented such a challenge seemed apt. 'The Manchester United thing was still the great barrier across our progress,' Allison recalled. As usual, he dispatched his players to the field before the game to applaud the United fans massed in the Stretford End. Predictably, the crowd bayed at their opponents and Malcolm noted contentedly that he had succeeded in creating an air of agitation that he hoped would project itself onto the United players.

Allison's game plan called for Tony Book to be employed in a man-to-man marking role on George Best, but such was the genius of the Irishman that it quickly became clear that the veteran was, for once, being overrun. Best scored in the first minute – after Book mis-hit a back-pass – and was threatening to take over the game. Allison accepted that Best was in irrepressible form and, not wishing to waste the extra dimension Book could give to the attack, shouted instructions that his captain should play his normal game instead. After 15 minutes, Bell equalised with a powerful shot past Alex Stepney.

This was one of those games Allison had had in mind when he had called upon Joe Lancaster several months earlier. He felt that City's better conditioning was the key as they overran United in the second half, power allied to panache producing two more goals. George Heslop got his lavish blond comb-over to Coleman's free-kick and Lee converted a penalty after Bell was felled in full flight by Francis Burns. Even the fact that Bell was stretchered from the field could not take the gloss off the night. Mercer wept tears of joy and Allison would recall, 'Years of humiliation had been, if not wiped away, at least eased. It was one of the great nights of my life.'

The result meant that the Division One title race was now a three-way tie. City won two of the next three but then picked up only a point from games against Chelsea and Wolves, failing to score in either match. Mercer and Allison took the team to Southport for four days, where Joe played the role of the hard man, giving the players what Mike Doyle described as 'the biggest bollocking' they had ever had from him. 'The championship is there to be won,' raged Mercer. 'Either you want to win it or you don't. You'll train together tomorrow and then I don't want to see you again.'

Never lost for words, Allison, on the verge of his greatest achievement in football, decided that his silence was all that was required on this occasion. Here he was, close enough to touch the vindication of his wrecked playing career – to erase the bitter taste of West Ham's refusal to award him a Second Division championship medal – yet his confidence in his players, the men he had nurtured and moulded, was such that he felt no need to say anything. He trusted them to get together, discuss Mercer's dissatisfaction and rectify the situation. If he was feeling the strain of the title race, he was handling it and hiding it. 'Malcolm never showed anything,' says Bell. 'He was no different whether we were playing Manchester United or Leicester. Every game was a big game, but he didn't want any nerves to rub off on the players. He instilled in your brain you would be good enough to win.'

City had four games left and knew it was unlikely that anything less than four wins would bring them the First Division title. At least Bell was fit again after missing four games with the knee injury he'd suffered against United. And fortune decided to spend a day with City. Sheffield Wednesday forward Brian Usher diverted Young's indirect free-kick into his own net for the only goal of a game in which City had the benefit of some indifferent refereeing. When the players returned to the Maine Road changing-room they discovered that Leeds had been beaten. The day's events left Manchester United only two points ahead of City, with Leeds sandwiched between them.

By the time City completed victory against FA Cup finalists Everton four days later, United had been walloped 6–3 at West Bromwich in one of those remarkable games that went out with black and white television. Apparently relaxed by news of United's impending defeat, City scored second-half goals through Book and Coleman to move to the top of the table. Two games to play, both away from home: Tottenham, where the City players always felt confident of getting a result, and Newcastle, where they didn't.

At White Hart Lane, Allison achieved what he modestly described as a 'brilliant tactical success'. He decided to go after the veteran Dave Mackay, who was slowing with age and would be leaving Spurs within the next few weeks. Lee was instructed to abandon his habit of cutting in from wide and instead hug the right touchline, keeping left-back Cyril Knowles occupied. Summerbee, meanwhile, was ordered to drift out to the left, making sure that centre-half Mike England went with him. That would unleash the powerful running of Bell into the wide open spaces in the middle of the field, where Mackay would be exposed. It worked like a dream, as Summerbee remembers. 'Malcolm decided to isolate Dave Mackay and we destroyed him. Colin ran him into the ground. It showed you how ruthless we were.'

After the teams had exchanged opportunities during the first 40 minutes, Book, Lee and Coleman combined to free Bell, who stepped past Mackay and put the ball beyond Pat Jennings. Young was denied by the Spurs keeper before half-time and after having an attempt cleared off the line shortly after the break, Bell crashed in a shot through a crowd of defenders. Summerbee took advantage of good work by Bell and Lee to make the game safe before a Spurs penalty made the final score 3–1.

United, 6–0 winners against Newcastle, remained level on points with City but with inferior goal average. If City won at that same Newcastle team on the final Saturday of the season, then the result of United's home game against Sunderland would be irrelevant. Any slip-ups and the cursed Old Trafford gentry would be poised to deny Allison's blue-collar workforce the prize they had chased for months; the reward for which they'd got their fingernails dirty and for which they'd had lumps kicked out of them by the likes of Coventry. The BBC's reaction to such a scenario, Malcolm discovered with incredulity, was to send the *Match of the Day* cameras to watch bloody Busby and his spoiled glory boys. The BBC might not have had faith in City, but Summerbee says, 'We never expected to lose away from home, partly because we knew we could dish it out as well as take it.'

Bell admits, 'There was obviously more pressure because you knew what the situation was and it was in the papers all week. And then I don't think I had ever been to Newcastle and won. That played on your mind, but you just had to get on with it.'

Summerbee and Bell were withdrawn from the England squad to play Spain to ensure their fitness and the day before the game the City squad – along with numerous pressmen and as many fans as could fit into the second-class carriages – took the midday train to Gateshead. A visit to the bowling alley adjoining the Five Bridges Hotel only partly succeeded in taking their minds off the next day's task. While the squad members were rising from their beds to take a Saturday morning walk in the crisp Tyneside air, a convoy of cars and coaches was making its way along the A1 from Manchester, transporting Maine Road's Kippax Stand into the heart of St James' Park. The journey from hotel to ground, which should have taken 10 minutes, lasted 45 as City's team bus fought its way through the throng of well-wishers.

In the changing-room, it was the usual routine. A few words from Mercer, a reminder from Allison that 'you are the best team in the League; the best players in the country', and then City went out to face the crowd of more than 46,000, close to 20,000 of whom had arrived from Moss Side. 'There must have been more than 90,000, judging by the people who have said they were there,' says Bell. 'The thing I remember is that they were even sat over the wall on the walk-round. There was no fencing up or anything, but everyone behaved themselves.'

A frantic opening found City ahead after 13 minutes when Doyle's low cross from the right was swept in by Summerbee. But only two further minutes elapsed before Bryan Robson was set free in the City area and put a strong shot past Ken Mulhearn. City led again after 32 minutes when Young lashed in a first-time shot with his left foot from the edge of the box, only for the home side to equalise quickly once more. Heslop – who, according to Allison, 'panicked every time the ball came near to him' – gave the ball away and it was knocked forward for Jackie Sinclair to plant another unstoppable effort in the

City net. Lee recalls, 'It was a wonderful game because every time we scored, they scored. It was backwards and forwards – marvellous to watch and play in.'

Allison couldn't believe how poorly his defence was performing, but he was not about to start making changes. Bell remembers, 'He would back the players to perform so he wouldn't make wholesale switches to tactics at half-time. He would have a go at one or two and maybe change one or two little things, just to get us going in the right direction.'

He was, however, ready to give his men a rollicking when he arrived in the dressing-room. 'But when I got there I could see that they were all so tensed up,' he explained. Instead, Allison told them, 'You've had 45 minutes to warm up and get used to the game, now go out and play like champions.'

Within three minutes of the restart Summerbee fed Bell, who cut inside two players from the right and saw his shot cleared towards the edge of the box, where Young charged in to drive the rebound low into the net. This time there was no immediate riposte from Newcastle. City, inspired by Bell, looked more assured, completely in control of their destiny. A further 15 minutes on, Bell threaded a pass to Lee, who slipped the ball past the keeper and stood arms aloft in front of the delirious City fans.

But it was still a little too early for happy ever after. Given the season City had gone through, it was inevitable that the title should be won in a high-scoring nail-biter of a game and, with four minutes to play, Newcastle centre-half John McNamee ventured forward to net a powerful header to pull the score back to 4–3.

The tension around the ground conveyed the long-suffering City fans' refusal to believe that United would not somehow stage a late recovery from being 2–1 down against Sunderland – a result that, if it stood, meant a City victory was not strictly necessary. When the final whistle arrived, City players leapt into each other's arms. Tears were shed on and off the pitch. Fully-grown, fully-kitted, men hurled themselves like excited infants into the team bath. City were Football League champions for the first time since 1937 and they had won the title themselves, not relied upon an unexpected United setback. Even when champagne gave way to brown ale on the coach journey home, nothing could dampen their party spirit. 'It meant so much to everyone at the club; to Malcolm and Joe; and to the players,' says Lee. 'No one in that side had ever won anything.'

For Allison, however, the moment of triumph was a draining one. In the immediate aftermath of victory, he mourned the loss of the need to plan and plot any more – the very life force that had driven him so energetically through the previous months. 'I couldn't catch the mood. The title had come to us on a flood tide. I think deep down I was a little stunned.'

That feeling did not last too long. At some point during the team's celebrations at the Cabaret Club that night, the sense of achievement began to penetrate Allison's emotional fatigue. Consistency, fitness, discipline, flair, teamwork – all had been bandied about in the players' post-game interviews. But it was the fact that the title had been won without aping the pragmatism of England's World Cup winners that did most to restore Allison's buoyancy. That and the champagne. Besides, within hours – after barely 60 minutes' sleep at a girlfriend's flat – he would be setting himself new targets, defining new goals for his team, and setting out on another journey.

Allison had never been one to accept victory in a quiet, understated manner. Whether it was buying champagne all round at Ascot, or piling all his winnings on a long shot at Hackney dogs, victory had to be marked by some act of extravagance. Malcolm put such behaviour down, not to simple showing off, but to a need to involve others in his good fortune. Now, if he couldn't buy all the City fans and the nation's football media a bottle of bubbly, he could at least include them in his moment of triumph by giving them a shot of his very own brand of bravado, served chilled at the following day's Maine Road press conference.

Those reporters who resented having to forego Sunday lunch with the family for this post-championship briefing were well rewarded as Allison announced to a packed room, 'I think we will be the first team to play on Mars. We have had more courage than the majority of teams in the League. The courage to play this game. We work at things and are consistently disciplined. Any side we play at home or away has got to be at their very best to beat us.'

Allison was warming up now, and there was one 'red cloud' on the horizon of his finest professional accomplishment that he found impossible to ignore. In a couple of weeks' time, Manchester United would be in a position to overshadow City's domestic success by winning the European Cup. However much his team might be the flavour of the week, he knew that City would soon be elbowed out of the headlines by tales of Matt Busby's destiny – victory from the ashes of the Munich air crash, which had decimated the great 'Busby Babes' side a decade earlier.

Allison was in no mood to play the good neighbour. As well as shouting over the garden fence about what his team could achieve, his comments were a not-so-thinly veiled dig at United's success. 'Manchester City will not play in Europe like some of the sides I have seen play Manchester United. I promise you City will attack these people as they have not been attacked since the days of the old Real Madrid. I think a lot of these European people are cowards. Their teams won in spite of their coaches, not because of them.'

He later admitted that the knowledge that United would, in due course, achieve a 4–1 win against Portugal's Benfica at Wembley would have 'spoiled that morning of triumph'.

The First Division trophy was presented two days later when City played a friendly against Bury, a game that, naturally, turned into a party. Even Allison took the field, replacing Heslop with ten minutes to play and prompting chants of 'Allison for England'.

But there was to be no relaxing summer on the beach, basking in the glory of the League championship. City were off across the Atlantic for the kind of summer tour that would be unthinkable in modern times – nine meaningless matches played over the course of five weeks, with only one game won. The absence of the team's leading players on England's tour of South America and others on England Under-23 duty meant that the remaining players were overworked at a time when they should have been recharging for the following season.

It was a shambles from the start. Tony Book picked up an Achilles tendon injury that would keep him out of the side for the first half of the following season. City ended a game against Dunfermline with only nine men on the field because of further injury, while planned matches against Mexican sides Atlante and America were cancelled – the first only hours before kick-off – because the home teams claimed City were breaking their agreement by not fielding the team that had won at Newcastle to lift the title.

City were beaten twice by the Atlanta Chiefs, one of the better teams in the fledgling North American Soccer League, whose player-coach was Phil Woosnam – a former Wales inside-forward who had signed for West Ham just as Allison's time at Upton Park was ending. Woosnam took great delight in beating his former colleague at a time when the standard of play in the NASL was higher than it would be in any season until the likes of Pelé, Beckenbauer and Cruyff found their way to the US in the mid-'70s. After an initial 3–2 defeat in Atlanta, Malcolm claimed that their opponents had been of Fourth Division standard and that such a freak result could not happen again. When the games in Mexico were cancelled, Allison happily accepted an invitation to play a second match against the Chiefs, this time losing 2–1. In the Chiefs team was former Aston Villa and Northern Ireland winger Peter McParland, who remembers, 'We wanted to beat them badly because Malcolm was shooting his mouth off and we thought we had better shut him up. We had something to prove.'

The tour was not without its moments off the field. Tony Coleman and Stan Bowles so upset American police with their rowdy behaviour that warning shots were fired into the pavement. Malcolm so impressed the female head of an Atlanta radio station that she attempted to persuade him to remain in the United States with her. Francis Lee stunned patrons of a bar in San Francisco by eating the flowers from the tables, while Neil Young and George Heslop witnessed two people being shot while they queued for a hamburger.

Back home for the new season, City found that English teams wanted to beat them as much as the Atlanta Chiefs had. The combination of their status as champions and Allison's boasting meant everyone was out to get them. Mike Doyle noted that 'we never picked up a newspaper without expecting to see some big words from the big fellow'.

Allison appears not to have appreciated that while a developing, inexperienced team had responded to the way he built them up – both privately and in the media – he should ease up a little now that they were established as England's champions. The more reserved players in the squad believed that Allison's outbursts were the equivalent of sticking targets on their shirts. Summerbee suggests, 'There was a little of the José Mourinho arrogance about Malcolm' – although Allison's comments were at least delivered with a cheeky twinkle in the eye rather than a chip-on-the-shoulder scowl.

Bell saw it as less of an issue, reflecting, 'He just did all that to get City into the papers and promote the game of football. I thought it was great. It was all for show and it didn't bother me.'

But it clearly disturbed some players, as Lee explains. 'It did put extra pressure on us and a few players did at times say to him, "Why don't you keep your bloody mouth shut? The game is hard enough without you sticking your oar in. It's all right you saying we are going to do this, that or the other, but you aren't bloody well playing." He just wanted everybody to believe we were a super team and he was a super coach. He felt people weren't writing about the club in the right way and it was all a PR exercise to get the club to the forefront.'

After starting the season with a 6–1 win against West Brom in the FA Charity Shield, Allison's promise about what City would do in the European Cup was put to the test in a first-round tie against Fenerbahce, champions of Turkey. Malcolm's comments had once again been tolerated by Mercer, who understood that it was part of his make-up and saw that it added excitement and panache to the game. Take that away from him and you would lose part of the spark that drove him towards such achievements on the field.

Besides, there was little danger of coming a cropper against Fenerbahce. At that time, Turkish football was regarded as something of a joke. Their club sides were mere early-round fodder for the bigger teams in European competition, while the national team would have considered the act of qualification for the World Cup finals cause for wild celebration. Anyone suggesting that, by 2002, they would be reaching the semi-finals would have been regarded as insane.

Allison and Mercer chose not to scout their opponents, relying instead on a report from former Doncaster Rovers manager Oscar Hold, who'd had a two-year stint as Fenerbahce manager. Neither was there an advance party sent to Turkey from the club to check on hotels and logistics. The tie was expected to be effectively over by the time City had played the first leg in front of their own fans, yet they were bereft of the drive and guile to break down a massed and well-organised defence. Confronted by a goalkeeper in great form, they were held 0–0.

Allison's words were already looking a little hollow, although in this instance Lee does not attribute the City performance to any additional pressure created by their coach. 'His quote was made specifically for us: to stop us being apprehensive at what was an entirely new venture to us, and to give us confidence. But we became too confident and they were so moderate that we dominated them so much in the first half we treated it like an exhibition game. At half-time Malcolm tried to get us to realise the game was slipping away, and told us to go out and score a hatful. But our chances had gone.'

Things got worse in the second leg. City were totally unprepared for what awaited them in the Turkish capital, Istanbul, where 55,000 crammed into the National Stadium, built for about 10,000 fewer than that. Book, who had made the journey even though he was still injured, recalls, 'I remember looking out of the hotel window at about half past eight in the morning. You could see the stadium down the hill and the fans were already queuing to get in. When we got to the ground the pitch was surrounded by soldiers with guns. It is hard to ignore stuff like that when you have not experienced it before.'

Bell continues, 'It was a complete culture shock. You felt that if they could have shot you, they would have. They kicked lumps out of us in the first leg but had picked us up, which was very nice of them. We went out there and they kicked us again, but didn't pick us up. They were spitting at us and there were fires in the crowd. It was the worst experience I have had on a football field. It was frightening.'

After surviving some early pressure on the bumpy pitch, City took the lead after 12 minutes when Tony Coleman seized upon defensive uncertainty to round the keeper. There were few scares for the away team in the remainder of the first half. But then, in what Allison would liken to 'watching a slow-motion horror film', the

Turks fought back to win 2–1. They scored inside a minute of the second half and a swarm of attacks finally produced a second goal with 12 minutes to play.

Allison was devastated. He had been convinced of his team's ability to triumph, a certainty built on the fact that even the European coaches he admired were, he felt, too negative, their ambition unable to match their technical expertise. Beaten and embarrassed, he said nothing publicly for 48 hours. Finally he admitted that 'defeat in Istanbul was the biggest disappointment of my whole career'. He felt that his team had adapted reasonably well to the problems of playing abroad in a hostile environment, but believed that the fact they had not been fully appreciative of the problems lying in wait for them meant that 'there was not enough urgency in the first game'.

Bell echoes that view many years later: 'We were out before we knew what had happened. Second time around in Europe, a year later, we knew what it was about a bit more. It was a learning experience for us and if we had got through that first round we might just have learned about European football as we went along.'

The European Cup upset was symptomatic of City's disappointing start to the season. They won only once in the first nine League games, by which time the only team below them in the table was newly promoted Queens Park Rangers. Lee admits, 'After we started the season by thrashing West Brom, I think we were a bit over-confident. We thought we were going to win every game by scoring a lot of goals.'

The title had been lost quickly and City would finish in 13th position, only a couple of places higher than their first season back in the First Division two years earlier. Whether or not Allison's statements had any impact on the team, one thing was for certain: he had spoken up once too often for the authorities' liking. In a bad-tempered match at Southampton – a description that could have applied to a good many games at The Dell in that era – Allison had been heard to direct 'abusive remarks' towards the linesman, earning the seventh summons of his career to appear before the FA's disciplinary committee.

In November 1966, he had been banned for a month from sitting on the touchline for swearing at the officials during a League Cup game. At the time he had predicted it would be 'the longest month of my life' but refrained from saying any more because 'they might hang me'. He had also been suspended from all management duties for a month for an incident in a match against Tottenham. Now it seemed likely that, given his previous, a more lengthy banishment from the dugout beckoned. Before the case could be heard, Joe Mercer announced he was enforcing his own sideline ban on his coach. 'You must sit with me in the directors' box,' he told him. A telephone link was set up between Allison and assistant coach Johnny Hart on the bench, while Malcolm made his view from the executive seats more rewarding by inviting American film star Jane Russell to watch a game with him.

If Mercer's action was intended to draw the FA's sting, it didn't work. The result of a 40-minute hearing was that Allison was fined £100 and banned from the touchline for life. It was the inevitable conclusion to years of Allison's verbal assaults on match officials but there was little sign of repentance as he ranted, 'Referees are just an occupational hazard because of their incompetence. The standard of some refereeing in this country, and some others, is so low it's pathetic. What's needed is a drastic overhaul of the system. There's been nothing done about the methods of training referees for 60 years, which is ridiculous. They should have to go to school for at least one month every year so that they keep up with what's going on.'

Inevitably, Allison was not the most popular figure among the community of match officials. Norman Burtenshaw, one of the country's leading officials in the '60s and '70s, felt that players such as Colin Bell carried their coach's confrontational attitude onto the pitch with them. 'Manchester City were a team I never liked having. They had the unenviable reputation of being the mouthiest team in the Football League. I think the players took it from their manager Malcolm Allison, who, when I had dealings with him, seemed to be an arrogant man, although I can think of no row between us.'

Burtenshaw described City versus Leeds as the game that no referee wanted and recalled Don Revie asking him to check City's studs before a game on a frosty surface after hearing a comment on television about them having special studs made. This was before linesmen routinely checked studs before matches and was indicative of both Revie's infamously suspicious nature and Allison's reputation as a coach who might try to pull a fast one. In his autobiography, *Whose Side Are You On, Ref?*, Burtenshaw wrote:

> After another City match I came out of the dressing-room and saw Allison talking to some reporters on the other side of the passageway. 'What about the shirt pulling?' he shouted. I was willing to have a civil conversation but not to join in a shouting match across a passageway.
>
> My next meeting with Allison was at a disciplinary hearing after I had booked Mike Summerbee for a late tackle. Allison looked at me as though I were an imbecile. City brought in film of the incident and played it in slow motion, showed stills and even played the film backwards. Summerbee lost his case. As Allison left the room where the hearing took place he said, 'It's a disgrace.' He was called back and lectured about his conduct.

Allison also managed to wind up Burtenshaw by taking his team sheet in to the officials without waiting for the opposition manager to present his list simultaneously. 'I can't accept that – you know the rules,' Burtenshaw would tell him. 'He was the only manager who used to come in on his own. Why did he do it when he knew it was against the regulations? Allison was never a conformist.'

Former Football League linesman Tony Ellis recalls Allison trying to use his status and personality to dominate match officials. 'He was an intimidating figure. I always felt he was lording it over you,' he says, although others saw Malcolm more as a 'loveable rogue'. Pat Partridge appreciated the fact that Allison would talk to him 'man-to-man in private' and recalled several such confrontations. 'His tongue is overworked and constantly in danger of getting him on the wrong side of officialdom, but despite our set-tos I believe he is good for the game,' he said. 'I like the man immensely.' He even claimed to have got on better with Allison than Mercer, with whom he fell out when genial Joe made disparaging comments about him in front of his wife.

Meanwhile, Allison's popularity was obviously growing among clubs eager to find someone who could create a winning team for them. In December 1968, Queens Park Rangers chairman Jim Gregory was on the end of the phone after the conclusion of Tommy Docherty's ill-fated 28 days in charge at Loftus Road. 'I haven't followed it up because I didn't fancy the job,' Allison told reporters.

Less than two months later, Coventry manager Noel Cantwell promised his old friend considerably more money than he was earning at City if he would team up with him at Highfield Road. This time Allison took some time to consider the tempting offer. 'If Malcolm leaves there's a transfer request coming from me and probably Colin Bell and Tony Book,' announced Summerbee. Touched by the urgings of his players and confident that loss of form in the League was only temporary, Allison was in a mood for compromise during a 50-minute meeting with the City board. Club secretary Walter Griffiths emerged to read a statement in which Allison was said to have 'apologised', resolved his 'very slight differences' with City and agreed to a new four-year contract.

From his new seat in the directors' box, Malcolm was to be rewarded for his decision by a grandstand view of many more City triumphs.

11

CUP KINGS

'If you start to take Vienna, take Vienna'

– French Emperor Napoleon Bonaparte

From the beginning of 1969 to the mid-point of 1970, Manchester
City took part in four cup competitions, winning three of them.
First, they lifted the FA Cup, and then became the first English team to
complete successful European and domestic trophy campaigns in the
same season by lifting the European Cup-Winners' Cup and League
Cup.[5] Those who had scoffed at City's premature European Cup exit
and dismissed their championship victory as a flash in the pan were
forced to admit that over a three-season span, during which they won
four different competitions, City had proved themselves one of the
finest teams in English football history. The continued achievement,
and the manner of it, brought Malcolm Allison to the attention of
some powerful men. So much so that he was almost not around for
what he would regard as his most satisfying triumph.

Floundering in the League and out of Europe early in the 1968–69
season, Allison's players recalled the challenge he had set them when
they attended the previous season's FA Cup final. Watching West
Bromwich Albion overcome Everton, he had announced, 'Look at this
lot here. We're better than these. We should be here next season.' By
the time City began their FA Cup campaign against Third Division

---

[5] Leeds United won the 1967–68 League Cup and European Inter-Cities Fairs
Cup, but had to wait until early in the 1968–69 season to play their two-legged
European final.

Luton, Allison was making an important positional change, placing Mike Summerbee back on the right wing with Francis Lee in the centre, where the coach felt his acceleration over ten yards could make him a lethal presence. It was a Lee penalty that settled the Luton tie after an unconvincing team performance. The fourth round sent City back to Tyneside, scene of their title triumph, to face Newcastle, who would end the season as winners of the European Fairs Cup. City battled to a 0–0 draw and Neil Young scored an early goal in the replay to put them on the way to victory, Bobby Owen sealing it with a second after half-time.

The scheduled fifth-round game at Blackburn Rovers was postponed four times – three times because of bad weather and once when the FA allowed the home team to defer because of an outbreak of flu. It was nearly four weeks since their last game by the time City took the field at Ewood Park. Allison had told his team that the Rovers defence played too square and could be beaten by through balls. Bell proceeded to split them apart with a pass for Lee to run onto and open the scoring, the first of his two goals in a 4–1 win.

The delay meant City already knew that an attractive home tie against Tottenham awaited them in the quarter-finals. The Spurs team that had succumbed so meekly on their last two visits to Maine Road, conceding four goals each time, were determined there would be no repeat. A team renowned for its incisive football displayed a blunt edge instead, but were beaten by Lee's late winner.

City fans were proclaiming a new hero after their semi-final win at Villa Park against Everton, the previous year's runners-up. The early-season loss of form suffered by George Heslop had persuaded Mercer and Allison to give a chance to Tommy Booth, a tall, dark-haired, skilful centre-half who had progressed from schoolboy City fan to captain of the club's youth team. Booth, who had been an inside-forward when Allison first saw him, looked at home from the moment he stepped in and the mid-season return of Tony Book from injury ensured that there was no need for the extra experience offered by Heslop. A somewhat dour semi-final turned out to be 19-year-old Booth's coming of age.

A day spent in Matlock before the game helped establish a light mood that lasted at least until a couple of hours before kick-off, when Allison delivered what he felt was one of his best team talks. Everton, like City, were earning renown for their positive instincts and in Alan Ball, Colin Harvey and Howard Kendall possessed the most revered midfield trio in the country. In the semi-final, though, they were unwilling to play with the freedom that would carry them to the League title a year later, preferring to concentrate on stifling City and hitting on the break. Allison was aware that they had employed such tactics successfully in semi-finals against Manchester United and Leeds in 1966 and 1968 respectively and was determined not to play into their hands by being too adventurous. 'We are going to close them up, absorb some punishment and then strike at them,' he told his team.

David Connor kept Ball out of the game after being deployed in one of his specialist marking roles and the result was a tense, tight contest. It seemed destined to end goalless, especially when Neil Young's shot ricocheted off the shoulder of keeper Gordon West in the last minute. Booth recalls, 'We all looked around at each other and shrugged because we felt that was probably our best chance gone, but we were all waved forward for the corner.' Young landed the kick on the head of Mike Doyle and the ball was helped on by Summerbee. It fell to Booth six yards out and he sent City to Wembley by smashing in a low shot. City had a surprise guest at their changing-room celebrations when Allison spotted West skulking in the corridor, afraid to face the wrath of Harry Catterick. 'We can't have that,' Allison told him. 'Come in our room.'

By the time the week of the final arrived, Book had been named as joint winner of the Footballer of the Year award – along with Derby's promotion-winning captain Dave Mackay – and his teammates were allowed to attend the Football Writers' Association dinner two nights before the final to see him receive his prize. Then it was back to the teetotal Oatlands Park Hotel in Weybridge. The tension on the team bus during the journey to Wembley was lessened by the distraction of the players looking out to pick up lucky mascot Paul Todd, the young schoolboy who had been leading the team out for three years. On arrival at Wembley, however, they walked headlong into a fierce battle between the two broadcasting networks.

The season had seen ITV position themselves as serious rivals to the dominance of BBC's football coverage with their successful Sunday afternoon highlights. The FA Cup final would be just as bitterly fought between the two stations as it would be on the field, with the BBC determined to underline their place as the pre-eminent network. The on-field interviews before kick-off – part of the ever-lengthening build-up to the game, which came to include such items as *Cup Final It's A Knockout* (BBC) and *Cup Final Professional Wrestling* (ITV) – were conducted in a relatively orderly fashion compared with what would ensue after the game. As technicians and producers battled to get players in front of their cameras at the final whistle, some punches were thrown. Allison was an ally of ITV and had helped them slip their men past Wembley security into the inner circle by handing out a few City tracksuits. During the game, while the BBC grabbed a few words with managers Joe Mercer and Frank O'Farrell on the bench, ITV would take advantage of Allison being forced to sit in the stand by placing reporter Paul Doherty next to him with a microphone up his sleeve, enabling Allison to give his views as the action unfolded.

In the changing-room before kick-off, City's players pulled on their change strip of red and black stripes. Allison loved the 'AC Milan-like invincibility it gave off' and had happily volunteered for City to give up their usual blue shirts because of the colour clash with Leicester. With kick-off approaching, City were summoned to the tunnel, yet Allison slammed the door in the official's face and told his team to sit down. He'd allowed them to relax with a tot of brandy as they changed and he didn't want them getting tensed up by hanging around listening to the closing bars of 'Abide With Me'. Having told his men to let the opposition stew, he also encouraged them not to show any tension when they appeared in front of the 100,000 crowd. 'I told them they must go out and play as I knew they could and that if they lost the Cup by taking my advice I would carry the can.'

Leicester were kept waiting three minutes in the tunnel, a tactic that Arsenal would adopt two years later against Liverpool, thanks to Gunners full-back Bob McNab getting to know Allison during the 1970 World Cup. 'He helped us win in a way. He told us not to go out in the tunnel too early. Also, he told me that when you walk out at Wembley you can see who is going to play well: they are the ones looking around and sniffing it, saying, "Yes, we are here." The others are looking at their toes. He said, "When you get out there, Bob, get your head up and look around like you own the place." I mentioned that to the players before the game.'

Allison finally sent his men into battle, feeling a pang of jealousy at seeing Mercer leading them out. 'I should be there too,' he told himself. Instead, he took his place in the second row of the stand, which because of Wembley's lay-out meant he was actually closer to the pitch than Mercer was on the bench.

City's line-up read: Dowd, Book, Pardoe, Doyle, Booth, Oakes, Summerbee, Bell, Lee, Young and Coleman, with Connor on the bench. They made a fast-paced start, with Doyle powerful and prominent in midfield and Summerbee posing problems for David Nish, Leicester's 21-year-old captain. Young shot over from the edge of the box and Coleman should have scored after Lee and Summerbee combined on the right. Dowd was called upon to make his first save, diving to his right after Allan Clarke, named Man of the Match, cut in from the left. Clarke was playing one of his last games for Leicester, who had paid Fulham £150,000 for him at the start of the season and, once relegation was a certainty, would sell him to Leeds for a British-record £166,000.

Leicester full-back Peter Rodrigues missed two swipes from close in as the ball moved back and forth across City's six-yard box, but the unrelenting tempo of the game couldn't force Allison's team to abandon their usual passing game and after 23 minutes they took the lead. Summerbee slipped defender Alan Woollett at the by-line, just inside the box, and pulled the ball back for Young to score with a high left-foot shot from near the penalty spot. The rest of the first half ebbed and flowed, and Leicester could have scored shortly after the interval when the balding centre-forward Andy Lochhead lashed wide.

The longer the game progressed, the safer City appeared. Booth was commanding and Leicester were running out of steam. Lochhead was bustled off the ball when put through with 15 minutes left and Bell had the best chance to add to the scoreline when he headed on the run into the arms of Peter Shilton. At the final whistle, there were few doubts that City were deserved winners.

While City fans swam in the Trafalgar Square fountains, the team enjoyed a victory banquet at the Café Royal before taking a special Pullman train home on Sunday. An estimated quarter of a million people stood on the streets to watch their bus make its way to Manchester Town Hall for a civic reception.

For once, Allison was not in a party mood. He had the opportunity of a lifetime weighing on his mind. Late in the season, he had been approached by an Italian journalist with an offer from Juventus to take the job of manager. Money, for himself and the team, would be no object. As usual, Allison was unhappy with his compensation from City and was spending more than he was earning. He'd just lost his car to a finance company. Here was the opportunity for financial security – if such a concept could ever be applied to Malcolm.

The follow-up came from the famous Italian agent Gigi Peronace, who had been responsible for taking the likes of Denis Law and John Charles to Italy and who was in the process of dreaming up the less than illustrious Anglo-Italian Cup. It was arranged for Allison to visit Turin after the FA Cup final to meet the club's owners, the Agnelli family of Fiat car company fame. If nothing else, he was determined to look the part and flew out in a shiny Italian-cut light blue suit, which he accessorised with white shoes. This was to be anything but a private visit, with reporters from England and Italy following his ten-day jaunt and watching him being driven around in a red Ferrari.

Allison was impressed by Juventus: its history, its facilities and its ambition. But he felt a strong emotional pull towards his City players, who he felt could achieve even more. He knew this could be his one big chance to cash in on his personal success and felt he was at the peak of his profession. 'I have seen all the best coaches in the world and, as a self-made instructor, I rate myself as good as any of them. I know my own value now.'

Yet something nagged at him about Juventus. Finding ways of spending the proposed £20,000-a-year contract would be no bother, but he sensed that the pressure to produce results would be immediate and he would have little freedom to do things his way if he failed to instigate an overnight transformation. He was suspicious of the Italian press, who pushed him hard to explain his master plan for restoring Juventus to the glory of the 1930s and who he felt would be quick to turn on him if he failed to deliver.

For once in his life the impulsive Allison hesitated over making a decision and asked for a few more days, during which he managed to become involved with a Hungarian striptease dancer at a Turin nightclub. The walks he took with her as she exercised her chihuahua in the middle of the night gave him the chance to ponder his decision. And as he strolled the streets down which Michael Caine's Minis had raced in the recently completed movie *The Italian Job*, he realised he didn't much care for the city. He also had his girlfriend, Jennifer, waiting for him back in England. He returned to Manchester, where he announced that he was turning down the Agnellis' offer – leaving Italian journalists accusing him of having simply grabbed a free holiday. Allison, though, was comfortable with his motives for the visit and would feel even more at ease with his decision when he heard that Juventus had fired the man they hired instead of him after only seven weeks. Meanwhile, his own team – despite modest League performances that would give them a tenth-place finish – were embarking on a journey that would result in a memorable cup double.

Following the Turkish trauma of a year earlier it was with some trepidation that City approached the first round of the European Cup-Winners' Cup. Drawn away in the first leg against the Spanish club Atletico Bilbao,[6] Allison and Mercer left nothing to chance, flying to watch the team play and checking on accommodation facilities. When City travelled to London to face Tottenham, they spent Friday evening in the ITV studios watching Bilbao's victory in the final of the previous season's Copa del Rey. Throughout their European campaign, the reserve team would adopt the tactics of Continental teams, such as man-to-man marking, in order to make training a more meaningful preparation for the battles ahead.

---

[6] The club is now known again as Athletic Bilbao, having reverted to its original name following a period, from 1941 to 1976, when General Franco banned teams from using non-Spanish names.

City's concerns appeared well founded when the home team, managed by former West Brom and England centre-forward Ronnie Allen, took a two-goal lead inside 11 minutes. After Young pulled one back, City went 3–1 down before half-time, but fought back to draw, Booth scoring another important goal and Bell harrying a defender into scoring in his own net. In the return leg, City achieved their first European victory, attacking from all parts of the Maine Road pitch and scoring second-half goals through Oakes, Bell and the young Ian Bowyer.

They had reached the first rung of a ladder that had proved unattainable a year earlier and were ready to climb all the way to the top. Belgian side SK Lierse, despite Allison's warnings to the contrary, offered little resistance in the second round, Lee scoring twice in the first half of the away leg and setting up a third for Bell. The return game was a formality, Bell and Lee scoring two apiece in a 5–0 win.

As the competition went into its winter recess, City's interest in the League Cup was growing. Third Division Southport had proved surprisingly stubborn on their rain-swept ground in the second round, with Lee recounting, 'We trooped into the field not tuned up to the game at all. I think we all felt that if the opposition got an early goal we could have easily chucked the game in.' Instead, they ran out 3–0 winners after a pair of saves early on by goalkeeper Joe Corrigan.

Along with Bowyer, who had inherited Coleman's number 11 shirt after the winger's October transfer to Sheffield Wednesday, Corrigan was one of two significant newcomers to the regular first-team line-up since the FA Cup win. Tall and prone to be on the heavy side, Corrigan had become an Allison project, given hour after hour of additional work by the City coach. Teammate Ian Mellor recalls, 'Every Friday Malcolm would take Joe and kick balls at him from all parts of the pitch, all different angles. It showed how much he cared about the game and the players. He just loved it.'

Mercer stated, 'Malcolm must take all the credit for Joe making the grade. I must admit even I had my doubts about him and once told Malcolm he might be wasting his time by persevering, but he was stubborn. He took three stone off the lad.' Francis Lee was another who thought Corrigan would never amount to a First Division goalkeeper, let alone go on to win nine England caps. 'He virtually manufactured Joe. But having spent so much time and energy and shown so much faith in big Joe, the honesty in Malcolm's make-up did not stop him dropping him and giving him a verbal lashing for being overweight.'

Corrigan himself, while disputing that he was 'manufactured', acknowledges Allison's considerable contribution to his development. 'He must have seen some raw ability and then he turned his knowledge towards trying to develop it. We worked hard on it together.' The most important decision Allison made on behalf of his goalkeeper was to loan him to Shrewsbury Town, where he had the opportunity to work with former Manchester United goalkeeper Harry Gregg, who was managing the club.[7] 'That was the biggest thing I did because I learned a lot from Harry. But Malcolm also brought in [former England goalkeeper] Bert Williams once or twice to work with me. These were the days before goalkeeping coaches so it shows how he was ahead of his time. As manager, Joe Mercer had the final say on team selection but Malcolm had a lot to do with me getting in the team because he had been working with me on the training field and obviously had a lot of faith in me.'

Having got past Southport, City would not have to leave Manchester again in the League Cup until the final of the tournament. Liverpool were the visitors in the third round, with Bowyer scoring what proved to be the decisive goal in a 3–2 victory. When Everton made the same trip from Merseyside, manager Harry Catterick opted to field a below-strength side and suffered a 2–0 defeat. Two goals by Bell in the first ten minutes set up a 3–0 win over Queens Park Rangers to produce the tie that had Manchester buzzing – City versus United in the semi-finals.

United were not the team they had been when winning the European Cup two years earlier. Matt Busby, now a 'Sir', had moved upstairs

---

[7] Jimmy Rimmer later benefited in a similar way when Manchester United loaned him to Swansea, where Gregg had become manager. It was a proud day for Gregg when both Corrigan and Rimmer made their England debuts in the same game, playing one half each against Italy during the Bicentennial Tournament in the United States in 1976.

a few months earlier to leave team affairs in the charge of Wilf McGuinness, an honest, decent man who never seemed anything but dwarfed by the job throughout what would turn out to be 18 unhappy months in the role. The only thing he would achieve was a near nervous breakdown and the premature loss of his hair, although a Wembley appearance early in his reign might have made a significant difference to his fate. Having already suffered a 4–0 League defeat at Maine Road, McGuinness took his team back for the first leg of the semi-final and the signs looked bad for United when Bell rounded off set-up work by Lee to score after 13 minutes.

Half-time arrived with the home team clinging to their lead but Bobby Charlton and George Best carried the game to City after the break, combining for Charlton to equalise. The League Cup, though, had not proved a happy competition for United centre-half Ian Ure. The big blond Scot with the chiselled jaw had been responsible for the mix-up that allowed Third Division Swindon to take a shock lead against Arsenal in the previous season's final, a mistake that precipitated his sale to United for £80,000 in August. Now it was Ure who helped City take an advantage into the second leg when, with two minutes left, his outstretched leg brought down Lee, who scored from the penalty spot. Referee Jack Taylor's decision so angered Best that he knocked the ball from the official's hands at the end of the game, an action that would earn him a six-week suspension.[8]

Before battle recommenced in front of 63,000 at Old Trafford, City lost Bell to a shoulder injury suffered while playing for England, but teenage sensation Bowyer saw City extend their aggregate lead after attempts by Young and Lee were blocked. United launched a spirited rally when defender Paul Edwards fired home from a Paddy Crerand pass. Midway through the second half, Best advanced on the City backline, fired in a shot that Corrigan could not hold and saw Denis Law seize the chance to level the tie at 3–3 overall. Extra-time seemed certain until City were awarded a late free-kick on the edge of the United box. Referee Jim Finney clearly raised his arm

---

[8] This was the suspension from which Best returned by scoring six goals in an 8–2 FA Cup fifth-round victory at Northampton, whose unfortunate goalkeeper was Tony Book's brother, Kim. United had earned that tie by exacting some revenge over City with a comfortable 3–0 fourth-round win at Old Trafford.

to indicate an indirect free-kick, but Lee, apparently unaware of the signal, blasted the ball towards goal. Instinctively, Stepney blocked the shot and Summerbee netted the loose ball. Stepney, who would go to Mexico as England's third keeper at the end of the season, was roundly criticised for not simply letting the ball go harmlessly into goal, although his split-second decision in the heat of the moment seems beyond reproach, even if his handling wasn't.

The traditional three months that elapsed between semi-final and final of the League Cup gave City the chance to pick up their European campaign. The timing was unfortunate, though, with a trip to Portugal to face student side Academica Coimbra in the first leg of the quarter-final coming only three days before the Wembley date with West Bromwich Albion. Allison had scouted the Coimbra area and knowing the importance of setting a relaxed tone in a potentially hectic week, booked the team into King's Palace, now converted into a hotel in a remote hillside area. The journey home from the central Portuguese town proved more problematical than a 0–0 draw in which City were rarely extended. A 13-hour flight delay because of bad weather meant that their journey from the sunshine of Portugal to the fog, snow and sleet of England was completed with only about 36 hours to go until kick-off at Wembley.

Allison ordered a Friday afternoon five-a-side to get the stiffness out of his players' limbs and then took them off to see *Butch Cassidy and the Sundance Kid* in the evening. With the game approaching, Allison told his men to ignore any lingering fatigue. 'Forget all about the hard week we had,' he told them. 'It's all in the mind. You can recover from anything in 36 hours.'

Having seen his team untroubled in Portugal, where Glyn Pardoe had played in midfield, Allison decided to play what looked an even more defensive system against Albion. Heslop would partner Booth in the centre of defence and, with Arthur Mann at left-back, Pardoe would continue to help Doyle and Oakes anchor the middle of the park. Young, the Wembley hero of less than a year earlier, was sacrificed – although somewhat consoled by being able to be present instead at the birth of his daughter. Bell would be relied upon to get forward to support Summerbee and Lee, and Allison's thought, relayed to his team, was that 'the Albion back four are not good enough to hold our front three'. Lee called it 'typical stuff from Malcolm, putting us in the right frame of mind'.

The formation might have looked as though it was built upon defensive intent but it provided the platform for an exciting display of attacking football. Wembley, going through its infamous period as a mud bath – aided by being used as a show jumping venue and, in this particular week, having been subjected to a snow blizzard – saw one of its most enthralling finals. As early as the sixth minute, City's decision to change the basic nature of their line-up appeared to have back-fired when they failed to clear a corner. Corrigan was unable to deal with the resulting cross by Ray Wilson and the ball was headed in by England international centre-forward Jeff Astle, the man who had won the FA Cup for Albion two years earlier. From that moment, however, Heslop barely gave Astle a sniff of a chance.

City players are now mostly in agreement that conceding an early goal was just the spur they needed to shake off the fatigue of the week. They quickly began to dictate the pattern of the play, with Oakes and Doyle commanding in midfield and Lee almost scoring with an acrobatic header. Colin Suggett wasted a chance to score a second Albion goal on the break, but it was no surprise when City equalised after an hour. Summerbee, back on his feet after suffering what proved to be a hairline fracture of the left leg, helped on a corner from Pardoe. Bell headed across goal and the unmarked Doyle arrived to bury the ball in the net.

Bowyer took the place of Summerbee; Book made a last-ditch tackle to deny Albion substitute Dick Krzywicki; and the 90 minutes ran out. After the week they had endured, another 30 minutes on a strength-sapping pitch was the last thing City wanted and as they took the opportunity to find an extra breath of energy Lee and Allison got into a row about tactics for the final half-hour. Lee, angry that his team had not wrapped up victory already, disagreed with Allison's desire to have him drop deeper and leave Bowyer alone up front. 'Never mind all that, Mal,' the striker yelled. 'Just give me the fucking ball. I'll win the game for us.'

Lee went out and did his own thing, continuing what many observers felt was the finest performance of his career. Tirelessly he continued to pressure the Albion defence, despite taking a physical

This Charlton Athletic team picture sums ups Malcolm Allison's career at The Valley. Standing in the back row in his street clothes, he is once again the odd man out. Allison, who has legendary goalkeeper Sam Bartram on his right, made only two first team appearances during five years with the club. (© Colorsport)

The paths of Frank O'Farrell and Malcolm Allison, pictured as teammates at West Ham, were to cross many times. They opposed each other in the FA Cup final, managed on opposite sides of the Manchester divide and, later, it was O'Farrell's Cardiff team that condemned Allison's Palace to relegation from Division Two. (© Colorsport)

Allison in action against Blackburn Rovers in an FA Cup tie in 1956. Note the modern cut of West Ham's kit compared with that of the opposition.
(© Colorsport)

West Ham manager Ted Fenton (left) and trainer Billy Moore, who, according to many of the Hammers players, were happy to let Allison get on with running the club. (© Colorsport)

Manchester City display the Second Division Championship trophy at the
start of the 1966-67 season. Back row, left to right: Tony Book, Glyn Pardoe,
Bobby Kennedy, Cliff Sear, George Heslop, Peter Blakey (physio).
Middle row: Walter Griffiths (Secretary), Roy Cheetham, Mike Doyle, Stan
Horne, Harry Dowd, Alan Oakes, Mike Summerbee, Malcolm Allison (coach).
Front row: Colin Bell, Neil Young, Johnny Crossan, Joe Mercer (manager),
David Connor, Ralph Brand, Johnny Hart (trainer). (© Colorsport)

Allison with Alan Oakes (left) and Colin Bell, one of the
City players he helped develop into an England international.
(© Colorsport)

Allison was rarely seen on the City training ground without his red tracksuit, which he wears with pride as he talks to Mike Summerbee, George Heslop and Tommy Booth. (© Colorsport)

Neil Young fires City's winning goal past Leicester keeper Peter Shilton in the 1969 FA Cup final, a game Allison was forced to watch from the stands after the FA banned him from the touchline. (© Colorsport)

Another Wembley triumph. Allison holds aloft the League Cup after City's 2-1 win against West Bromwich Albion in the 1970 final. (© Getty Images)

The famous ITV World Cup team of 1970. Presenters Jimmy Hill and Brian Moore are standing behind the revolutionary four-man panel of Bob McNab, Pat Crerand, Derek Dougan and Malcolm Allison. (© Rex Features)

Joe Mercer might be smiling but the cracks in one of football's most successful relationships can be seen on the face of Malcolm Allison as City prepare for the 1970-71 season. (© Colorsport)

Allison at the head of his Crystal Palace team of 1973-74. He tipped them for promotion but saw them relegated to the Third Division. The players are (from back, left to right): Bobby Bell, Andy McBride, Jim Cannon, John Jackson, Paul Hammond, Mel Blyth, Bill Roffey, Iain Phillips, Frank Lord (coach), David Payne, Derek Possee, Charlie Cooke, Paddy Mulligan, Alan Whittle, Bobby Tambling, Don Rogers, Tony Taylor. (© Getty Images)

Malcolm's good looks and flamboyant lifestyle took
him from the sports pages into the world of celebrity
photographers like Terry O'Neill, who took this shot in
1973. It's hard to imagine Don Revie in such a pose!
(© Getty Images)

Allison celebrates one of his most famous Palace
victories, the 3-2 FA Cup win at Chelsea in 1976.
(© Colorsport)

The Middlesbrough reign of Malcolm Allison, pictured in the
dug-out with caretaker coach Cyril Knowles, began with smiles
all round but ended in acrimony and a court battle.
(© Colorsport)

Malcolm's public appearances became rare in later life as he slipped
into the grip of mental illness. But he remains a hero at many of
his former clubs and is pictured here acknowledging the cheers
of the Crystal Palace crowd. (© Colorsport)

battering, most notably from Doug Fraser, who Lee felt 'used me as a punching bag'. He thought that Fraser had 'lost his rag because of the pressure'. Inevitably, it was Lee who helped set up the winning goal with nine minutes remaining. Confronted by two defenders, he clipped the ball forward to Bell, who back-headed towards goal. Pardoe stuck out an eager leg and hooked the ball past Osborne. Another trophy was won and another party began in Trafalgar Square, concluding the next day on the sleet-soaked paving of Manchester's Albert Square.

City's European quest continued with a hard-fought win against the Portuguese students, who appeared to be majoring in gamesmanship as they kicked and cursed their way through 120 bad-tempered minutes at Maine Road. City, sticking with their Wembley formation, struggled to create chances against a team intent on securing the goalless draw that would have seen the tie decided on the toss of a coin. City weren't helped by the loss of Bell to an ankle injury and Book must have been deciding whether to call heads or tails when, in the final minute of extra-time, Young's cross was cleared to the edge of the box and blasted back into goal by 17-year-old substitute Tony Towers.

German team Schalke 04, reportedly Hitler's favourite team during their golden period before the Second World War, were the semi-final opponents. They tried to get one over on City when they gave them one ball to warm-up with before the first leg in Germany, but Allison warned home team officials, 'Here, one ball. Manchester, no ball.' They got the message.

In heavy conditions, it took a piece of individual excellence by the best player on view, German winger Reinhardt Libuda, to win the game when he beat Pardoe and Derek Jeffries on his way to firing past Corrigan. Allison gave his players an easy week before the second leg, stepping up the work in the days immediately prior to the game and placing the emphasis on movement around the opponents' penalty area. The result was what might well have been the finest performance City produced during the Mercer–Allison era. With the familiar formation restored, their play was powerful and penetrative, with the golden boys, Lee, Bell and Summerbee, outstanding and Young back to his goalscoring best. They wiped out their opponents' first-leg goal within eight minutes when Doyle converted a deflected shot by Oakes and scored again when Young controlled in the box and fired in off the post after build-up play by Oakes and Bell. The inspired Oakes played a part in yet another goal before half-time when Lee dummied his pass for Young to score on the run.

At half-time, Allison instructed Corrigan to stop kicking the ball into the vicinity of the dangerous Libuda and, with their best player having been starved of possession, there was no way back for Schalke. By the time Libuda did score a late consolation Lee had rounded off some neat teamwork for the fourth goal and Bell's cross had found its way in for number five. The final 5–1 scoreline was a perfect reflection of the brilliant manner in which City had become the fourth English team to qualify for the final of this competition.

The venue of the final made City's achievement all the more poignant for Allison. Two decades earlier, the Prater Stadium in the Austrian capital of Vienna was where the eyes of a young soldier had been opened to the way it was possible for football to be played. The circle would now be completed. Preparation for the final saw Allison employing Booth as a sweeper against the City attack to get them accustomed to the system they would be facing. Their final training session was in Vienna on the eve of the game, when Allison got lost in the woods after being tailed off behind the two groups of joggers ahead. He ended up running nine miles instead of three.

With rain lashing down as kick-off approached, Mercer warned his players that the crowd would be small. Few Polish fans were in attendance because of the difficulties of travelling from eastern Europe, while the locals were likely to stay in the dry comfort of their living rooms. Concerned that City only performed at their best in front of big crowds, Mercer said, 'You will have to create your own atmosphere.'

Allison's talk to his players echoed his favourite theme about European sides. 'Often they don't know what to do when a team attacks them. They cannot believe it when we take the play to them. So pressurise them and don't give them a chance.'

Wednesday, 29 April 1970, was a historic night for English football. A record British television audience for a club match was achieved when a combined total of 29 million people watched BBC's and ITV's simultaneous coverage of Chelsea's FA Cup final replay victory over Leeds at Old Trafford. The same bad luck that had led to City's title being overshadowed by Manchester United winning the European Cup weeks later meant that this was the night City chose to win the European Cup-Winners' Cup. The lack of live television coverage meant that what Allison and Mercer considered to be their greatest triumph is possibly the most overlooked European triumph by an English team. Hardly anyone saw City's clash with Polish side Gornik Zabrze in person, either. Only 10,000 of the 80,000 places in the stadium were filled, about 3,000 of them by City fans.

The Poles, who had needed a coin toss to beat a horribly negative Roma side in the semi-final, were a dangerous team on the break but appeared to focus too heavily on trying to contain this City starting line-up: Corrigan, Book, Pardoe, Doyle, Booth, Oakes, Heslop, Bell, Lee, Young, Towers. The nagging leg injury of Summerbee kept him on the sidelines, while Oakes played through the pain of a calf injury. Doyle lasted only 17 minutes before being carried off to be replaced by Bowyer, causing Bell to take up a deeper role.

Gornik's tactics were undermined by conceding a goal in the 12th minute. Again, Young was the man for the big occasion, pouncing on a rebound after Lee had sliced between two defenders and shot against the post. It was a sweet moment for the player who had been left out of the League Cup final. Two minutes from half-time, Young took possession away from defender Florenski and was in full flight towards goal when keeper Kostka sent him flying, allowing Lee to convert the penalty via the goalie's legs. City seemed comfortable, but a goal midway through the second half by Oslizlo, set up by the dangerous Lubanski, made it a nervous finish. In typical Allison style, City never sat back, continuing to play fluent football in search of a third. It didn't arrive, but nor did the Polish equaliser and the final whistle sounded on another City triumph. A year behind schedule maybe, but Allison's men had shown that they could dominate in Europe.

'This was our moment of triumph,' he said. 'This was the moment that I knew the [Helenio] Herreras and their like are not in the same league as us. We go out and throw ourselves at teams, going for goals all the time.'

This time, the City party went on through the night, starting at Vienna City Hall and ending up with Lee dancing in his underpants on the piano at the team hotel. As Allison ordered bottles of champagne, the establishment's manager voiced concern that he had ordered too many. 'Don't worry. I've got £500 to spend,' Allison insisted. It kept the manager happy even if it was a white lie.

Reporter James Lawton recalls, 'One of my fondest memories of Malcolm is after the final in Vienna. James Mossop and I had gone for a glass of champagne in a club somewhere and had got skimmed by them. Malcolm came in a little later and asked how we were doing. Jimmy said, "Actually, Malcolm, we have just been skimmed." Malcolm just put his hand in his pocket and pulled out a roll of Austrian bank notes and said, "There you are, boys. Go and have a drink on me." That was typical of Malcolm and his expansive nature.'

Allison watched dawn break over the city that meant so much to him and was joined at his hotel by Lawton. 'I went to his room to do a column with him. He was still with Beth then and she was doing the packing. He was out on the balcony smoking a cigar and he turned to me and said, "What a great feeling to be in Vienna having won a big title. I feel like Napoleon this morning."'

None of the City fans seemed to mind that they were kept waiting at Manchester Town Hall because of the team being late for their departure from Vienna airport. Allison had flown home with hopes soaring for his team and for himself. He saw another five or ten years of domination stretching ahead. Yet he would never win another trophy with an English club. Big Mal, however, was about to be unleashed on the world.

12

THE BIRTH OF BIG MAL

'I beheld the wretch – the miserable monster whom I had created'

– Mary Shelley, *Frankenstein*, 1818

John Bromley, then the head of ITV sport, would not have realised it, but at the moment he sat down to plan the network's coverage of the 1970 World Cup he became a television Frankenstein. When ITV went on-air at 5.15 p.m. on Sunday, 31 May with its coverage of the opening ceremony and the Mexico–USSR match, the monster of Big Mal was brought to life. All that was missing was the lightning bolt striking the castle tower.

Events in Mexico changed the face of televised football. For those who had upgraded their sets, there was a glorious parade of colour, making the brilliant football of the Brazilians even more vivid and vibrant. For those tuning in to ITV, there was placed before them a new way of discussing football on television. Here were blokes sitting around arguing and wise-cracking about the game in the way the average viewer did with his mates at the pub. Those who had spent the earlier part of that Sunday afternoon watching the rapid-fire delivery of Bob Monkhouse fronting the popular game show, *The Golden Shot*, would scarcely have seen the join.

Brian Moore had been asked to anchor ITV's coverage in the London studio instead of taking his place behind the microphone in Mexico, with Jimmy Hill placed in charge of a revolutionary new feature – the 'World Cup Panel'. Giving their views on the action unfolding before them were Wolves and Northern Ireland centre-forward Derek Dougan, Scotland international wing-half Pat Crerand and England full-back Bob McNab, who had been among the six men sent home by Alf Ramsey from his original travelling squad of 28. Alongside them was the undoubted leader of the gang, Malcolm Allison. The next three weeks would change the course of his life.

This was the moment that 'Big Mal' became more than just a convenient nickname applied by the media when they needed a snappy headline. Big Mal was now a living, breathing personality. He became the Mr Hyde to Allison's cerebral, innovative Dr Jekyll. Having won four major trophies in three years, Allison did not win a single thing in English football after the birth of Big Mal, despite two decades of trying. It seems to be more than coincidence.

Allison's profile away from the field was already growing, having been introduced by Derek Ufton to the agent Bagenal Harvey, the man who turned Denis Compton into the original 'Brylcreem Boy'. Ufton recalls, 'I was working with Bagenal and when Mal went to Manchester City I got him involved. Bagenal was a great guy. He was the first agent and he suffered because people didn't really know what that meant, so people used to call him Mr X. I said to Bagenal, "You have got to get Malcolm on the books because he has so much to offer and he is bound to be wanted by the media." Malcolm was two hours late for their first meeting, which didn't go down well. Bagenal wanted to be the top guy and the one who set the timetable.'

Newspaper columns and some work with ITV followed. It was natural, therefore, that the call would go out to Allison when Bromley, who had also been represented by Harvey, decided in the spring of 1970, 'We need some people who can actually talk lucidly about football.' Originally, he had planned to use his panellists individually, but once they had been assembled and were wondering what exactly their roles would be, Bromley informed them that they would be placed on screen together. It was an approach Allison understood, like throwing his team into all-out attack without responsibility for covering at the back. The resulting analysis was lively enough to complement the unforgettable action on the field; loud enough to match the fashionable shirts the protagonists wore instead of the traditional sensible jacket and tie. It was noisy and it was unscripted – a far cry from the speak-when-you-are-spoken-to BBC style.

Bromley recalled, 'Crerand, the tough little Scot, and Allison, the hard-nosed Cockney, were the baddies, and the charming Dougan with the lovely McNab were the goodies. The whole mix was absolutely right and it took off and they became folk heroes in four weeks.'

McNab adds, 'People had never seen anything like that before. The BBC was very stuffed shirt. John Bromley was brilliant and I really liked him.'

Brian Moore, who sat as a somewhat detached observer as mayhem swirled around the studio, explained, 'We suddenly realised we had hit the jackpot,' putting the success down to employing 'attractive men with a knowledgeable, knockabout style'. He added, 'They gave football punditry a fresh intoxicating sparkle that has never quite been matched since. For the first time during the coverage of sport on television, we had passionate, controversial, confrontational discussion, sometimes outrageous, even bigoted.'

According to Dougan, 'The chemistry was right and we used to spark off each other. Not once did we have a rehearsal. Malcolm was the only guy that I have ever worked with who could drink an excess of champagne and go on there and not slur his words. I used to admire him for doing that because I wouldn't try to do it.'

McNab has similar memories: 'We all stayed at the Hendon Hall Hotel and Malcolm would be ordering Riesling with wild strawberries for lunch and talking about which wines he was going to try the next day. Then we went in the green room and I had to be careful because I was never a great drinker – and they were obviously trying to loosen your tongue. They did ply you with drink, but Malcolm seemed to be able to cope with it. I can't say drink had any influence on what he said or did on screen.'

It was the survival of the fittest once the cameras started rolling, with Allison, puffing cigar smoke over Dougan in the next seat, revelling in the competition. 'Jimmy tried to control it, but Malcolm used to try to control Jimmy,' says McNab. 'Jimmy was taking his job very seriously, which he had to do, and Malcolm would take the piss out of him unmercifully.'

McNab also recalls Dougan becoming a target of Allison's mischief making. 'Malcolm would say stuff to Derek off-camera to set him up, hoping that he would copy him and say something silly on air.'

The basic rule of the panel was that the loudest opinion was usually the one that got heard, with McNab – himself not exactly shy and retiring – playing the role of the quiet man on the end of the desk. At one point the producers suggested giving him a bell to ring when he wanted to make a point. Allison was clearly the star of the show, as Moore recalled in his autobiography *The Final Score*:

Of all the men I have met in my football travels, none was bigger, brasher, brighter or more likeable than Big Mal. He looked striking enough on our panel to fit the James Bond image, and in no time he had captured every female heart – well, almost. The only time I saw him come off second best was when, in our hotel one lunchtime, he tried to chat up that stunning actress Diana Rigg, who was passing through. She gave him a haughty once-over and in five seconds turned on her delectable heel and left him for dead.

The effect of the panel was exactly what Bromley had hoped. For the first time, ITV was pulling in numbers for its sports coverage to compare with, and on occasions beat, the BBC. This group of good-looking, fast-talking, stylishly dressed men were making football more accessible than it had ever been. At a time when the sport was still a fiercely male preserve, even female viewers, who, as Moore put it, 'didn't know an overlap from an underpass', were drawn into the tournament.

Fan letters poured into the ITV studios and the panel members suddenly found that they were household faces. Shopping or eating in public became a long round of autographs. McNab says, 'It really promoted Malcolm and he took to it like a duck to water. He loved going out and being recognised in restaurants. One night we went to eat in the White Elephant restaurant in Mayfair. Michael Caine came in with a group of people and he came over and bought us a couple of bottles of champagne. He told his people to go and get themselves some drinks "while I have a drink with the lads". He said he loved the show. Malcolm took over then. He was the leader and Michael Caine seemed pleased just to be with us.'

Allison quickly realised that he was proving to be worth far more to ITV than his basic fee, which was £500 for three weeks. One day the Hendon Hall Hotel manager approached Bromley nervously with Malcolm's bill, which was rapidly growing thanks to the regular orders for the best champagne and expensive cigars. Bromley took one look, weighed up the value for money Allison was offering to his programme, and assured the worried man that all was in order.

In among all the discussion of Pelé, Beckenbauer and Alf Ramsey, another name cropped up on a couple occasions – that of Malcolm's old flame Christine Keeler. McNab recounts, 'We went out to Tramps in the middle of the week and it was as dead as a dodo. All we were doing was sitting and drinking in the end. Malcolm wouldn't give up and it got to about 4.30 and he said, "Do you know Christine Keeler? She is a friend of mine." I told him she would go bananas and suggested we just went home, but he said, "No, let's go and have a drink with Christine." So Malcolm, Paddy and I got in a cab and pulled up outside this apartment in a mews-type house. He was banging on the door and shouting, "Come on, Christine, let's have a drink." This window opens upstairs and she shouts out, "Malcolm, why don't you fuck off?" She slaughtered him. I was trying to disappear under the car seat.'

Another time, Allison had the panellists worked up into a frenzy when he slipped into conversation that he was meeting Christine for lunch and that anyone was welcome to join them. Tongues hanging out, the crew turned up on the appointed day dressed to kill – even Jimmy Hill – only to find that Ms Keeler had sent her apologies.

On screen, it was inevitably Allison's comments that created the biggest ripples, especially when he referred to Russian and Romanian players as 'peasants', resulting in calls of complaint to the ITV switchboard. Says McNab, 'I couldn't relate this to anything specific, but I think Malcolm was cute and clever enough to say something to cause a reaction. He was highly capable of that.'

England's hopes of retaining their trophy ended in the quarter-finals when West Germany came back from two goals down in Leon. The defeat gave City striker Francis Lee the opportunity to point out an interesting comparison between the Ramsey regime and the methods of Allison at Maine Road. Describing the scene heading into extra-time, he said, 'We trooped off the field to Sir Alf and I was expecting the team would get a real roasting. I suppose my club background took over here. But I know if we had let the management down at Maine Road like this there would have been no punches pulled. If the same thing had happened in an FA Cup tie, we would have been bawled out, and justifiably.'

Back in the studio, it was Allison who was the fiercest critic of England's performance. While McNab was sensitive about making negative comments about players who had been his teammates until a few weeks earlier, Allison let rip. He felt that Beckenbauer was too slow to play as an effective sweeper and could have been frightened if attacked. Individually, he focused on Tottenham midfielder Alan Mullery. He made no bones about stating that his own player, Colin Bell, should have been in the team from the start instead of coming on as a second-half substitute when Ramsey decided to save Bobby Charlton's legs for the semi-final.

While reviews of the panel, and Allison in particular, were generally favourable, some felt the criticism of Mullery, given his efforts throughout the tournament, had gone beyond reasoned thinking. In *The Times*, John Hennessy wrote:

> Allison's prejudices in isolation would be unbearable. How a man could fail to salute Mullery with enthusiasm rather than grudging reluctance after his match against Pelé is beyond me.

Sensing the opportunity for some must-see television, Bromley invited Mullery on air upon his return to England to confront Allison. Mullery agreed as long as the discussion was aired live. The debate that ensued was exactly what Bromley had envisaged, gradually becoming more personal as the two men warmed up. Allison, who had pointedly ignored Mullery in the pre-show hospitality area, began by criticising Ramsey and then took up the theme of Mullery's own performance. The Spurs man responded by asking Allison, 'How many caps did you win?', before delivering the *coup de grâce* by taking one of his own out of a carrier bag and tossing it at Allison. 'I've got 30 of these,' he said. 'This one's spare. You have it because it's the only way you'll ever get one.'

Moore, whose job it was to prevent events degenerating into fisticuffs, noted, 'In its way, it was all pretty unpleasant.'

Jimmy Hill would recall, 'His stand against Alan Mullery as a class England player, against which he argued to the death, turned a lot of people off him. It would have been easier to coat his criticisms with sugar. But obstinately, his brain kept telling him truth was more important than diplomacy. It is almost as if the bigger the audience he has, the more important he feels it is to reveal his innermost thoughts to all of them. The truth for him has to be stated at all costs. Football is too precious to lie.'

It was an early example of the kind of brutal made-for-TV approach that has worked so successfully for the likes of Simon Cowell. And it all added to the Big Mal legend – even if, on this occasion, he was on the receiving end of the knockout blow.

For coverage of the final between Brazil and Italy, the panel were decked out in dinner jackets. It meant that Allison, tall and handsome, cut quite a dash when the team arrived at the Brazilian Embassy for a post-game reception. Predictably, he caught the eye of a beautiful young Brazilian girl called Claudia, beginning an affair that continued for two years. They would meet up when he was in London, or arrange rendezvous at hotels in Manchester, and Malcolm admitted it was an affair that revolved around his availability – until she announced to him over dinner that she was to be married.

It was Malcolm Allison who checked in at the Hendon Hall early in the summer, but it was Big Mal who arrived back in Manchester. Life would never be the same again and Allison seemed uncertain whether he wished to be a serious football man or a show-business celebrity. Results, and the testimony of those around him, suggest that the latter was more often than not the case. Bob McNab, who saw the transformation close up, says, 'I think the other side, the opposite of that professionalism he had, came out more after the World Cup. He took to that celebrity thing. He loved it. He got that in him and he wanted to be in front of the camera.'

Mexico '70 set in motion a vicious circle from which Allison was unable, or disinclined, to break free. Unleashed upon the general public, the more extreme the Big Mal character became, the less successful was Allison the coach. And the more games he lost – and the further his footballing credibility waned in the ensuing years – the more outrageous he would have to become in order to be heard and noticed.

Allison was to be a regular feature on television over the next few years, appearing once again on the ITV World Cup panel in 1974, by which time he had Brian Clough lining up alongside him following a transfer from the BBC. And his column in the *Daily Express*, launched in 1969, would become required reading. 'He had a good sense of what would catch the eye in print,' recalls his ghostwriter, James Lawton. 'But he was very genuine about football in his opinions. He was a playboy and a self-publicist but no one could question his passion for the game.'

The prescience of one of Allison's columns particularly sticks in Lawton's mind. 'After that dreadful World Cup in 1990, FIFA were so concerned about the stultifying football that they brought in the rule banning the back-pass. Not many agreed at the time, but everyone would agree it has immeasurably improved the game. But I had written with Malcolm a big splash almost 20 years earlier suggesting exactly that. Everyone said he was mad, but he was explicit about how it would make defenders honest, make them think about playing the ball and open up the game. He said it would kill off the coaches who played route-one football. To me, that is one of the most dramatic examples of a man who is ahead of his time.'

Pointed attacks on England managers and the English football system were to become a staple of Allison's media appearances. He argued that Ramsey was a good coach of a bad team, but couldn't extract the maximum potential out of a good side, which was why he failed in 1970 with what was considered to be an even stronger squad than that of four years earlier. After Ramsey named his squad for a 1973 friendly against Yugoslavia, Allison stated, 'Ramsey lives in his own football world. He picked Manchester City players who are completely off form.' Ramsey's successor, Don Revie, could do little right in Allison's eyes, while Graham Taylor, two decades later, was described as 'arrogant and a tactical disaster'.

In the mid-'70s, Allison was claiming that Trevor Francis and Alan Hudson were the only potentially world-class players in the country and that the likes of Johnny Haynes, Bobby Charlton, Stanley Matthews and Tom Finney had been great players in spite of the English system. None, he said, had been coached to greatness in the manner of Hungarian players like Puskas and Kocsis. 'In England we have been too sloppy,' he said. 'We do things out of habit and without properly enquiring about their value.'

Friend and journalist Jeff Powell argues that Allison eventually came to appreciate that Ramsey's World Cup winners had not been such a total anathema to his own preferred style of football, but applauds Allison's continued stance against 'functional football'.

Powell says, 'Graham Taylor made a silk purse out of a sow's ear at Watford, but Malcolm said that the long-ball type of football promoted by him and people like Charlie Hughes at the FA should not be involved with the England team. They were all about getting the ball into the corners and winning free-kicks or corner-kicks. Malcolm had views that the geometricians of football couldn't cope with. He offered something bigger, something on a more major scale. Their brand of football was pretty horrible compared to Malcolm's great vision.'

Allison had seriously held beliefs and had been expressing them ever since he was a young player at Charlton. The difference now was that he knew the impact they would have when they came from the lips of Big Mal, a character Lawton believes had always been lurking not far below the skin of the man with whom he developed a long-standing friendship. 'Big Mal was a self-generating phenomenon, partly due to his zest for life. I never felt that it was a performance – not like Ron Atkinson, who, without being offensive to him, was aping Big Mal when he became Big Ron.'

Gradually, however, that side of Allison's character would soon be threatening to win possession of his soul. McNab comments, 'We had become very close and I thought the world of Malcolm. I enjoyed him. He was flamboyant and devil-may-care, but he was self-destructive. He was a genius, but he was flawed. He loved his football, but I wonder in the end if he would even jeopardise that for a good night out.'

There were, of course, plenty of good nights out in Big Mal's life – enough to fill a book on their own. He got himself into enough scrapes that when Joe Mercer was stopped in his car by police for speeding, his first thought on seeing the blue light pulling him over was, 'Christ, now what's Malcolm done?'

A few times Allison's escapades landed him in trouble, although most were harmless high jinks. Like the time City played a testimonial game in London for former QPR player Frank Sibley and one group of players were out until six in the morning. As they approached the hotel they saw Francis Lee staggering along the road with what appeared to be a large sack over his shoulders. His burden turned out to be Allison, who was left sleeping in his room as the team headed back to Manchester.

Another London visit ended, after a detour to the Playboy Club, in a bar where Allison's group encountered James Last, the pianist, composer and orchestra leader who had sold millions of records around the world. Allison persuaded him to play something for them, before Summerbee, Lee and Rodney Marsh hijacked his performance and had him playing accompaniment to an old-fashioned English knees-up. Allison sent four bottles of champagne over as a thank-you.

Marsh, who signed for City in 1972, also tells the story of a game in France, after which Allison was ordering champagne and holding court in the hotel bar. He was interrupted by a sheepish head waiter who nervously informed him that the bill had reached the equivalent of £1,000. Allison took a long drag on his cigar and barked back, 'Is that all? Don't come back until it is double that.'

Another time, Allison and a couple of his players began an afternoon session that eventually turned into a full-scale party, in which 23 bottles of champagne were uncorked. With only the final bottle in the crate left to be opened, Allison said to the owner, 'I'm not going to have the 24th bottle. I don't want people to think I am a flash bastard.'

Don Rogers, who would play for Allison at Crystal Palace, remembers him as 'the champagne man' and recalls attending a boxing awards dinner with him at the Café Royal. 'I happened to be the one chosen to sit next to Malcolm at ringside watching the boxing. I was sat there and the next thing I know he is delivering a bottle of champagne to me under the seats – while the fights were on.'

He continues, 'One time, we were in Italy in the Anglo-Italian

Cup. There was just me, Alan Whittle and Malcolm sat round the table – everyone else had gone to bed. Malcolm called the waiter and asked for a bottle of champagne. The waiter said he was very sorry but they only had two left and they were both about £25, which in those days was very expensive. Malcolm said, "We will have both please." I thought it was just class.'

And Allison would never lose his love of a social occasion. Frank O'Farrell could be telling a tale of teenage buddies instead of two men in their 70s when he says, 'The last dinner I was at with Malcolm was up at Nottingham. We stayed up late having a few drinks and I remember putting him to bed well pissed at about three in the morning. I had to take his tie and shoes off and put his coat over him. He didn't know where he was. The chamber maid let me in next morning to check he was all right. I just left him in peace.'

One of the consistent aspects of stories of Allison's partying is the fact that he was so often to be found out on the town with players who, by daytime, were in his charge. Clearly, he never felt that such a situation would undermine his authority within the club. As Rogers comments, 'You don't see that very often; our previous Palace manager, Bert Head, wouldn't have done it. But the next day he was the boss again. You knew where you were. You could have a good laugh and drink, but then he was coach again and you were the player.'

Colin Bell has the same memories. 'He was a good chap away from the game, but once it was football, it was football 100 per cent. If you mentioned anything else he would chew your head off.'

Jeff Powell even remembers Malcolm's girlfriend, Serena Williams, falling foul of that rule. 'Malcolm used to hold court in Sam's Chop House in Manchester, especially after European games. We would come back to London together and then I would drive him to the Playboy Club, where he was seeing Serena. Bobby Moore would join us and Serena would ask, "Can't we talk about anything else but football?" Malcolm would say, "Bobby's here. No we can't."'

Lee continues, 'Malcolm created a great club atmosphere. He could have a few drinks with the lads and could voice opinions to individuals over a drink. You could have your say back. It wasn't all, "Yes, sir. You are right, Malcolm." There were plenty of times when people argued back and told him he was wrong and it created a fair bit of communication between management and players.'

Powell agrees that Allison could turn social events into further education. 'Because he knew a lot he wasn't afraid of being embarrassed by players coming in with opinions so he didn't exclude them. He was one of the few who could have a social relationship with the players without losing their respect and if someone gave him their opinion, he would not dismiss it, but say, "Why do you think that?" He would take little bits from everyone. If property is about location, location, location, Malcolm was about information, information, information.'

Mike Summerbee never felt that having Malcolm along on nights out with him and George Best was a compromise of Allison's position. One such evening produced an often-repeated tale that Powell recounts. 'Malcolm had ended up with George in a casino. It was the night before a City–United game so instead of telling George he should be at home in bed Malcolm plied him with drink. In his team talk next day he said, "You will be all over George Best today, boys. I left him at six o'clock this morning and he was paralytic drunk." By half-time United were about three up and Best was scoring goals and setting them up. When Malcolm walked in the dressing-room, Colin Bell piped up, "Do us a favour and don't take Bestie out on the piss again."'

The incident did little to diminish respect for Allison, feelings that had grown when players realised that their boss trusted them to behave like professionals. The City players were allowed to have a bottle of brandy on the dressing-room table and could have a nip before the game. They could also invite friends to visit the inner sanctum, and Lee described show-business figures like Kenny Lynch and Matt Monro, boxer Johnny Prescott and even the odd beauty queen being present on match day. 'The management know they can trust us and anything that is good for a laugh must be OK,' he said.

Bell continues, 'When players went out and had a pint he treated them like men, not like kids on a school trip. If players had a bad game after breaking the rules then he let them know. But if they performed and gave 100 per cent he probably wouldn't say anything to them. Once their form dipped he would say, "I know you have been out. Watch it."'

Tony Coleman, the wild-man winger Allison persuaded Mercer to sign, had finally outstayed his Maine Road welcome late in 1969. In the end his antics had become too much for even the tolerant Allison and he was sold to Sheffield Wednesday. On one occasion Malcolm was tipped off that Coleman was out in the Cabaret Club after midnight and having tracked him down, he slapped his face. Coleman was ready to fight but Allison got him out of the nightclub and before long, out of City. 'I could not afford to let anyone get away with it,' he said.

Allison's relationship with young forward Stan Bowles was another stormy one, again coming to blows. With Bowles's wife due to go into labour, Mercer had excused the player from a two-day training trip to Southport, leaving him to practise with the reserves. When the first team returned to Manchester, Allison barked at Bowles, 'Why the bloody hell weren't you at Southport?' Bowles explained that Mercer had excused him, but Allison shouted back, 'I'm in charge of this team and I decide who stays at home.' Bowles's account has Allison starting to push him and, when the player refused to back down, throwing the first punch. Reserve-team coach Johnny Hart intervened to separate the two men, who barely spoke after that incident.

Having made a goal-scoring impact in his first couple of games in 1967–68, Bowles had played only one game the following season. His appearances in 1969–70 reached double figures but he knew Allison would not allow established first-teamers to lose a permanent place through injury. Bowles was reprimanded for missing a flight to Amsterdam as his relationship with Allison became more fraught. The coach felt that his young forward was falling in with the wrong crowd in the wrong parts of town – a typical case of 'don't do as I do, do as I tell you' because Bowles found that 'wherever I went, it seemed Malcolm had already been there'.

Bowles acknowledges Allison as a creative, passionate and innovative coach, but has no regard for his man-management skills. In his autobiography, he argues that, unlike the avuncular Mercer, Allison was unapproachable for players with personal problems. 'He might fly into a temper at the slightest provocation.' That view offers an interesting comparison with the unconditional love and respect dispensed by most members of the championship-winning team.

Bowles was duly suspended by the club, then shipped off on loan to Bury, before ending up at Crewe. He felt his unhappy experience with Allison came back to haunt him when Crewe were trying to cash in on his good form by selling him. He believed that Allison was giving unfavourable character references, forcing his former coach to declare, 'I have personally not dealt with any inquiries about Stan. We want him to get on, he has a lot of ability. Let's hope his past is behind him now.' Even that statement could have been read as carrying an implication of trouble. But in later years Bowles came to believe Allison had done him a favour by kicking him out of City, giving him a determination to succeed that propelled him to eventual stardom at Queens Park Rangers.

Meanwhile, other young players were trying, with various degrees of success, to force their way into the successful City side as the first full season of the 1970s heralded in the age of widespread colour television coverage of football and contrastingly dismal performances by the England team. The esteem in which Allison was held by the senior players helped smooth the newcomers' transition from the reserve and youth teams.

Winger Ian Mellor, who made his City debut in 1970–71, explains, 'When you went into the side everyone tried to help you because they knew you were good enough, otherwise Malcolm wouldn't have put you there in the first place. Malcolm believed in giving the kids a chance and a lot of us came though – Willie Donachie, Frank Carrodus, Derek Jeffries, Tony Towers.'

Mellor and his counterparts experienced the motivational powers that had pushed the likes of Bell, Summerbee and Lee into the England team. 'He was the best I had ever come across. He was very passionate about what he believed in, about how he wanted things to work. If you weren't trying to do it right he would be really angry and frustrated.'

Allison appeared on the touchline during the first half of Mellor's first-team debut, shouting, 'If you don't fucking sort yourself out, I will have you off at half-time.' But by the interval, Allison had reappraised his approach. 'He had simmered down and we had a little chat about certain things, he had collected himself because he had been frustrated. But I would have run through a brick wall for him. Everything he did was positive. He said to me, "If you are in the final third and you are up against a defender you take him on, or you pass the ball forward. If you can't, you pass the ball square and only as a last resort do you pass the ball back." Another time we played Leeds and I remember him saying to me, "If you get one-on-one with [goalkeeper] Gary Sprake, put it to his left because he is slower going down to that side." He had actually worked it out in that sort of detail.'

Mellor also remembers Allison looking after the financial concerns of young players. 'When I first turned pro, I had a two-year contract with a two-year option with a basic of £18 a week and £35 if I played in the first team. After I had played about 10 or 15 games someone said I needed to go and see Malcolm about my contract. He said, "No problem. I will put you on a one-year with a one-year option and put you on 50 quid a week, no matter what." He was a players' man.'

But while the likes of Mellor were being looked after by their inspirational coach and others, like Bowles, were falling out with him, Allison was about to become embroiled in a much bigger battle – one that would change the very nature of his relationship with the club he loved.

13

THE END OF THE AFFAIR

'I'd had enough of being patted on the head. I thought that if I was not going to be given what was my due, I would attempt to take it for myself'

– Malcolm Allison

If a relationship counsellor had gone digging for the origins of the 'irreconcilable differences' that led to the break-up of Malcolm Allison's footballing marriage to Joe Mercer, the obvious starting point would have been that triumphant night in Vienna. Success in the Cup-Winners' Cup was the sixth trophy born of the partnership – if one includes Division Two and the FA Charity Shield – but the season that followed was to see them effectively sterilised by a domestic dispute. At its root was Allison's belief that he should have inherited full control of the Manchester City team after victory in Austria.

As Allison had celebrated in the rain, he couldn't help thinking back a few months to the moment when Mercer, following the League Cup semi-final victory, had said to him, 'This year will do me, Mal.' He had heard a similar comment before – Mercer's 'two years' before their first game together – but 'the times had been so good, so rich, and fulfilling, that I never pressed the point'.

Allison's enjoyment of City's latest achievement was all the more intense for his faith in Mercer's intention to execute a seamless transfer of power. He later recalled:

I thought my time had come. We had towels over our heads, the rain slanted in cold on our faces, but it was a warm feeling that spread through my body. I had slogged for five years and now I was ready to receive real status. I didn't want to clamber over Joe. I wanted recognition of my work with the team. I wanted to be the team manager. Joe could have any title he wanted.

I still valued him highly and I imagined we could work together as closely as before. Now I was to get the acceptance of a manager in my own right. It was a good feeling I took back to the old luxurious hotel near the Hapsburg's palace.

Once he had emerged from the summer with his national profile, not to mention ego, considerably enhanced by his World Cup television appearances, Allison felt even less inclined to settle for continued status as number two. Yet it did not take long for him to experience the sinking realisation that Mercer had either forgotten, or was ignoring, what had been said. Allison was forced to accept that Mercer had simply not appreciated the extent of his ambition, while he himself had been guilty of underestimating the hold that the sequence of success exerted over his boss.

Malcolm was enough of a junkie for the glory of the game to understand Mercer's reluctance to go cold turkey. What angered him was his belief that Mercer had twice reneged on his commitment about the future. Had Mercer never said anything to build up his hopes, Allison believed he could have continued to work together effectively with him – although it is still likely he would have possessed only a finite amount of patience in such a situation. Allison couldn't help thinking that the original comment on the bus to Middlesbrough was Mercer's way of taking advantage of his ambition and naivety, dangling a carrot that might never materialise.

Mercer did indicate that Allison could have the title of team manager, but made it clear that he would still make the final decisions, a superficial tinkering with job titles that Allison dismissed by saying, 'He threw me a sprat.' And he explained, 'I suppose it was then that I decided to organise a takeover of Manchester City.'

So it was that the 1970–71 season was played out against the backdrop of a debilitating battle for control of the City boardroom. By the end of it, it was unclear whether Allison had advanced closer to his goal of taking complete control of the team. What was certain, though, was that he'd come perilously close to becoming a victim of the power struggle, while his relationship with Mercer had suffered irrevocable damage.

Allison's impatience led him to conclude that a new group of directors might help to progress his ambition. He also recognised that the needs of the modern game required a more businesslike approach than that of the current board and felt that there were too few men of commercial vision supporting the chairman.

It is a view shared, then and now, by Ian Niven, whose introduction as a director was drawing near and who had got to know many of the City players after taking over the Fletcher's Arms pub in the Manchester suburb of Denton. He offers valuable insight into the workings of the club at that time. 'I thought the board were not adventurous or forward looking. Boards consisted of older men who I thought were fuddy-duddies and out of touch, although they were not bad people. I originally had no pretension of joining the board but I used to write to the club a lot.

'The hierarchy of the club were very old-fashioned and Malcolm wasn't their cup of tea. They didn't like his attitude or his lifestyle. He was in command of himself and was so forward looking. I felt the club secretary at that time, Walter Griffiths, had been allowed to run the place. He was the kingpin and was a good administrator, but he was jealous of Malcolm. We didn't have our own training ground and Malcolm got frustrated about things like that. When people like me heard about it we got frustrated too. We wanted the club to move on, but there were murmurs from the club that they thought they could manage without Malcolm.'

One incident sums up the stifling bureaucracy of City's boardroom. Former club stalwart and Wrexham manager Ken Barnes had quit his job as boss of Bangor City after being invited by Mercer to join his staff, but instead ended up spending most of his days at the Fletcher's Arms. 'The board wouldn't countersign the appointment, so he was unemployed,' Niven explains. 'I wrote to the chairman, Albert Alexander, and mentioned Ken's situation.'

Niven warned that the outcome could be more bad publicity after a recent court case in which a director had been removed from the board. He was soon receiving a call from Alexander, who stated calmly, 'We have a problem. The board makes the appointments, not the manager.'

Having pointed out that this was a position on the football staff, not in the offices, Niven was informed, 'He has to write and apply.'

Niven continues, 'Ken was his own man, not influenced by others, and he said, "I am not bloody writing a letter. I have got the job." Eventually I wrote the letter, took Ken into my office and almost had to guide his hand to sign it. He got the job.'

In Allison's opinion, Mercer had been too much in awe of the board to challenge their retarded outlook and officious methods. Mercer had what Malcolm felt was 'an excessive respect for the establishment', whereas Allison thought that the duo's success gave them the right to be bold in their battles with the directors. He wanted to take them on over the signing of new players, improved contracts and upgraded facilities. His view was that Mercer enjoyed the power and glory, but craved an easy life to go with it.

When it became known that vice-chairman Frank Johnson was ready to sell £100,000 worth of shares, Allison saw his chance. Whoever bought those shares would be close to taking control of the club. He identified a possible buyer in Oldham-based double-glazing tycoon Joe Smith, who asked Ian Niven if he could set up a meeting with Johnson. 'I knew Joe from my pub,' says Niven. 'I thought it was great that we had someone new who wanted to get on the board.'

Smith had been a City fan for as many of his 51 years as he could remember, although Niven says, 'He had done well in life and saw it more as a business. He'd moved from selling encyclopaedias to windows, had spent time in Canada and was ahead of the game in double glazing in this country. I think he saw City as a bit of an ego thing.'

Having agreed a deal with Johnson, Smith went to see Albert Alexander to explain his plans for the club, although he was hardly welcomed with open arms. An indignant Alexander said, 'I hadn't had my breakfast when he called on me. I told my wife to ask him to wait while I washed and shaved.'

Smith was soon declaring that he and his partners had bought

Johnson's 521 shares, claiming that the main reason behind his involvement was to safeguard Allison's future with the club. Saying he had no desire to remove Alexander as chairman, he added, 'I will do my utmost, everything in my power, to cooperate in any way in any project with Mr Allison to better the club. He is the greatest man in football.' According to Allison, Smith promised him a 20-year contract with City if he took control of the club.

Tony Book recalls becoming aware of something brewing when he arrived for a game to see a gleaming new Rolls-Royce pulling into the Maine Road car park. 'Someone said to me, "You will have to be watching that car soon." It turned out to be Joe Smith's.' The newspapers made sure that the players didn't need to keep their eyes peeled in the parking lot to know that a major shift in the club's balance of power was taking place. According to Book it was 'a trying time'.

By 24 November, the day of what proved to be a stormy board meeting, the takeover group – Smith, Niven, Chris Muir and existing shareholder Simon Cussons – were reported to be ready to complete amicable negotiations. Johnson, however, said he had changed his mind about selling 510 of his 521 shares to Smith, claiming he didn't know the consortium included Muir, the director who had been asked to resign a year earlier. Smith responded by insisting he had a signed agreement.

Meanwhile, the board had gone to Mercer after hearing of Smith's bid and asked him bluntly, 'Whose side are you on?' Mercer, as Allison would have expected, was with the board. 'How do you hijack a football club in full flight?' he said.

Allison's role in the plot, and his undisguised support for Smith, was by now making the directors uneasy. Alexander emerged from the boardroom with a warning. 'We don't go around with our eyes closed and I would like Malcolm to know that.'

Another board meeting was planned three days later, on the Friday of the same week. The rumour mill predicted the sacking of Allison, whispers that got back to Malcolm. The players, preparing for a difficult game at Leeds the next day, had, according to observers, shown signs of hostility towards their coach. Battles between directors might have been beyond their sphere of influence or interest, but it was different when the familiarity of their footballing infrastructure was threatened. Allison recalled Francis Lee, Mike Summerbee and Colin Bell approaching him to ask why he wanted to change something that had been so successful. It was not so much an 'Allison or Mercer' situation as it was a desire to keep together their partnership. But the two men now appeared to be on either side of an unbridgeable divide.

As training concluded, Mercer fell into step alongside Allison and said, 'You are on your own now, Malcolm.'

Allison replied, 'That doesn't bother me, Joe. I have always been on my own.'

Goalkeeper Joe Corrigan says that most players had been so focused on their own jobs that they were unaware that Allison's ambition and desire for public acknowledgement were creating a rift with Mercer until they started reading about it in the newspapers. 'We knew there were things going on in the background and talk of a takeover, but we didn't really know anything about Joe and Malcolm. Things like that didn't really affect us. I was only interested in playing.' Summerbee agrees, saying, 'I was quite shocked when it came about. I think Malcolm listened to the wrong people at the wrong time.'

The view of many players was that Mercer made sure Allison received plenty of credit for his contribution to the club's achievements. That partly explains the reports of their hostility towards Allison's actions at the time – feelings that have admittedly been forgotten and forgiven. But it still does not take into account Malcolm's burning ambition. Being a coach, no matter how much his influence was recognised, was no longer the role he wanted.

Lee points out, 'Malcolm was probably one of the best coaches the game has ever seen and at that time he was probably the best in the world. But the moment he hit the big time and things started to go really well he wasn't happy to be the coach, he wanted to run everything. The same thing happened years later when he went to Portugal. He won the championship, but ended up wanting to be president of the club, running everything. That was his biggest problem.'

Upon returning to his former club to join the coaching staff, Ken

Barnes explained that 'it only took five minutes to see the relationship was under strain'. He continued, 'Anyone at the club could see what was happening. Malcolm wanted to be the manager no question about it. My first impression of him was that success had gone to his head a bit. He had a bit of a swagger, a bit of a swank about him.'

For younger players who had not been at the club in the early days of the Allison–Mercer double act, any shift in the balance of the roles and relationship appeared purely cosmetic. While the senior members of the squad recall the regular presence of Mercer at training in the early days, youngsters like Ian Mellor saw the manager purely as a figurehead. 'All the time I was in the first team squad I never saw Joe Mercer,' he says. 'He came on the training pitch once in his shoes and it was embarrassing. He was a great PR man, but the modern game was changing and he was getting too old. To see him in a coaching situation seemed like being in a time warp. You thought, "This isn't your place." Malcolm ran the show.'

Some players had been given the opportunity to see first-hand evidence of a possible conflict between the club's two leading men. Striker Chris Jones, for example, had – as far back as the summer of 1968 – voiced concerns to Mercer that Allison didn't rate him and therefore he had doubts about his future at the club. Mercer's reply was, 'I don't care what Malcolm thinks. I'm the boss here.' Yet when he approached Allison, he was advised to accept a transfer to Swindon to make way for Bobby Owen, whom Malcolm planned to sign from Bury. Jones decided that Allison held sway and accepted the move.

Barnes recalls another incident when a fan asked Allison, 'How's Joe?' To which Allison barked back, 'Joe who? I run the team.'

Now, at that Friday night board meeting, Allison was asked where he stood in the takeover and how he saw his role at Maine Road. He informed the directors that he had the interests of the club at heart but that penny-pinching could stop them becoming truly great. He spoke of the 'small-time attitude of the board', a comment he sensed had made it easy for them to fire him. But whatever was decided after Allison left the room remained among those present as City prepared for their trip across the Pennines.

On the team bus to Leeds the next morning, Mercer once again appeared next to his lieutenant. This time he indicated to Allison a change of heart. 'I have thought it over. It is you and me together. We are this bloody club.' If Mercer expected Allison to fall into his arms, he was disappointed. Instead, Allison nodded and remained aloof, still stung by Mercer's apparent abandonment of him the previous day.

The game at Elland Road mirrored the disappointment of much of City's previous two months. Having started the season with six wins and two draws in the first eight games to top the First Division, a 1–0 defeat against new leaders Leeds meant they had won only two of the subsequent ten games. They had also gone out of the League Cup at Second Division Carlisle United.

At six o'clock, the pleasantries in the home team's boardroom having been dispensed with, chairman Alexander approached Allison in one of the corridors under the Elland Road stand. 'Malcolm, the board want to sack you,' he reported.

Allison, who had great personal affection for Alexander, put his arm round him and said, 'You do what you feel you have to do.'

The words were still hanging in the air when, like the shopkeeper appearing from nowhere in the Mr Benn cartoons, Mercer materialised to announce, 'If he goes, I go.' Allison, for now, had been saved.

Niven witnessed the scene, although unaware of its significance. 'I remember seeing Malcolm coming down the stairs inside. The chairman had his arm round him. They were having very close discussions and the chairman didn't look very happy. Later that night I got a call saying Malcolm had been sacked and I realised I had probably seen it.'

What Niven didn't know was that the City directors had hurriedly re-grouped in the Leeds boardroom and instructed Allison to report for a meeting with four of them at the Piccadilly Hotel in Manchester. There he was reinstated and given a 'final warning' about taking sides in the boardroom battle – although Allison was never going to be frightened into silence by a bunch of old men.

It was made clear that Mercer's intervention had been Allison's salvation, but that couldn't erase his simmering resentment at the two unfulfilled promises to hand over power. Allison no longer felt the close bond with the man for whom he had originally been so eager to work. Their relationship had even reached the point where a general conversation in a hotel bar about 'power and men' had turned into a stand-up row, the subject matter having been, according to Allison, 'too close to the bone'.

The battle was far from over and for neutral observers it was painful to watch. 'Malcolm wanted to be an institution at City and it damaged his reputation,' says journalist James Lawton. 'As an observer I felt very torn at that time because I identified with Malcolm as his journalistic contact but Joe was an irresistibly attractive man in his own right. I loved Joe but I do think there were some seeds of truth in Malcolm's frustration that he didn't step aside. Joe latched onto Malcolm as a brilliant ramrod and coach but he wasn't ready to hand over the glory.

'It was sad because when they were good, they were very warm together. I remember going on a scouting mission to Coimbra with Joe and Malcolm in the season they won the Cup-Winners' Cup. After a few drinks in Lisbon, we went up country on the train and went out to dinner in a little restaurant and then to a nightclub. When we got back to the hotel Joe was pretty paralysed and when we got him into his room he said, "The fucking room is spinning, Malcolm." Malcolm replied, "Joe, it is not a problem. Just put one foot on the floor and it will stop." Joe put his foot on the floor, this great look of relief crossed his face and he said, "You are a brilliant man, Malcolm."'

While Allison and Mercer continued to undermine such moments of harmony, Joe Smith completed his haggling with Johnson, agreeing a price of £110,000 for his shares. The existing board members, however, threatened legal action, claiming Johnson was obliged by covenant to have offered his shares to current members of the board before selling to an outsider. It was an argument they would subsequently lose.

In the meantime, another proposition had been placed before Allison. Rainwear manufacturer Ralph Levy approached him while the Johnson–Smith negotiations were in progress with the revelation that he had £500,000 to invest in the club if no deal was done. Having realised that his arrival on the scene was too late for City, he was intrigued when Allison told him he had heard that Bolton Wanderers could probably be bought for £50,000. Levy asked Allison if he was interested in being manager at Burnden Park and becoming a director of one of his companies. Allison was briefly tempted, but felt that Bolton was a 'rundown club' and he was disinclined to go through the kind of regeneration programme he had completed at Maine Road.

Allison was not prepared to compromise. He didn't simply want to be the number-one man at any club: that club had to be Manchester City. He felt he had earned the right. Had he been willing to move elsewhere to achieve his aim of being undisputed manager, there would have been any number of opportunities. But that was not Allison's way.

Besides, with the Smith deal having gone through, Allison appeared on the brink of achieving his ambition. As he wrote his cheque and took his seat on the board, Smith asked Allison exactly what he wanted. It was an easy question to answer: a new contract and to be the manager. Smith assured Allison that there would be no question of who was in charge. But Mercer was sticking to his guns. He would relinquish the title of team manager only as long as he retained the final say.

Allison's wishes weren't about to be granted. He was offered a new contract – one that his solicitor proceeded, metaphorically, to tear to pieces. Allison reported to the board that his contract was worthless. And Mercer was still in charge. 'I felt terribly frustrated,' said Allison, who admitted finding it difficult to focus on coaching. 'I had lost the drive and strength which had carried me – and City – into such a position of strength.'

On the field, City's campaign was meandering. In the middle of January, they began a run of ten League games without victory. The game that ended the sequence, a 3–0 home success against Everton, would be their only win in the final 19 matches. By the end of the season home crowds were dipping below 20,000 and it was only their fast start that enabled them to finish in the top half of the table.

The FA Cup offered City the final hope of maintaining their sequence of domestic success and they were drawn away in the fourth round to holders Chelsea. Without the injured Francis Lee and Glyn Pardoe, whose leg had been broken in a tackle with George Best during City's derby victory in December, City were comfortable 3–0 winners, with Bell grabbing a couple of goals.

The fifth round paired them with title-chasing Arsenal, the kind of disciplined team whose organisation Allison could admire while condemning their lack of flair. The one player in the Gunners team who contradicted their workmanlike, professional personality was the young, long-haired Charlie George. By the time a waterlogged Maine Road had forced the game to be pushed back four days, Allison and George were the focus of attention in the Arsenal dressing-room. Gunners centre-forward John Radford explains, 'Frank McLintock goaded Charlie into winning the game for us. Frank went to Charlie and told him that Malcolm had been in the papers saying that he was just an upstart, that he wasn't as good as everyone said he was. Well that was it for Charlie; he went out and had a blinder.'

On a wet and foggy night, George scored two individual goals, a free-kick from the edge of the box and a spectacular run from the halfway line, against a solitary reply by Bell. 'After Charlie scored he was running along the touchline signalling at Allison,' Radford recalls.

The Football Association, meanwhile, were preparing their own retribution for the outspoken Allison. The touchline ban had done little to soften his attitude to authority and at the end of March, he was up before the FA again for 'bringing the game into disrepute' – something Malcolm felt the game's bosses were themselves guilty of on an almost daily basis. The latest misdemeanour had come in December when he directed an outburst at Bolton referee Bob Matthewson, the former professional player, during half-time of a game at Burnley. Allison accused him of favouring the home team, although he later claimed that 'the remarks were intended to be light-hearted'. This time his sentence was to be banned from active participation with the team for 12 months and fined £2,000. Ten months of the sentence was suspended until the end of 1973, which meant he had effectively been placed on probation for the best part of three years. A furious Allison argued that he had been victimised, saying, 'Anyone else would have got away with it.'

The punishment meant that Allison was not allowed to work with his players or even watch games at Maine Road. He could go to away games if he bought a ticket. The situation with Mercer was to come to a head during Allison's absence. As the programme of Easter games approached, City's season now hung entirely on their defence of the European Cup-Winners' Cup, where they had recovered from an unimpressive start to face Chelsea in the semi-finals.

Having beaten Linfield, the Northern Ireland part-timers, by only a single goal at home, they had then, embarrassingly, lost the away leg 2–1, relying on Lee's away goal to send them through at the end of a night that saw goalkeeper Joe Corrigan pelted with bottles.

Lee was on target again in each of two wins over the Hungarian side Honved, results that meant a lot to Allison given the influence that country's footballers had over his professional development. In the quarter-final, City found themselves two goals down after a first leg in Katowice against the Gornik team they had beaten to win the trophy. With key men missing through injury, they levelled the aggregate scores in the second leg and – these being the days before penalty shoot-outs – took the tie to a third game. The day after the FA had passed sentence on Allison, goals by Young, Booth and Lee earned a 3–1 win in Copenhagen, an admirable performance by a side missing half its regular members. Even Arthur Mann, a capable replacement defender, had been left at the airport in Manchester after tranquillisers failed to combat a pre-flight panic attack.

City now faced three First Division games in four days over Easter before playing their semi-final after a break of only two days. Allison felt it was impossible to ask the first-team players to go through such an arduous programme and still be physically ready for Chelsea. After defeats against Nottingham Forest and Huddersfield, he urged Mercer to rest key players for the Easter Monday game at Newcastle. But with Summerbee, Oakes, Pardoe and Heslop already set to miss the Chelsea game, and Derek Jeffries having suffered injury on Good Friday, Mercer stubbornly played the strongest possible team in a 0–0 draw. Allison believed that Mercer's selection had been motivated by his fear of losing three in a row. Mercer, according to Malcolm, thought people would see another loss as proof that he could not succeed without Allison at his shoulder. Midfielders Bell and Doyle duly suffered injuries that would end their seasons, while Corrigan would be forced to face Chelsea with his left eye virtually shut after suffering a blow to the face. Allison told Mercer to his face that his ego had undermined the season.

It was this understrength City team – including 17-year-old Jeff Johnson – that took the field at Stamford Bridge: Corrigan, Book, Connor, Towers, Booth, Mann, Donachie, Johnson, Hill, Lee, Young.

Chelsea had also suffered over Easter, losing centre-forward Peter Osgood, and City performed with courage and conviction – although a defensive lapse allowed makeshift striker David Webb to set up South African Derek Smethurst for the only goal.

Summerbee's return for the second leg was countered by the absence of Corrigan and Booth and Chelsea again scored the one goal of the contest, stand-in keeper Ron Healey fumbling an indirect free-kick by Keith Weller into his goal. The somewhat farcical manner of City's relinquishing their trophy seemed entirely in keeping with the events of the season.

The rumblings around the club continued throughout the summer. The newly constituted board now included not only Smith and Niven, but future club chairman Peter Swales, who had joined in April. Swales was supposed to be playing the role of peacemaker and many felt he quickly seized the power in the boardroom. 'He was a very good businessman and a very hard man,' says Niven. 'I gathered that he and Malcolm didn't get on. They were two very ambitious people. Peter had one ambition only, which was to be chairman.'

Existing chairman Albert Alexander wrote of the events in the boardroom in the match programme for the first game of the 1971–72 season, against Leeds. 'All these problems of the club have now been amicably solved in what we all trust will be the best interests of Manchester City,' he chirruped. Tellingly, he neglected to make mention any of the new board members.

Mercer remained in overall charge of the team, and his cautious attitude in the transfer market caused yet more friction between him and Allison, who was desperate to add Rodney Marsh, the flamboyant Queens Park Rangers forward, to the City line-up. The two clubs appeared to have settled on a fee of £140,000 but a disagreement over whether that included VAT or not ended with Mercer advising the board not to pay any more.

The clock was ticking on the Mercer–Allison partnership. Finally, following a 3–0 League Cup defeat at Bolton early in October, zero hour was reached. After a three-hour board meeting, club secretary Walter Griffiths declared, 'The board is pleased to announce the appointment of Malcolm Allison to the position of team manager with full responsibilities to the board for all team management. Mr Joe Mercer will continue as manager of the club.'

While expressing his public support for Allison's elevation, Mercer made sure to point out, 'I still believe I have a lot to offer.' And his lack of confidence in the practicality of the new arrangement could not have been much more obvious when he said, 'I'm a tactician not an administrator and don't really see myself as a general manager.'

Within the next few weeks, further changes at Maine Road would be revealed, with 38-year-old Eric Alexander succeeding his father as chairman and Smith becoming vice-chairman. Colin Bell was installed as team captain, with Tony Book taking the title of club captain.

Allison's first game as manager was a 1–0 win against Everton. As he spoke to the press in the boardroom after the game, cigar in one hand and glass of champagne in the other, he was asked how good a manager he would become. Such a question to a publicity seeker like Allison was like offering a drug addict the keys to the pharmacy. 'Probably the best there ever was,' Allison replied, certain of the headlines such a comment would create. 'And I'll tell you something else. It will be nice to walk out at Wembley ahead of the Cup final team.' But he was honest enough to admit, 'Today has been so different for me. Doubts arose that had never been there before purely because of the new situation I was in. It was a strange feeling.'

Asked about his future relationship with players to whom he had been so close, he shrugged off potential problems. 'They can call me what they like. "Sir" and "boss" are for the establishment.'

The other obvious question was whether the additional responsibility as figurehead of the club would bring a change in Allison's confrontational manner. 'People think that carrying the full title of team manager will help keep me out of trouble,' he said, before lapsing into convenient memory loss. 'That side of my football life is behind me anyway. I haven't been involved in any real clashes with authority for three years now. There is no need these days. Before it was a lot of frustration trying to get myself and the club noticed.'

The players' view of the new dynamic between Allison and Mercer – albeit one sanitised for public consumption – was offered by Francis Lee in his column in Manchester's *Football Pink*:

It's pointless to argue which needed the other the most. They needed each other and we all benefited. It is certainly true that while Malcolm worked brilliantly with the players, he needed Joe at times to put a restraining hand on him. Malcolm's early years in Manchester were studded with forthright and controversial outbursts.

He doesn't have too much regard for the establishment and not being a sufferer of fools gladly he has had his brushes with authority. I suppose he will never be a diplomat like Joe Mercer or Sir Matt Busby, but he has learned a great deal of control and I think the time is right for him to have the full responsibility of manager.

If the changes were meant to mean the end of the unrest at the club, someone miscalculated badly. No one was about to live happily ever after. As City chased another First Division title, Mercer no longer felt close enough to the team, while Allison thought Joe was too involved and would end up describing him as 'a sort of shadowy presence'.

Niven explains, 'We [the new board members] were big supporters of Malcolm, but we weren't anti-Joe Mercer. Joe wasn't happy about the new situation. He didn't want to be director or football consultant or anything like that. The board didn't want either of them to go, but it turned out to be a compromise that satisfied neither of them.'

By the end of the season, chairman Eric Alexander would be forced to admit, 'Since Malcolm took over as team manager [he and Joe] have not hit it off.' He offered the trite explanation that 'it is probably because they come from different eras', ignoring the reality that their differences were far more to do with a conflict of ambition than a generation gap.

As the postscripts to the 1971–72 season were being written, the City board sat down to address Mercer's job description, one that would likely have been centred on public relations and ambassadorial duties. Before any resolution had been reached, Mercer saved them the bother by announcing that he was to take the job of general manager at Coventry City, where he would form a new partnership with the young team manager Gordon Milne. Mercer knew that Allison didn't want him and sensed that the club directors weren't bothered what happened to him. As well as losing his title, he claimed his parking space had been taken away and his name removed from the door of what he thought had been his office. According to Swales,

'The board had to choose between Malcolm Allison and Joe Mercer – and we chose Malcolm Allison.'

Mercer felt he could have been accommodated on the board in the manner of Busby at United. Perhaps the sight of subsequent managers Wilf McGuinness and Frank O'Farrell being intimidated and undermined by the continuing influence of Busby at Old Trafford convinced the City board that it wasn't such a good idea. Mercer, however, was not quite the powerful patriarch that Busby was, while Allison was much more independent and thick-skinned than McGuinness and O'Farrell.

Mercer's parting comments left no one in any doubt about his sorrow over the situation at Maine Road. 'The humiliating part of this sad affair is that at one time the board were saying there was a job for life. But I finished up by being offered a three-year engagement plus a thirty-three and a third per cent cut in salary. However, the thing that hurt most of all was that they just didn't know what to call me. All my life I have been known as Joe Mercer the footballer or Joe Mercer the manager. Then suddenly they can't find a title for me. That was when my pride was hurt most of all.

'I always wanted [Malcolm] to have the job but at the same time I wanted to retain some control, although that can only be done on a mutual understanding. I did not want to be shorn of all authority, but unfortunately it was not to be. I am the sort of person who has got to be involved in the footballing side of football, helping to create and build teams, making and taking decisions and formulating policy.'

Alexander's response to Mercer was, naturally, to defend the club's actions. 'We have been cast as villains of the piece and it is simply not true. The fact is that we have bent over backwards to create a situation in which Joe and Malcolm would not clash. It has to be admitted that the pair are not compatible.'

Contacted in South Africa, where he was involved in coaching courses, Allison didn't do himself any favours by showing little compassion towards his former mentor. 'Before I left Manchester to come to South Africa I told Mercer all there was to be told. He knew exactly where he stood. Why must these questions be brought up again? Mercer knows how I feel. In effect he was relegated to opening the mail.'

If Allison had been that blunt to Mercer's face in letting him know 'where he stood' it was insensitive and disrespectful. Yet he had simply gone beyond the stage of being able to trust Mercer's ambition. Malcolm now had what he wanted, but it was not in his nature to be a gracious winner. The manner of his former boss's departure and his reaction to it undoubtedly diminished Allison in the hearts of fans who had previously worshipped both men. Sympathy for Mercer was strong and the club's supporters' association pointedly invited him to their annual dinner dance.

Mercer was too clever in the field of public relations to be drawn into a slanging match. Instead, he said, 'Never let anyone forget the contribution Malcolm Allison has made to City. Never let anyone undervalue what he has done.' But he couldn't resist offering Allison a word of caution. 'There are more things to managing than coaching. If I could offer him a piece of advice it would be to listen. Please yourself what you do afterwards, but do listen to others first. For when you stop listening you stop learning.'

Allison would write in 1975 that 'I no longer care one way or another whether I ever hear from Joe Mercer again'. Looking back on their partnership he said:

> I suppose the best thing is to say there is nothing owing from that relationship. We gained so much from it personally, though in the process we lost the thing which made all those successes happen, an implicit friendship and understanding. My complaint, my bitterness, flows from a feeling that the relationship was always tilted subtly in Joe's favour.

Part of that final point was Allison's recognition that Mercer had been careful to depart from Maine Road with his legacy untainted and his place in the affection of the supporters secure. 'Joe had controlled his personal position with great skill. He had come out smelling of roses.'

Meanwhile, Allison would now have to prove himself to the City fans all over again. Not only was he seen by some as being responsible for Mercer's eviction, he was being held personally accountable for having thrown away the 1971–72 League Championship after one of the most gripping title races in English football history.

14

SINKING FEELING

'It was the greatest 12 of all time. No one's going to remember the Open in five years from now – who won, who lost – but they're going to remember your 12. My God, Roy, it was . . . why, it's immortal'

– Molly Griswold (Rene Russo) to Roy McAvoy (Kevin Costner), *Tin Cup* (1996)

In the climactic scene of the golf movie *Tin Cup*, Kevin Costner's down-and-out driving range pro, Roy McAvoy, finds himself in contention to win the US Open at the final hole. Instead of playing safe with a seven-iron down the fairway, he goes for a near-impossible shot across the expanse of water protecting the green. For McAvoy, winning with caution is not winning at all. Victory with style is the only one that counts. 'This is everything, ain't it?' he muses as he selects a three-wood from his bag. 'This is the choice it comes down to. This is our immortality.' He swings the club and sees his ball sink, along with his dreams.

With the end of the 1971–72 First Division title race in sight, Rodney Marsh was Malcolm Allison's three-wood into the lake.

City were closing in on the championship, with daylight between them and their challengers, when Allison decided it wasn't enough to continue playing the way that had left his team on the brink of success in the season when he had finally become team manager. Big Mal craved the spectacular. Marsh, one of football's great individual talents, was bought for £200,000 and City barely won another game.

In the movie, McAvoy fails with four further attempts to make his shot until, with his final ball in play and disqualification staring him in the face, he clears the water and lands the ball straight in the hole for an unforgettable 12. Allison even had his own equivalent of that belated moment of justification – when Marsh played magnificently to inspire a victory over eventual champions Derby in the last game of the season. And as Rene Russo's character assures her man, the glorious folly of defeat can sometimes be remembered more clearly than victory itself. To those outside of Derby, the 1971–72 season will always be the title that Allison threw away.

Of course, the difference in golf – fictional or otherwise – is that one man's implosion affects only himself and his nearest and dearest. Allison was left to answer to the City fans and the rest of the team, most of whom have no doubt that the season would have ended very differently without Big Mal swinging for the green.

City's one significant signing for the start of the season had been Wales centre-forward Wyn Davies, who arrived from Newcastle for £60,00, almost five years after Allison and Joe Mercer had first tried to sign him. Davies's physical presence had been an important part of Newcastle's march to an unlikely triumph in the European Fairs Cup of 1968–69 and he gave City's attack an aerial dimension to add to the cut and thrust of Francis Lee and Mike Summerbee.

The fitness of his players had been occupying Allison's mind since the club's hopes in the previous season had been undermined by their string of injuries in the spring. He had seen Leeds' battle-weary players blow the League, FA Cup and European Cup in a whirlwind of late-season fixtures in 1970, while Arsenal had just been forced to play 64 games to win the League and FA Cup. The physical demand on players was forcing itself to the top of football's agenda in the days when a 'rotation' applied only to crop farming.

Allison had his fitness advisers come up with a programme that would bring them to a peak at mid-season. 'The normal approach by clubs is to have everyone going flat out from the word go,' he explained. 'This often means there are periods of tiredness and lethargy in the winter. We aim to finish in a sprint.' Fewer, more varied, training sessions were ordered.

As well as a new centre-forward and an updated training plan,

City had a lush green pitch to replace the previous season's bog, two yards wider than before, and a new, covered North Stand to replace the old Scoreboard End. The team responded by losing their opening home game against Leeds but were beaten only twice more before the end of November. To Allison's consternation, it was Manchester United who were setting the pace in Division One. In his first season in charge, Malcolm's old West Ham buddy, Frank O'Farrell, steered them to a five-point lead, losing only two games before Christmas. Allison, however, remained unconvinced that it was anything other than a brief last hurrah for an ageing team. He offered the opinion that United would soon be found out. When seven consecutive defeats in the New Year duly saw them slide out of contention, Allison didn't bother trying to contain his satisfaction.

The 1971–72 season was memorable for the clampdown on foul play by referees, who, on the Monday after the season kick-off, had received a Football League memorandum instructing them to adopt a zero-tolerance attitude to offences such as handball, obstruction, tripping and most significantly, tackling from behind. Some forwards had taken to wearing padding on the backs of their legs to protect them from the assassins who masqueraded as defenders, but now they were to receive protection from new guidelines that pointed out the virtual impossibility of tackling from behind without making contact with the opponent first.

The 'Refs' Revolution', as it quickly became labelled, led to a sharp rise in bookings – although numbers were still negligible compared with the modern era. When seven players were booked in a game between Tottenham and Newcastle two days after the letters dropped on the referees' doormats, Newcastle captain Bobby Moncur commented, 'The referees are turning it into a game for cissies.'

Players threatened to strike if early-season bookings counted against them when they had not been forewarned of the new regulations, while referees warned of similar action if their decisions were overturned. Once the initial hysteria had died down what emerged was a season in which elegant footballing teams like City and Derby prospered. Even Leeds seemed to have thrown off the shackles, producing 5–1 and 7–0 wins in successive games against Manchester United and Southampton that were utterly sublime. And then there was the story of George Eastham, who was able to bring back his dainty style of inside-forward play from exile in South Africa to help Stoke City win the League Cup.

The First Division title race was to prove one of the closest and most exciting for many years, with City, Leeds, Liverpool and Derby eventually separated by a single point. And the four-way battle was a tabloid headline-writer's dream, contested by the four most extreme characters in the First Division: Allison, Revie, Shankly and Clough – Big Mal, The Don, Shanks and Cloughie, pioneers of the cult of the manager that had resulted from the ever-intensifying media coverage of the sport.

City's charge was led by Lee, who couldn't stop scoring, although he is remembered as much for the fact that he converted a record 13 penalties as his overall tally of 33 goals. Early exits from the two major cup competitions meant there were no distractions. Nor was there any disturbance from the Texaco Cup, the short-lived '70s competition that was supposed to reward the best teams from England, Scotland and Ireland to have missed out on European qualification. For a team like City, experienced in the real thing, it was a waste of time. They fielded a virtual reserve team for the second leg of their first-leg tie at Airdrie, at a time when such a stand was still frowned upon, and cared little that they were beaten 2–0 to go out of the tournament. The Scottish press accused City of 'cheek and arrogance' and 'cheating' the 14,000 fans. City's £1,000 fee for entering the competition was withheld, but Allison responded, 'We just can't afford to be in these second class competitions – especially in Scotland, where the rules of the game seem to be slightly different from anywhere else in the world.'

Allison hadn't seemed to hold such a low opinion of Scottish football a couple of weeks earlier when he expressed an interest in taking on the job of managing the national team on a part-time basis following the summer sacking of Bobby Brown – a job that eventually went to Tommy Docherty.

By March, the contenders were positioning themselves for their final push. At Derby, Clough announced he had signed the Nottingham Forest and England winger Ian Storey-Moore and staged a contract signing on the pitch before a home game. Forest, however, said their signature was not on the forms and that Storey-Moore was still their man. Three days later they sold him to Manchester United for £200,000.

Spurred, some believe, by the need to match United's extravagance, Allison moved quickly and two days later, with the hours ticking away to the transfer deadline, he paid a similar amount to QPR for Marsh and introduced the player, dressed in a long brown leather coat, to the press. Significantly, Allison used another United reference to justify his spending. 'He could blossom into English football's biggest crowd puller. I maintain that he can give more consistent pleasure and more feeling of involvement to the fans than even George Best.' Allison was pained that his successful team could still not draw the crowds that a declining United were able to command and would admit later that his motivation for signing Marsh was the feeling that his 'touch of theatre' could break United's stranglehold on Manchester.

Allison explained that he'd had to 'bully' his directors into writing the cheque and had assured them that Marsh, who had scored 17 League goals for Rangers that season, would get 10 for City before the campaign ended. But it was a deal that upset both Mercer, watching from his detached position, and Rangers manager Gordon Jago, whose team had just seen their promotion hopes hit by losing three successive games without scoring a goal.

'I had told Malcolm Allison previously that we would not sell while we were in the hunt for promotion,' says Jago. 'Once we lost a few games Malcolm called me and said, "You are out of it. Sell me Rodney." I swore loudly. I felt Rodney had been tapped up. City were top of the League and he wanted to go there, I could understand that. But the manner in which City conducted business was not professional and it affected Rodney. He knew if we were out of the hunt we would let him go and he was affected by that.'[9]

Meanwhile, Mercer, who had baulked at spending considerably less than £200,000 for the player a few months earlier, looked on in bemusement. 'I thought Mal stopped listening. Mal loved the

---

[9] QPR would remain unbeaten in their final 12 games following Marsh's departure, but finished in fourth place, two points out of the promotion places.

Marshes. I didn't want the back-heelers. I didn't want players who played at other people's expense.'

Proof, if it was needed, of Allison's alignment with the game's more colourful on-field characters came the following week when it was announced he had teamed up with Marsh, Alan Hudson, Geoff Hurst, David Webb, Alan Ball, Terry Mancini and Terry Venables to launch 'The Clan'. Allison, who missed the initial photo-shoot at which the players were pictured by Terry O'Neill dressed up to the nines, described the group as 'an exclusive academy, where all the talk and theorising will be about the greatest game in the world' and maintained that they were 'committed to improving the image of the game'. As an attempt to improve their own image – and earnings – within and around the game it was short-lived, although in recognising the opportunities that were there to be pursued in the wake of football's growing public profile, it was arguably ahead of its time.

Back on the field, Marsh made his debut in a 1–0 home win over Chelsea, but struggled with the pace of the game and was eventually substituted by the man whose place he had taken, Tony Towers. The result left City five points clear at the top of the table, but three games without a win followed before Marsh scored his first two City goals in a 3–1 victory against West Ham. For the time being, however, Allison had seen enough of Marsh throwing up in training sessions and, with a trip to Old Trafford next on the schedule, announced he was dropping Marsh for 'no less than three games' because he was 'not fit for top-class football'. Marsh still managed to grab the attention by warming up on the sideline in a gold tracksuit top before coming on to volley the third goal in another 3–1 win, producing what Allison would describe as 'the most dazzling 20 minutes of his career'. After missing a draw at Coventry, Marsh was back in the starting line-up, but a defeat at Ipswich left the title out of City's reach.

No one, not even Marsh, doubts that it was Allison's late-season profligacy that was the turning point in City's season. Tony Book says, 'It was maybe the biggest mistake he made – not the signing itself, but making the change when the team was settled. Rodney was not up to our fitness and I honestly feel we would have gone on and won the title without him. He loved to run at defenders, hold the ball and do a bit extra, but at that time we didn't play that way. We moved it fast.'

Marsh's more languid style of play did indeed seem to run counter to Allison's well-advanced theory of playing the ball at speed. In *Soccer For Thinkers* he had written of the importance of players doing so automatically.

Watch a good First Division team play a weaker side. The good side play the ball about quickly, appearing sometimes to make unnecessary passes. This is a habit with them, whether the opposition are 15-year-olds or a Fourth Division reserve side. If they begin to play it slowly their level will often sink to that of their inferior opposition.

Why is quick play so important? It changes the situation all the time. When the ball stops, the defender's task is suddenly easier. He can weigh up the situation, pick up his man in relation to that situation, organise cover and even anticipate the next move.

Colin Bell offers this view of the Marsh signing. 'If he was going to come I couldn't understand why he didn't come in the summer instead of when we were sailing on quite nicely. It was too much to expect to bring in a player and get him used to your formation and your team in a few games.'

And Summerbee suggests, 'Malcolm could have kept Rodney back until the next season when he was fully fit. At that time, it was the wrong decision and Rodney knows that. It could have been anyone coming in then and not being the right player. But Rodney made a great contribution the season after and was very popular with the fans.'

The point to stress is that it was Allison's signing of Marsh, not Marsh himself, that derailed City. Marsh believes that the distinction has become blurred over the years. 'If City hadn't signed me, they would've gone on to win the League, but I'm not the manager. The manager buys the players and if they want to sign me from QPR for £200,000 that's their decision.' He also goes along with the idea that keeping him on the bench for the remainder of the 1971–72 season might have ensured a title victory. 'Everyone would have lived happily ever after. I feel it's wrong to keep making me the fall guy 30 years on.'

Meanwhile, Mercer, having observed City's collapse, couldn't resist a swipe at Allison, saying, '£200,000 is a lot of money to spend to throw away the championship.'

But there was one final game left, in which Marsh showed what Allison meant when he had said, 'I know I have secured one of the elite group of players who bring a thrill every time they touch the ball.' On the final Saturday of the season City returned to the top of the table with a 2–0 win over Derby, although the chasing teams' remaining fixtures meant that it was impossible for City not to be overtaken. As the club's official publication put it, 'It was like arriving at the winning post and then having to nonchalantly lean there waiting for the rest of the field to overhaul you.' Marsh, socks around his ankles, strutted around the pitch, pulled all the strings and made the two most telling contributions to the action. In the first half, he picked up a long ball on the right touchline, cut inside two defenders with a swivel of his hips and advanced into the area to drill home a low right-foot shot. Later in the game, he juggled the ball to bring it under control on the left wing, sped past Colin Todd and was upended in the box by Terry Hennessey, giving Lee the chance to score yet another penalty.

Even though City would finish in fourth place, Allison was at least able to say later, 'I felt a sad sort of vindication that afternoon.'

15

OUT OF THE BLUES

'Malcolm's brilliance was as a coach. If it was to do with a ball or motivating players, that was his speciality. He wasn't a manager because he couldn't manage a club. He was to finance and balancing the books what Sweeney Todd was to hairdressing'

– Former Manchester City forward Francis Lee

Manchester City began the 1972–73 First Division season with five defeats in six games – four without scoring a goal. Despite his concern, Malcolm Allison did not agree with those who felt the team would, or should, break up. He felt there was still too much quality in the squad for that.

City fans had been waiting to see how Rodney Marsh would adapt to the team's methods with the benefit of a full pre-season of integration. Allison crowed, 'We shall use him to some extent in midfield, but his greatest value will be coming through on the left flank. This allows us to set up different points of attack and will help us to stretch defences more. He'll find more room than he was previously used to because he is no longer the centre point of everything. Give him 20 games and you'll see the real Rodney.'

City had been invited to contend for the FA Charity Shield against the previous season's Division Three champions Aston Villa, winning by a single goal at Villa Park. But when they found themselves stuck in the bottom two of the table several weeks into the League season, debate began over whether Allison was losing his powers and his drive. Jimmy Hill wrote that Lee and Summerbee had commented to him,

'Malcolm's gone soft and has nearly become part of the establishment.'
Hill's article in *Goal* magazine continued, intriguingly:

> I cursed the limitations of time with the television interview when
> discussing Manchester City with Allison recently. At a point where
> I had no time left, Malcolm astonishingly said, 'Winning is not as
> important as it was before.'
>
> He was explaining why he thought he would behave in ex-
> emplary fashion on the touchline if the FA decided to lift the ban
> on him sitting there. The statement was so extraordinary, because
> one would have thought that, since he and Mercer separated,
> Allison would have been even more determined to make City
> tick.
>
> A bad start to the season will be taken by Allison's critics as a
> sign that he is losing his grip or that he never was the genius his
> supporters made him out to be.

He was at a loss to explain the poor start. 'You look at players. You
know what they can do and there is no way that they can make the
sort of mistakes which are getting us into trouble. Yet those mistakes
are there in every game. Bad passing, bad running, defensive errors.
We've always been a confident team, but look at us now.'

Allison could bemoan the form of the players, but results were
suggesting that, even if he had not quite lost his powers, the new role
of manager was making it impossible for him to use them in the way
he once had. Early in October, City went to Fourth Division Bury in
the third round of the League Cup, but the players had seen nothing
of him since their League game the previous Saturday until he showed
up in the Gigg Lane dressing-room shortly before kick-off. Following
a 2–0 defeat, they glimpsed him only briefly after the match, although
he did appear in front of the press long enough to accuse his players
of being 'non-triers'. The comment led reporters to seek out reaction
from the board. Peter Swales, whose ambition to become chairman
would be realised with the imminent resignation of Eric Alexander,
confirmed that Allison had said nothing to cause them concern.

The board themselves were being watched closely, with Swales,
the 39-year-old millionaire businessman, already being described by
one article as 'the power behind the throne'. Asked whether there

were pro- and anti-Allison camps developing, Swales commented, 'You could say that when you have a board of eight people you have eight camps. To suggest that the harmony of Manchester City has been destroyed, and that the team has been affected, is bunkum.'

He stopped well short, however, of giving Allison's leadership a ringing endorsement. 'It was a unanimous decision to appoint Allison. In view of this season's results I suppose it would be ridiculous and untrue to deny that there must be someone who has the odd doubt now.'

The most obvious explanation for Malcolm's problems is that he was simply not cut out to be a manager. Colin Bell points out, 'It is down to individuals to know what role you want to be. For me there was no one better as a coach and motivator than Malcolm Allison, but to shift to being a manager and to organise things is completely different. You couldn't see him sitting behind a desk.'

Ken Barnes, who was asked by Allison to help him coach the first team, suggests in his autobiography, 'Sometimes [Malcolm] disappeared up his own arsehole with his theories, but Joe was there to rein him in if he went a bit too far. For all his qualities, Malcolm couldn't or wouldn't accept that he was better in combination with Joe than he was on his own. Perhaps it was pride, or ego or both.' Barnes's blunt assessment of Allison as team manager is, 'Let's face it, he made a right balls of it.'

Tony Book, who had seen Allison falling foul of directors during his management days at Plymouth, adds, 'He was at his best when he was a free spirit. All of a sudden you take on a manager's job and you have to be on your best behaviour. Malcolm loved a good time. That didn't go down well in some people's eyes as a manager. You have to behave yourself, be cleaner than clean and be disciplined. If there is a board meeting at a certain time you have to be there. That wasn't Malcolm. He would roll up an hour late and they wouldn't stand for that. I had a feeling it wouldn't work. Knowing him over the years, he was an out and out coach.'

Allison might not have been showing up for board meetings on time, but neither was he always on the practice field when he should have been. Players recall that loyal club servant Johnny Hart was frequently left in charge of training sessions and that when their manager did eventually return there was no explanation about where he had been.

The disaffection Allison was feeling was further compounded in September 1972 when the FA turned down an appeal to have his lifetime ban from the touchline rescinded. He claimed that it was impossible to properly discharge the duties of team manager without being close to the action, but it would not be until 1979 that he was allowed back into the dugout on English grounds.

In later years, Allison would admit to the pressure he felt during this time. 'The most frightening period of my life did not occur when I was out of work or even when I was in a sanatorium suffering from tuberculosis. It came at the height of my success at Manchester City. I had given them years of extremely hard work and the strain was affecting me more than I realised. I withdrew into myself and began doing the job from memory.'

Meanwhile, one of the immutable laws of football began to take hold: that when a team is doing well, everyone gets along famously – but when things go wrong, cliques, resentment and accusations of manager's favourites begin to fester. Mike Doyle claimed that players began to question Allison's relationship with certain players, noting that he socialised with internationals like Mike Summerbee and Francis Lee to an extent that disturbed troopers like Alan Oakes, Glyn Pardoe and himself. 'Mal, Mike and Franny were the champagne set; we were the black-and-tan brigade,' he said.

The view of Doyle, whose support of Allison was tested by his being left out of the odd game, is refuted by Bell, who states, 'Malcolm had no favourites. His best eleven were his favourites and that eleven could change depending who was playing well.'

Bell argues that there was a difference between playing favourites and picking a settled side, something that had been a feature of the championship side but was now missing – 20 players having been used in the first three months of the season. Recalling the successes, Bell says, 'It was happy families. If everybody was fit everyone knew who would be playing and even the subs didn't mind because they knew we were a good side. They accepted it without aggravation or nastiness and they knew that Malcolm would stick them in if somebody wasn't playing well.'

Yet Doyle insisted in his 1977 book, *Manchester City: My Team*:

I believe that if Malcolm had restricted his relationships with individual players in the team . . . he might still have been the manager. His involvement with a section of the players, rather than with the whole, didn't show on the park but we talked about it among ourselves.

Two players had fallen out of favour with Allison sufficiently to have been transferred to Preston at the beginning of 1972: Neil Young, whose important goals had contributed so much to City's big-game victories, and David Connor, the unsung man-marking expert. Young felt he had been sacrificed to raise cash for Marsh at a time when he was going through personal trauma, having suffered the loss of his brother to cancer, and had shed tears after leaving the club. Both men claim that Allison had promised testimonial games in return for accepting the move, but no such games were ever forthcoming.

Once again, it was the FA Cup that offered City their final opportunity of salvaging the season as they struggled to force their way into the top half of the table. Hopes were high after a fourth-round triumph against a Liverpool side on their way to winning the title in their penultimate season under Bill Shankly. Allison claimed to have 'psyched out' Liverpool by writing in his *Daily Express* column, 'We will bury the myth of Liverpool.'

Ghostwriter James Lawton explains, 'Everyone was saying it was a bad draw for City, but Malcolm said, "I fancy that. Let's face it, Liverpool are just trial horses these days. When was the last time they won anything?" It was the back page lead in the *Express* and at about 7 a.m. the next day I was woken up by a call from Bill Shankly. It was like a pneumatic drill on the other end of the phone. "That fucking man is a lunatic and you are a disgrace for printing it." He had got under Bill's skin and they got a well-played draw and then turned Liverpool over at Maine Road. Game, set and match to Malcolm.'

Allison had suggested that the Liverpool side – being refashioned into the team that would dominate the next decade and a half of English and European football – had an inflated reputation and that City would expose their limitations. Allison, never slow to point out his own genius, recalled: '[Bill] may have recognised an element of truth in what I said. That was a piece of the old psychological warfare.'

After a niggardly 0–0 draw at Anfield, Allison responded to suggestions that his team had been too physical by suggesting that Durham referee Pat Partridge had been intimidated by the home crowd. Partridge felt that Allison was merely laying down a marker for some favours in the replay and even Lee disagreed with his manager's comment. 'The referee kept a firm grip and if he hadn't this game could have ended in a brawl.'

City won the replay 2–0 with goals by Colin Bell and Tommy Booth and according to Partridge, 'Allison was all sweetness and light.' Writing several years later, Partridge used the episode to illuminate Malcolm's personality.

> That's him. He can say things and sometimes get away with things you would strongly object to from other managers because there is so much honest emotion which bubbles over, yet so much genuine friendship under the surface. There's no undercurrent of malice which sometimes prevails in others.

Second Division Sunderland put paid to Allison's hopes of eventually leading his team out at Wembley, holding City to a 2–2 draw at Maine Road before beating them 3–1 in the replay at Roker Park. It was a result that was to have extreme consequences. A prolonged FA Cup run could have prompted a different response from Allison to the events of the next few weeks. Instead, he stated, 'That, I suppose, brought the curtain down on me at Maine Road.' It needed one final push, however, to send him through the doors.

City had remained dormant in the transfer market since the signing of Rodney Marsh a year earlier. Players like Frank Worthington, David Nish, Jeff Blockley and Ted MacDougall, twice, had all made headline-grabbing moves for huge sums. City's most significant activity had been to send Wyn Davies across Manchester for £65,000. Swales, still not chairman but undoubted spokesman for the board, outlined the reality that buying new players needed to be balanced by selling. 'We are a club which has spent £200,000 on one player and almost £500,000 on a new stand. If you are talking about spending another £100,000 or £200,000 we could find the money, but in the long term we would be looking towards balancing the books.'

Until 6 March, winger Ian Mellor had been as memorable for the stick-like figure that earned him the nickname 'Spider' than for his 30-odd appearances in City's first team. The events of that day ensured his permanent synonymy with the end of an era.

Three days after losing the League Cup final to Tottenham, Norwich City went shopping for a new wide man. Their offer of £65,000 to City for Manchester-born Mellor, accepted by the Maine Road board, could not have been better timed. 'Malcolm had been ill and Johnny Hart was in charge for a while,' Mellor recalls. 'We got battered 5–1 at Wolves and although I was one of the best players on the field I was dropped for the midweek game at Southampton. I was seething and when one of the directors asked me if I would like to talk to Norwich I said, "Of course I fucking would." I was so naïve, I signed for Norwich the next day. I should have said no but I was frustrated at being dropped for one of the big names and probably thought I was better than I was. Malcolm was seething because they had gone behind his back. Basically, I was the straw that broke the camel's back. I was an excuse for him to say, "Sod it."'

Allison quickly made his feelings known. 'My directors have gone against my wishes and my advice,' he complained. 'My row with the directors has gone right to the heart of football's greatest problem. It's been about money – the need for it, the balancing of it against such assets as young First Division-class players. My directors insisted that we sold a player of striking potential. But I will not resign.'

Despite his public statement, Allison was disillusioned with life at Maine Road and the breakdown of his relationship with the board. He felt they had 'dragged their feet' over a new contract and admitted that 'the urgency and thrill had gone out of my work'.

Meanwhile, his relationship with Serena Williams had been deepening. 'London called,' says James Lawton. 'There was the romance with Serena and he loved the big-time. He couldn't have been happier in Manchester those years when the team was doing well but there had been a general disintegration. London was part of him, part of his life.'

It so happened that there was a club ready to give Allison an escape route and the final destination he craved. Three weeks after his insistence that he was staying at Maine Road, he was introduced as the new manager of Crystal Palace.

Previous Palace manager Bert Head had spent every season since the club's arrival in the First Division four years earlier trying to keep a grip on their elevated status in the football world. His primary tactic had been to accumulate discarded big-name players like a schoolboy swapping surplus *Soccer Stars* stickers. The club's spending had become as eye-catching as their kit, changed in 1971 from claret shirts with light blue pin stripes to white with a broad claret and blue band down the front.

For the 1970–71 season, he had shelled out £100,000 on midfielder Alan Birchenall, unable to get a place in Chelsea's FA Cup-winning team. He had also added Bobby Tambling, the west London club's record goalscorer, and Liverpool full-back Peter Wall. There appeared to be no shortage of cash at Palace and stories emerged that their players could pick up £300 a week, higher than any other club in the First Division, if win bonuses were factored in – which they weren't very often.

Head delighted in being able to say that 'we have bought instant footballers' and the autumn of the following season saw another substantial turnover of players. The incoming group included John Hughes and Willie Wallace, members of Celtic's European Cup-winning squad in 1967, Blackpool stalwart John Craven and experienced midfielder Bobby Kellard. Another quick-fire burst of spending 12 months later saw winger Don Rogers – the hero of Swindon's 1969 League Cup upset of Arsenal – join for £150,000, while former Scotland winger Charlie Cooke and Irish full-back Paddy Mulligan became the latest players to make the short trip from Stamford Bridge. Another six-figure sum was spent on Iain Phillip, a 21-year-old defender from Dundee, and a further £65,000 outlay bought the little blond whirlwind Alan Whittle, whose late-season burst of goals had helped secure the 1970 League Championship for Everton. An additional forward arrived in the shape of Millwall's Derek Possee.

Whittle's debut was in a 5–0 Selhurst Park victory over Manchester United in December 1972, the most famous day of Palace's tenure in the First Division. A rampant Rogers scored twice, but the result proved more indicative of United's impending doom than Palace's hopes of a revival. In fact, it was the last straw for the United directors, who responded by firing manager Frank O'Farrell as manager. Allison's former West Ham colleague had seen his team collapse the previous season and with George Best having gone into his latest 'retirement', the manager's removal was being demanded by the Old Trafford fans.

O'Farrell, incidentally, recalls fondly the show of support he received from Allison at a time when he was not exactly the local population's favourite son. 'Malcolm was very kind and he invited me out for lunch in public in Manchester. He was very sympathetic.'

Allison had been quick to seize upon Best's disappearance from Old Trafford to declare an interest in bringing him back into football at Maine Road, saying 'all my players would welcome George in the dressing-room'. There was never any real chance of such a turn of events and Eric Alexander slapped down his manager by saying he had been 'talking out of turn'.

Meanwhile, Head was proving no more popular in the Palace boardroom than O'Farrell and Allison in theirs. Ray Bloye, a front man for the business consortium Matthews Holdings, had been installed earlier in the season as vice-chairman. Despite his insistence that 'when I joined the club as a director, I had neither the ambition nor the intention to become chairman', by November the old chairman, Arthur Wait, had become a 'life vice-president' and Bloye's boys were running the club. On 20 March, with Palace just above the two relegation places, Bloye announced that Head was to be moved to general manager, explaining unconvincingly that he was to perform a liaison role between the team and the board. It was Joe Mercer all over again. 'Within the next few weeks it is our intention to appoint a first-class team manager, who will set about planning for the 1973–74 season,' Bloye declared, apparently ignoring the fact that there was still a relegation fight to be won in the current campaign.

Aware of Allison's unrest, Bloye made known his interest in bringing him back to his native south-east London. Unsure whether it was the right move, Allison agreed to meet Bloye – and was immediately impressed. 'I liked his approach, which seemed to me to be bigger than almost any other football director I had spoken with. I couldn't imagine him putting the sort of petty, day-to-day restrictions on his manager that I had been suffering.'

Allison confided in Rodney Marsh and was told, 'You've got to do what your heart tells you is right.' His heart was directing him to Crystal Palace. Staying in Manchester and being a good little boy by selling players when the board told him was not his style. He despised colleagues in the profession who were happy to prolong their employment by doing just that. He also sensed that he had taken his men as far as he could. After seven years with many of the same players, familiarity was turning into complacency, on both sides. It seems ironic that such a feeling should take root in Allison so soon after he'd secured the job he wanted above all others. Or maybe that was the point: having ascended to the position of manager, his ambition was diluted.

He informed the City directors of his decision. Their reaction was to promise more money for players and suggested that his contract would be reviewed. But their magnanimity came too late and Malcolm 'drove away from Maine Road without glancing back'.

By that time, the City players were not exactly stunned by the news. Lee claims, 'When Malcolm ran out of enthusiasm for something, he would move on. He had the wanderlust. Towards the end of his career at City he was having too many nights out and he was knocking around nightclubs in London and the lads got the feeling that he had just lost the edge and his appetite for being at City.'

Board member Ian Niven, a staunch supporter of Allison, says, 'It was all down to the relationship between Malcolm and Peter Swales. They just didn't gel. Peter didn't show any sorrow, so it must have suited him. On the morning Malcolm went, Peter said to me, "Your mate's leaving." I asked what the problem was and he said I'd better go and ask him, but Malcolm wasn't in the mood for conversation. He just left.'

Allison duly arrived in London in the early afternoon of 30 March, spent an hour finalising details of his new deal, and was unleashed upon London's football media. 'I'm back home after spending eight years in the provinces,' he announced. 'I had some happy times in Manchester but recently my relationship with the players has soured – I couldn't motivate them. Palace is a club with vast potential and I am looking forward to the challenge. I would not be here if I thought it was too late. I see this as a good job.'

Allison's move had taken the football world by surprise. The Palace players were more shocked than anyone, as Don Rogers explains. 'We were surprised when Bert got moved upstairs and then we were told we would soon be meeting our new manager. We didn't know who it was going to be and I remember sitting in the dressing-room when Malcolm walked in the door. We were flabbergasted. Straight afterwards, everyone was saying, "I didn't expect that." He was the last person we would have thought. We didn't think we would have someone so well known. I'd been quite happy with Bert because I started off with him at Swindon, but I was pleased it was Malcolm because I knew he always had good footballing sides. We knew what he'd achieved at City.'

As Alan Whittle puts it, 'We all thought, "Hang on a minute. This is big time."'

With a compensation payment to City of £20,000 agreed, Allison took charge for the game against Chelsea and was introduced before kick-off to a Selhurst Park crowd of 40,000. It was former manager Head who was responsible for presenting his replacement to the masses but, symbolically, the two men sat apart in the stands, chairman Bloye and England manager Sir Alf Ramsey separating them. Head, who had greeted Allison's appointment by saying that 'Malcolm and I will have to have a chat before I know what's what', would quit the club at the end of the season.

Allison spoke to his new players for half an hour before kick-off and in keeping with their manager's instincts as a showman, they responded by scoring a goal in each half, the second via a header by young Scottish defender Jim Cannon on an impressive debut. The 2–0 win was Palace's first success in a London derby since being promoted. Muhammad Ali might have been silenced that same weekend by having his jaw broken by Ken Norton, but one of British sport's own most accomplished talkers was ready to fill the newspaper columns in his stead. 'There is no danger of us going down,' Allison bragged. 'The potential is ten times better than when I first arrived at Manchester City.'

The financial rewards were also a lot better. Palace had reportedly offered the kind of long-term contract Allison had been unable to get the Maine Road board to finalise, five years at £13,000 a year. The money would be welcome, being – as always – in short supply. While Palace fans were still celebrating victory in Allison's debut game, stories broke that Allison owed William Hill £1,300, the result of a gambling spree at Sandown races more than a year earlier. A spokesman for the bookmakers claimed that Allison had been warned off all racecourses until the debt was paid. Allison denied that part of the story, although not the existence of the debt. He also took the opportunity to criticise the bookmaking industry for encouraging such arrears to be accrued. 'Nobody should be given credit. It's like taking dope. Once you are hooked, you are hooked.' The sound of Allison asking to be protected from his own excesses earned him little sympathy, although once Bloye had paid his debt for him Malcolm claimed to have been given 'a sort of public reminder that a reckless streak could still lead to much self-damage'.

On the field, Allison was quickly discovering that he had not been blessed with the riches he had believed. A 4–0 defeat at Leeds left him complaining, 'There are players in the side who don't know how to run. They're lacking something as basic as that and they are playing in the First Division. Incredible.'

One point and one goal in the five games after beating Chelsea meant that defeat at Norwich in the penultimate fixture would send Palace down. With the score level at 1–1, an injury-time goal by David Stringer won the match for the home team and sealed Palace's fate. Defender Mel Blyth quickly spoke up for the new manager, saying. 'Malcolm came too late. If he had come sooner we would have stayed up. He instils confidence in you. He's that type of bloke.' And Rogers still argues, 'We should never have gone down. It was just luck. If your luck is out that year you have had it.'

Allison's immediate reaction was to take his players to a restaurant in Norwich, arrange the tables in a long line and have a relegation banquet. Rogers explains, 'Malcolm's attitude was, "It's happened, we can't change it, let's focus on next season."' But there was a sour taste to the soup and even a 3–2 win at Maine Road in the final game of the season, keeping Palace off the bottom of the table, couldn't cleanse Malcolm's palate.

16

CRYING GAME

'It was a great social life under Malcolm. But the football was crap'

– Former Palace striker Alan Whittle

Malcolm Allison escaped from the prospect of Second Division football by returning to South Africa for a second summer. In 1972 he had accepted the invitation of the Cape Town City club to organise six weeks of coaching clinics – an experience he found rewarding and, thanks to the natural beauty of the country and his hosts' hospitality, highly enjoyable. It was different when he went back in 1973. This time he was exposed to what he described as the 'harsh and terrible sadness' of apartheid, the political system that had led to South Africa's suspension by FIFA and attached controversy to any kind of visit by foreign sportsmen.

With the North American Soccer League not yet offering the summer opportunities it would in future seasons, several Football League stars took paid vacations in South Africa. As well as more coaching duties, Allison was invited to combine those players with some of his own choice and manage them in a series of 'Test' matches against local representative teams. Allison was able to call on Rodney Marsh, Frank McLintock, former England captain Johnny Haynes and several of his Palace players, including Don Rogers, for a series that he felt the local press blew up into grudge games. 'I didn't realise how much trouble and abuse I would be letting myself in for,' he said.

The media jumped all over Allison's usual habit of making sure his team enjoyed themselves between games and after one night out English football legend Sir Stanley Matthews, who had settled in South Africa, was quoted as saying he was 'ashamed' of the players. Allison claimed that what was described as an all-night session had been nothing more than a harmless evening of swimming and snooker at a local millionaire's mansion. After a 3–2 defeat in Johannesburg, the media stated that the approach of the English team was an insult to South African sport. 'The result was that the South Africans suddenly had some very angry and very talented players on their hands,' said Allison.

One of the tourists' critics was Allison's former West Ham teammate Eddie Lewis, who had ended his playing career in South Africa and stayed to become a well-known television commentator. 'When Malcolm's team came out here, Marsh was walking out with the sleeves cut off his shirt and there appeared to be no discipline,' he remembers. 'They came out for a big jolly. And when I made some comments and was mentioned to Malcolm, he said, "Eddie Lewis? Who the fuck is he?"'

Comfortable wins in Durban and Cape Town followed and the final game saw a victorious return to Johannesburg, where the tourists won 3–1. Allison's satisfaction at silencing the hysterical press with those wins over teams of white players was soon forgotten when he took his team to play the all-black Orlando Pirates. Rogers recalls, 'There were just a hundred white people in the middle of the stand and everyone else around was black. It was a full house. Driving to the ground, you didn't see a white face.' Allison was shocked to see hundreds of police circling the stadium and then roughly searching the black fans as they approached the turnstiles. Later in the day, he was equally disappointed to find that the South African Football Association had refused to attend an official post-game reception, where the black players clearly relished their rare opportunity to rub shoulders with visiting dignitaries.

On the field, even though his team won, Allison was impressed by the carefree football of the opponents and charmed by their use of nicknames like 'Card Shuffler'. Never one to turn his back on a potential gimmick, he decided to give his Palace players similar monikers. 'He had them printed on the back of our tracksuits,' says Rogers. 'I was Trouble Maker.'

Allison also brought back an elevated opinion of Rogers, whom he had used in a more withdrawn role. 'He even mentioned my name in the same breath as George Best. Malcolm was very good at making you feel as if you could play. He was lovely to play for because you could just go out and express yourself.' Allison predicted Rogers would appear for England and saw him as a key component of a team for which he confidently predicted an immediate return to the First Division.

However, it was a season in English football where very little went according to the established order of things. Leeds United would fail to succumb to their usual First Division collapse, landing a second championship under the stewardship of Don Revie; Brian Clough would quit Derby, pitching up at Brighton and Hove Albion just in time to get spanked in the FA Cup by non-League Walton and Hersham; and England would be eliminated from the World Cup in the qualifying stages by an inspired piece of Polish goalkeeping at Wembley, a result that within a few months had cost Sir Alf Ramsey his job. Allison lost little sleep over Ramsey's fate, while his only regret about Manchester United being relegated to the Second Division only six years after conquering Europe was that he wasn't in the city to gloat.

Yet Allison would miss out on the opportunity to resume hostilities with Manchester's 'red cloud' because Palace would themselves be leaving Division Two – in the wrong direction. The season, according to Rogers, was succinctly previewed in the very first game, a home defeat by Notts County. 'We absolutely annihilated them, especially in the first half. We hit the bar about three times and the post twice and were only one up. They scored right on half-time because of a mistake and we ended up losing 4–1. And the year seemed to go like that. We were nowhere near the worst team, yet everything seemed to go wrong.'

Allison appeared confused about how to rectify Palace's problems. Having urged the groundsman to widen the Selhurst Park pitch to encourage more wing play, he had it narrowed again. Alan Whittle explains, 'He thought it would work for us because we had quality players at the side. But it just meant other teams could lump the ball into the corners and thrash us.'

It took until 11 September for Palace to pick up their first point when they eked out a goalless draw against Aston Villa. Other cosmetic changes had been made, with Allison switching the team's colours to red and blue stripes. But Palace were no Barcelona. By October, having played ten games without winning, they were five points adrift at the foot of the table. Even Allison had to admit that his position should be reviewed if things had not improved by Christmas.

After a 1–0 defeat in a League Cup tie at Stockport, Allison accused his players of 'cheating'. Director Dick Varey insisted, 'We support and admire Mr Allison one hundred per cent. We admire his honesty. He has had a lot to deal with since he arrived here and he hasn't flinched. We believe Mr Allison is trying to solve our problems in the right way. This is a time to keep our nerve and not to resort to panic stations.'

Allison's justification of Palace's problems was unconvincing, implying that the Second Division was below the true level of his team. 'It's a joke. Nobody can pass a ball. The quality is not as good as it should be. Long hopeful punts are not football; everyone is running around like a cavalry charge.' Allison was still clinging stubbornly, perhaps misguidedly, to his beliefs in the way the game should be played. Pragmatism was anathema to him in football, as in life.

He also made the mistake of assuming his Palace players could be quickly taught to play the City way. He had forgotten that even City had been made into a tighter, meaner unit before he allowed them to become the personification of his romantic, attacking instincts. Rogers explains, 'From the day I first met him to the very last day when I left, all he wanted was for people to play football all over the pitch. That was his philosophy. There was no kick and rush. In our situation, we probably went too much that way too early, instead of getting rid of it and playing in their half. The fact that Malcolm changed too much too quickly had a lot to do with our problems, but you couldn't argue with it at the time because he'd had such success.'

Allison could see that his team needed major reconstruction and would talk later of the club set-up having been 'diseased' when he took over. Ideally, such an overhaul would be the kind of effortless regeneration achieved by a succession of Liverpool managers during the 1970s and 1980s. Allison, however, felt like a surgeon obliged to get to work on a patient struggling to survive on a life support machine.

He offloaded veteran goalkeeper John Jackson, who had lost his place to Paul Hammond in what was seen by some as a symbolic break from the past, along with a group of Bert Head signings including Iain Phillip, Charlie Cooke and Bobby Tambling. He went back to Maine Road to sign defender Derek Jeffries for £110,000 and midfielder Jeff Johnson, and added defenders Ron Barry from Coventry and Stewart Jump from Stoke. Home-grown youngsters like midfielder Nicky Chatterton, striker David Swindlehurst and the Hinshelwood brothers, Paul and Martin, were given opportunities and before Christmas an amazing total of 30 players had appeared in the team. That number included Allison's most significant Selhurst Park signing, winger Peter Taylor, bought from Southend for £120,000 in early October.

Taylor, who spent 2006–07 as the next in the line of Allison successors as Palace manager, remains a staunch supporter of his former boss, having 'loved him even before I met him'. He explains, 'I had watched him doing games on TV with Brian Moore and he was always interesting and controversial. He said what he felt and didn't hold back, so I was quietly nervous when I got the call to go and meet him. But from the first second he relaxed me and made me feel wanted. He said, "I have finally got you. I tried to sign you seven times in the past." He asked me what money I was on and I told him it was £42.50 a week. He said, "I will give you £100 a week, plus £40 per point." I thought I was a millionaire.

'I had the time of my life at Palace. I just hope players enjoy training with me as much as I did with Malcolm. I was a little bit of a moaner if training wasn't right, but it was always interesting and there was always thought in what we did – even down to having a pre-match meal of peaches and cornflakes instead of big fillet steaks.'

Taylor became the latest player to be administered a large dose of Allison's positivity. 'Every time I walked out of the office I felt I was the best player in England. He was willing to help anyone he knew was trying. I was delighted for him that things turned out well for me at Palace because I was in Southend's reserves when he bought me, so for him to spend that money on me was a gamble. I was pleased that I had three excellent years at Palace.'

Allison would soon be raving about Taylor in public, saying, 'He is being groomed to do everything Mike Summerbee can and did do. He is the nearest thing to Summerbee I have seen and he can shoot with either foot.'

Palace fans might not have cared much for Allison harking back to City, especially when the defeats kept coming. A loss at Nottingham Forest had taken Palace's run to 15 League games without a win. It was then that chairman Ray Bloye chipped in with the dreaded, 'I have complete faith in Malcolm Allison and the way he is doing it.' Remarkably, he appeared to mean it.

Having at last achieved victory when a goal by Whittle beat Bristol City, Palace were still rock bottom when, at the end of the year, Allison prepared to defend himself before a meeting of the club's shareholders. He also revealed that there was a clause in his contract that allowed the club to release him in March on the anniversary of his arrival. 'I'm ready to go if that's what the club wants,' he said.

But as 1973 gave way to the New Year, Palace started winning. A run of five unbeaten games lifted them off the foot of the table and they went on to lose only two out of thirteen. Even with this being the first season of three-up, three-down in the top divisions, they looked as though they could secure safety. Meanwhile, Taylor was already attracting attention from most of London's big clubs.

Then it all went wrong again. Inside a week, Palace lost at Millwall and at home to Fulham and Hull. Even after beating Swindon they went to Cardiff, managed by Frank O'Farrell, needing a win to have any chance of survival. A scrambled first-half goal by Jump gave them the lead, but a 1–1 draw sent Palace down again. 'It should never have depended on tonight,' said a dejected Allison. Rogers remembers, 'Nobody at the club could believe it – a year earlier we had been one of the most entertaining sides in the First Division.'

Taylor admits. 'I cried my eyes out after the Cardiff game. It was for Malcolm because he was doing his best as manager and I couldn't believe that with his ability we had gone down. He was an out and out football man and we probably played too much football for the division we were in. Maybe now, with the new rules on bookings and sendings off, we would have been more dangerous because most teams didn't let us play in the correct way. That might have been a slight excuse for us not doing so well. In this day and age we would have had more room.'

Whittle is a little more pointed in his belief that Allison has to take much of the blame. 'It wasn't Malcolm's fault that we got relegated from Division One, but it was his fault we went down to the Third Division. He thought that he could get us back up purely on his charisma, but you have to be able to transfer that on to the park. Malcolm thought he was still at Manchester City – he didn't evaluate the club he was coming to. I remember doing the same thing when I arrived from Everton. I thought that every club had the kind of set-up we had there but things at Palace were abysmal in comparison. Mal was a great coach but had no success as a manager. He needed someone to manage him and maybe Bert Head could have done that. But Mal went there to be the number one. He could have been our own worst enemy in the end because his personality meant that he was a big scalp for other teams in that division. We got raped by them all. Malcolm thought we could get through with pure skill, but he should have realised he needed a little more.'

There were more than a few smirks at Palace's fate. Allison, despite having dropped a division, remained one of football's most visible personalities, always a ready-quote for the media. In January, he'd made headlines by suggesting London clubs should play on Saturday and Sunday on a rotation basis[10] and he continued to appear regularly on ITV football shows. It meant that he was there to be shot at, and

---

[10] Earlier that month, four FA Cup ties had been played on a Sunday as a way of combating the ongoing power emergency during the infamous winter that would cost Ted Heath and the Conservative Party their government. The imposition of a three-day week had reduced the supply of electricity and Sundays were able to offer greater guaranteed access to power for football stadia.

some journalists were quick to take aim. An article written by John Anthony in *Football Digest* late in the season appeared under the heading, 'Is Allison Just a Big Mouth?' It pointed out Allison's fall from his position as the one rival to Brian Clough in the public's choice as next England manager. Noting that 'the very people who a year ago would have ushered him into Ramsey's seat now dismissed him as a raucous second-rater', the article read:

> Possibly the most instructive sound to emerge from our football grounds this season is the hum of satisfaction which runs through a crowd when it hears the latest score from Crystal Palace. As the news from that depressed area has grown worse, the general satisfaction has become more tangible.
>
> Malcolm Allison has given more pleasure to more people with one season of failure than ever he did with all of those years of triumph. It is not a pleasant state of affairs, but given the national attitude towards extroverts, it is an inevitable one.

Ironically, it would not be Clough nor Allison, but Joe Mercer who was given the opportunity to lead England during their summer programme of matches before Don Revie's appointment as full-time successor to Ramsey. In 1996, Allison would claim he had turned down the chance to work alongside Mercer with England, although he never mentioned it in his 1975 autobiography, at which time he was still saying that he never cared whether he ever spoke to Mercer again.

Allison as England coach does not seem such a crazy idea from a purely footballing standpoint, but in truth it had even less chance of happening than Clough's appointment to the job. Both men had opened their mouths wide enough and often enough to get themselves into trouble. Allison had been a frequent critic of the FA's coaching infrastructure and philosophy and had fallen out with Harold Thompson, who went on to become chairman of the Football Association, as long ago as his stint at Cambridge University. After his success with the Light Blues, Allison had been offered by Thompson the chance to coach Pegasus, the combined Oxford and Cambridge team. Blunt refusal followed, however, when Thompson indicated that he himself would handle team selection. 'I told Thompson, in effect, to stuff Pegasus,' Allison recalled.

Both Clough and Allison liked a drink, although the former's weakness emerged only later in his career. But while Clough kept his boozing off the tabloid news pages, Allison was an unashamedly public carouser – hardly what the FA was looking for.

Another relegation severely tested Allison's ability to look at life through the spectacles of an optimist and lose sight of his troubles through the glass of a champagne bottle. He claimed to take comfort in having modernised training methods and cut the Palace wage bill, but he took the first real failure of his career deeply to heart. He would describe himself being 'crushed' by defeats that 'came like a succession of hammer blows'. He found himself pacing his Kensington flat in the early hours of the morning, making cups of tea as he anguished over ways to make Palace win. Rogers comments, 'He must have found it very difficult, more than the rest of us, having had the success he'd had. We were just getting worse and worse as the season went on and he was frustrated, although he tried not to show it.'

When Allison attended the end-of-season Footballer Writers' Association dinner, he hated the looks that were cast in his direction – varying from the pity of friends to the sneers of those who enjoyed his comeuppance. As his discomfort grew and the alcohol worked its way into his system, Allison needed his companions to hold him back from storming the top table to give an unscheduled lecture about the fine margins between great success and horrid failure. He had now experienced both. He later wrote about the contents of the speech he never made:

> I would have said that there were a lot of compromisers and cowards in football and that often the system, which beneath a thin veneer of respectability is incredibly cynical and sometimes corrupt, most favoured those who were ready to be two-faced and even dishonest. I would have made it clear that I didn't have too much respect for the criteria of success and failure in the game, or the majority of the men who occupied positions of most power.

It is as well those words remained unsaid. The football community doesn't go in much for sermonising by someone who has been quick to revel in his own previous successes. In the cold light of day Allison at least had the grace to recognise that his speech might have sounded like 'the self-justification of a condemned man'.

Palace's performances in the latter half of 1973–74 had at least raised, once more, hopes of immediate promotion when the new season began. But despite playing reasonably well throughout they made only a few fleeting appearances in the top three and wound up fifth after winning only four of the final fourteen games. At one point Allison blamed his team's diminishing returns on the state of the winter pitches, asking, 'How can you expect an artist to work in these conditions?'

There were encouraging performances from the former youth-team players, notably Swindlehurst, who finished as the club's top scorer, while Taylor was selected regularly for the England Under-23s. Stewart Jump is forgiving of Allison's performance at Palace, saying, 'Ultimately, it has to come down to the players – you have to bear responsibility for not getting results. We had some good talent and sometimes it didn't gel.'

Some would argue that ensuring against any lack of cohesion was the coach's job, but Jump highlights Allison's continuing ability to improve players as the reason for the progress being made by the younger squad members and development in his own game. 'His genius was in giving you confidence. He thought about the game more than any coach or manager I had worked with and he made you think about it; talking to you about the guy you were up against and pointing out what he could or couldn't do.

'Even though he had a bit of a reputation away from football, nobody second-guessed his soccer knowledge. I was definitely a better player for having been with him and I still remember the things he taught me when I coach kids now, trying to make them more aware and asking themselves why they are doing certain things and how they can get the opponents to do what they don't want to do.'

There wasn't quite the turnover of players in 1974–75 that there had been a year earlier but Allison still managed to use 28 of them during the season. One who had hoped to be in a Palace shirt was Bobby Moore, released by West Ham in March 1974 after winning the last of his 108 England caps earlier in the season. Having previously indicated his interest in Palace to Ray Bloye he was convinced Allison would attempt to sign him. 'I believed Malcolm could give me the lift and the appreciation I needed to go on playing well, raise my game again. I wanted Malcolm to tell me where I went wrong and to pat me on the back when I did well. I wanted to play for Malcolm so much I decided in my mind that if Palace were a bit tight for money I would take £5,000 less on my contact to go there instead of any of the other clubs.' Allison didn't make a move and while he was attempting to steer Palace out of the Third Division, Moore was helping his new club, Second Division Fulham, to an FA Cup final appearance against his former team.

While Mel Blyth, the last stalwart of the Bert Head era, was sold to Southampton, the most significant transfer development of Palace's season came when Don Rogers, marginalised by the impact of Taylor, moved to Queens Park Rangers. Travelling in the opposite direction were the 22-year-old Welsh central defender Ian Evans and the former Chelsea and Tottenham midfielder Terry Venables, who was then 31. Venables had remained good friends with Allison and had even asked for his advice on the football novel he had co-written. Allison, meanwhile, saw someone who shared his modern thinking, his technical vision – and someone with whom he could enjoy a good night out. Venables was almost gone within a week, however, when QPR chairman Jim Gregory sacked manager Gordon Jago and approached Venables about the job. Allison told Rangers it would cost them £10,000 and Gregory changed his mind.

Venables appeared in only 14 games in Palace's midfield before Allison called him into a New Year's Eve meeting that set in motion events that helped shape English football history. Allison was typically blunt. 'You're finished. You are not going to be able to give of your best on the field, particularly as you have lost a bit of pace, so you're going to stop playing and work with me on the coaching side instead.'

Taken aback, Venables replied, 'I wouldn't take this from anybody else. I'm not even sure I am going to take it from you.'

'Listen. You are finished,' Allison continued. 'Come on the coaching side and you'll be more benefit to us than you will as a player. You're going to be a good coach. Go away and think about it and then come back and start doing it in the morning.'

Venables marched grumpily out of the door, but then turned, knocked and went back into Allison, who looked up, resigned to an argument. 'Happy New Year,' said Venables, turning on his heels. The future England manager had been born.

17

CAT IN THE HAT MEETS THE BIRD IN THE BATH

'If you behave "badly" in terms of what is traditionally good behaviour, nobody minds it when you are doing well. But as soon as you are not doing well they point the finger and say, "That's the reason."'

— 1976 Formula 1 champion James Hunt

If the years from 1968 to 1970 represented the pinnacle of Malcolm Allison's professional achievements in England then 1975–76 was the season that did most to inscribe the legend of Big Mal permanently into the lore of the game. It began with Terry Venables being formally installed as Crystal Palace's chief coach and Allison turning down an ambitious offer from Stockport County to become manager at Edgeley Park. Palace rewarded him with their best-ever start to a season, reeling off five wins and establishing themselves as early pace-setters in Division Three.

By the time they began their FA Cup campaign in November, Palace had lost only one of 18 games, so it was some surprise that they needed a solitary goal by newly arrived forward David Kemp to edge past Walton and Hersham of the Isthmian League. It was the only time they would be drawn at home in a Cup run that was to become one of the stories of the season and would keep Allison in his favoured place in the sporting spotlight. David Swindlehurst's goal helped Palace take

Millwall back to Selhurst Park for a replay that they won 2–1 with another Kemp goal and a penalty by Peter Taylor.

Before facing non-League Scarborough in the third round, Allison failed in his attempt to bring his most infamous former signing back to London. Rodney Marsh had fallen out of love in a very public way with Manchester City and was preparing to throw in his lot with the North American Soccer League. Allison made a request to the Football League to take Marsh on loan from the Tampa Bay Rowdies until their summer season started, but the governing body blocked the kind of arrangement that would soon see players flitting between teams on either side of the Atlantic like businessmen building up their frequent-flyer points.

It was on a train station platform that Allison revealed the headwear that was to become the symbol of Palace's Cup run and would be identified with Big Mal for the rest of his days. Waiting to change trains at Crewe on their way to Yorkshire, Allison, standing a few yards from his players, unzipped his holdall and plonked a wide-brimmed fedora on his head. 'Serena bought it as a Christmas present for me,' he would explain. 'I always liked that sort of hat, always loved to wear them.'

Allison's intention was to 'have a laugh' and as the players responded with a mixture of delight and derision, he piped up, 'We are going to win the Cup with this hat.' Allison had remembered Portsmouth manager Jack Tinn leading his team to a Wembley victory wearing 'lucky spats', while Dave Sexton had continued to sport the same overcoat during Chelsea's successful FA Cup run and Don Revie favoured a lucky suit. None of those sartorial statements were quite as photogenic as Allison's fedora, though, and when he took his seat in the stand, the photographers ran from their positions behind the goal to gather below him. 'What do you think of that cunt,' one Scarborough player was heard to say. 'The only chance we'll ever get of getting some publicity and he wears that fucking hat!' The home team were also denied any giant-killing headlines when goals by Taylor and Evans beat them 2–1.

The draw for the fourth round was made while the Palace party were stuck on a train and when Allison saw his messenger approaching he sensed from his gloomy facial expression that it must be bad news – possibly a First Division team, probably away from home. He quickly whispered instructions to Terry Venables, 'When he tells us which team it is, get very excited, say what a lucky ground it is for you, and really give it some hype.' When the words 'Leeds away' pierced the carriage, Allison punched the air and Venables announced what great success he'd enjoyed at Elland Road. Players looked at the pair as if they had gone mad. Leeds, although no longer under the iron grip of Don Revie, were second in the table and had been unlucky to lose the European Cup final against Bayern Munich a few months earlier.

As the game approached, Palace's players feared that Allison's traditional pre-match prognostications of success could be like prodding a bear with a sharp stick. Taylor says, 'Leeds were such a good team that we said to Mal, "Let's not give it the big 'un. We believe we can beat them, but let's keep it low key." We woke up in Leeds on the morning of the game, picked up the paper and there's Malcolm saying we will win 3–0! And actually, it could have been.'

Allison restored Alan Whittle to the Elland Road line-up in place of Kemp, and made another important tactical decision, explaining, 'We decided to play a sweeper at the back with four markers, and to break whenever we could. So it became a competition between our defenders and their strikers and we outplayed them.' The only goal of the game was headed in by Swindlehurst, meeting Taylor's first-half free-kick with a late run to the far post. Swindlehurst stung David Harvey's palms with a long-range free-kick after half-time and the Scottish keeper did well to keep out an Evans header. Palace were so comfortable that at one point Stewart Jump turned toward the bench and mimed smoking a cigar, as if to indicate the ease of the victory. 'That is a special memory,' Jump recalls. 'With a few minutes to go I shouted to the bench to find out how long to go and I just wanted to portray to them how very, very easy it was for us. They didn't even come close to scoring.'

Jump puts that down to Palace's preparation. 'It was a very intense week. Every day we played against the reserves and they were pretending to be Leeds. We developed a great confidence in the system we were playing and believed we were going to play well.'

The bandwagon was up and running. The fifth-round draw sent

Palace to Stamford Bridge to face Chelsea, and the resulting hype reflected the exciting prospect of Big Mal back on a major London stage in front of 50,000, rather than the thought of a contest between a mid-table Second Division team and one a division below. Cheap replica fedoras flew off the traders' stalls in and around Selhurst Park and the players even went into the recording studio. The match lived up to its build-up, the stadium crackling with more excitement than it had experienced in the previous two or three years of Chelsea decline. 'It is the game I always remember in that Cup run,' says Taylor. 'Every game was away from home but at least at Stamford Bridge we had a lot of our fans there. It was an incredible day and I still look at the tape every now and again. It was a great atmosphere.'

Palace silenced the home fans in the first half, with Taylor showing too much close control for the big, blond centre-back Steve Wicks. He teased and tormented him on the right edge of the box before firing against the underside of the bar, giving Nicky Chatterton the easy task of turning in the rebound. Taylor dragged Wicks wide again but instead of turning outside him he played the ball square to Chatterton and met the return pass with a low left-foot shot into the corner of the net. Up in the stand, Allison waved his hat in celebration before jamming it shapelessly back on his head.

After the teams changed ends, Chelsea mounted a comeback. Ray Wilkins – still hirsute and known as 'Butch' in those days – fired in from just inside the area and an ecstatic Wicks headed home a corner. With the crowd in the kind of frenzy that is absent from most grounds in the new all-seater era, especially for devalued FA Cup games, Palace were awarded a free-kick 25 yards out in a central position. Taylor stepped up to curl the ball round and over the wall to clinch a thrilling Palace victory.

Sunderland, a team who knew all about the romance and magic of the Cup, stood between Palace and a place in the last four. Having soaked up 45 minutes of pressure from the home team, who were playing with a strong wind at their backs, Palace left Roker Park with a 1–0 win after Taylor set up a goal for Whittle. The sense that perhaps fate was on Palace's side grew when they avoided Manchester United and Derby in the semi-finals and instead, drew Second Division Southampton. 'We were very confident,' Jump remembers.

Allison recognised the great opportunity that now lay ahead of him. The tough times he had endured since the end of his partnership with Joe Mercer had, on occasions, borne down heavily. The sleepless nights, the near-outburst at the Footballer of the Year dinner, were evidence that, for all his bluster, Allison had a need for approval. His bravado, his outrageous behaviour, was often no more than a clumsily constructed shield for the hurt and self-doubt that failure had planted within him. To the Palace fans, such humanity and vulnerability assured their loyalty. Chants of 'Allison out' had been scarce during Palace's free-fall through the divisions. And looking back, players such as Taylor appreciate the way Allison internalised his anxieties. 'Where he was so good was, even when we were under pressure, that he never let it get to us. He took it all on his own shoulders.'

Now Malcolm had his men on the threshold of Wembley, exactly the kind of performance to which he had alluded when, a few months earlier, he'd said in his autobiography, *Colours of My Life*:

> I have at the back of my mind an achievement which will really knock some people sideways. I want people to acknowledge that I have gone into a tight situation, fought it, and then say, 'He's a man among boys; he knows what he is doing and where he is going.'

Allison's quest to prove himself once more had even led him to express interest in managing 'Team America', the NASL representative side that would take on England, Brazil and Italy in the Bicentennial Tournament in the United States in the summer. In March he vowed, 'In a month coaching the best players in America, I could teach them more than they have learned in the history of the game there.' He wouldn't get the chance to make good on that promise, the job being given to New York Cosmos head coach Ken Furphy, the former Watford and Sheffield United manager.

Of course, the feat of becoming the first manager to lead a Third Division team to the FA Cup final would do more to restore his credentials than leading the likes of Bobby Moore and Pelé in a summer sideshow. 'How one ached for him to get to that final,' recalls James Lawton. On the strength of their impressive list of scalps, Palace were considered by many as favourites to beat Southampton at

Stamford Bridge. Allison predicted a Palace–Derby final and expressed his excitement about returning to the European Cup-Winners' Cup. The only negative note he sounded in the build-up was his anger at Millwall manager Gordon Jago for refusing to postpone the clubs' Division Three meeting four days before the semi-final.

Yet Palace's hopes on their big day were hit when Taylor was unable to display the form that had recently earned his first full England cap as a substitute against Wales. 'Everyone expected Peter to do more against Southampton,' says Whittle. 'But he was tied up by Peter Rodrigues and it didn't happen. Malcolm probably put too much on the boy.' The rest of the team appeared nervous without their talisman producing the goods. Taylor adds, 'We played hopeless in the semi, and Southampton played just as badly.'

It was hard to see where a Palace goal would come from and Southampton were comfortable 2–0 winners, through Paul Gilchrist and a David Peach penalty. It turned out that the Saints were the team of destiny all along, beating Manchester United 1–0 in the final.

The downside of all this Cup excitement was that Palace lived up to the old truism of teams being distracted from their primary objective of winning League games. In December, after their second-round win, they lost four successive games. They still retained top spot at that point, but slipped to third during a run of seven games without victory. They went almost four months without a Selhurst Park victory and failed to regain momentum after their Cup exit, winning only one of their final eight games to finish fifth. The fans might have retained their patience and affection, but that of the Palace board had run out.

In sport, winning can buy you the licence to behave in any way you wish. Tales of high jinks during a run of success are indulged and celebrated; the same stories during a fallow period frowned upon and condemned. Even in the good times, Allison tiptoed precariously close to what constituted the boundary of acceptability. But with the FA Cup run in full swing, he had plunged headlong down the waterfall of poor taste.

With training drawing to a close one day, a Rolls-Royce pulled up. Who should emerge but a tracksuited Allison, accompanied by 'actress' Fiona Richmond, resplendent in a fur coat. Fiona was the shining star of the early-'70s phenomenon that was the British soft-porn film industry. A household name and face even to those who were not aficionados of her work, her credits in films with such titles as *Exposé*, *Barry McKenzie Holds His Own* and *Not Tonight, Darling* sum up her career quite neatly. The players completed their exertions, retreated to the changing-rooms and flopped wearily into the communal bath. Barely a step behind them, however, with a photographer in tow, came Malcolm and Fiona. Before you could say 'no sex please, we're British', the pair of them had stripped off and joined the players in the tub. Allison would explain, 'She said, "Do you mind if I get in the bath?" So I said, "Yeah, why not?"'

Others could have answered that question rather easily. Venables recorded, 'I was out of the bath like lightning when I saw the photographer lurking around. Malcolm later told me he had never seen me move as fast on the football field.'

Stewart Jump says, 'Malcolm had announced that somebody was coming to training, a model or somebody. We didn't think anything of it. But when we came in after practice things started happening and the next thing she is in the bath and Malcolm jumps in after her. It was quite a spectacle and a typical Malcolm thing. Anything to get in the papers.'

Alan Whittle remembers that he and Peter Taylor were responsible for Fiona ending up in such hot water. 'Mal had said earlier that she was getting in the bath with us. After training she was in the physio's room and Peter picked her up and threw her in the bath and took her shoes off.'

Taylor claims no such part in the events, saying, 'Malcolm and I got on well and he had told me in advance what was going to happen so I was nowhere.'

However Fiona came to be naked alongside the Palace players, and however many of the players either saw the funny side or claim to have been nowhere in the vicinity, the truth was that there were few smiling wives – or club directors – when pictorial evidence of the escapade emerged. Allison had yet to meet a photo opportunity he didn't like and he pointed to the exposure, so to speak, that he achieved for his club as justification for the stunt. Yet friend Bob

McNab states, 'That sort of behaviour was idiotic. I remember saying to myself, "Malcolm, what the hell are you doing? That is not the publicity you want."'

The escapade was typical of Allison's ability to speak or act on occasions without giving full thought to the consequences, a trait that, in some ways, had a charming innocence about it. James Lawton says, 'Don Revie once described him as an embarrassment to the game but I don't go along with that. No one could ever claim on his behalf that he was modest but he wouldn't be self-serving in the way of José Mourinho. He could say something unguarded, and the incident with Fiona wasn't particularly well calculated.'

The real problem at Palace was that the daft headlines and the tabloid tales of his private life were starting to outweigh the victories. As bizarre as his behaviour with Fiona Richmond had been, if he'd given Palace three seasons of success instead of underachievement, the directors would probably have been lining up to soap her back. Instead, as he would recount, 'I had a good young team coming through, maybe the second-best I ever had after City, but then Fiona Richmond got in the bath and the FA said I brought the game into disrepute.' And in what became a well-rehearsed line, he added, 'It was a real disappointment to me because when she got in the bath I realised she had plastic tits. It wasn't worth getting the sack for.'

Allison was dismissed in mid-May, two weeks after a meeting with chairman Ray Bloye appeared to have determined that he would be staying at the club. Fiona had been the last straw. As well as disappointing results, Allison had angered the board by refusing to consider a £300,000 offer for Taylor from Leeds – funds the club needed badly[11] – and disappearing to the Cannes film festival with Serena Williams instead of staying at home to discuss the matter. He had also sailed close to the wind of the FA's disciplinary committee when, in defiance of his continuing ban, he had appeared on the touch-line to shout at his players during a loss at Rotherham.

As usual, the official statement released to explain Allison's departure spoke of him leaving the club 'by mutual consent'. Yet the directors had, quite simply, reached an unavoidable verdict: Malcolm

---

[11] Four months after Allison's departure, Taylor was sold to Tottenham for £200,000.

had lost it. He could no longer inspire and innovate in the manner that had shaped Manchester City's great run of achievement. His increasingly extreme lifestyle appeared incompatible with that of a successful manager.

His old friend and protégé, Bobby Moore, commented to his biographer Jeff Powell in the mid-'70s, 'Malcolm's had a great life but he has left some question marks behind him en route. As a manager I would still want to be part of my players. But only up to a point. I wouldn't even think about taking them out to night clubs. How else could I hope to discipline people? I would have told Mike Summerbee he had it in him to be the greatest winger in the world and to go out and prove it to me every game. If he failed, he would have to get in the reserves and prove he was still in good physical condition. I don't know if Malcolm leaves himself the right to do that.'

It seems sad that, in the space of a few months, Fiona and the fedora had helped to create a legacy for Allison that would overshadow his football achievements in the consciousness of the public in decades to come.

Taylor suggests that, just as Allison would have thrived in the environment of the modern English football club, where the manager is free to focus on coaching duties, so the contemporary lifestyle of the game could have shielded him from his own inclination to overindulge. 'Malcolm was a little bit unlucky. If he was managing now, when players take things so professionally and don't drink a lot, he wouldn't be out there so much with the champagne and cigars and people would take him more seriously.'

The flip side of that, of course, is that had Allison followed the same pattern of off-field behaviour in the modern celebrity-driven age the tabloids would never have left his doorstep. In 2004, with Sven-Göran Eriksson's latest fling being plastered across the front pages, he told James Lawton, 'Nothing changes in men chasing women. What's different is the way people are judged. In my time performance was everything. The trick was to do your work as well as you could in public and your pleasure in private – and try not to hurt anyone.'

Yet even in the less sensationalist days of the 1970s more than one club felt they were being hurt by Allison's antics, while undoubted self-damage was being inflicted by his apparent addiction to his celebrity status. He appeared unable any longer to rein himself in, even if he did feel it would have helped on the pitch. He certainly would never have done it just for the sake of decorum. By now some of the headlines that he was attracting were ones that even the most devoted publicity-seeker could have done without as his life away from football was played out in public like a cheap soap opera.

He lost his father, who was 65, to a heart attack in 1974, an event that hit Malcolm hard. 'My father's death came in the middle of a particularly hectic time at Crystal Palace,' he said. 'It was a shock and I deeply regretted that I had been unable to spend more time with him.'

On a seemingly happier note, he had set a date to be married to Serena, who commented, 'We have both played the field but now we just want each other.' She said that Malcolm had taken to wearing a pendant saying, 'No longer me, but we.' But the engagement lasted only a few months, the end reportedly coming soon after a row about money during a holiday in Spain, where Allison ended up getting into a fight with a barman. His face all over the news pages, he had returned to England in a depressed state.

At the end of December 1975, he was stopped by police while driving his Daimler the wrong way on the outer ring road of Regent's Park. He was found to have twice the legal limit of alcohol in his system and was subsequently banned from driving for 12 months and fined £125, plus costs, after pleading guilty to driving while unfit and failing to provide a blood or urine sample. A reflective Allison commented at the end of the year, 'I'm not saying I've lost pride in myself or my ability to do certain things, but in the last month or so certain things have happened to really make me think.'

The new year began with notification by a credit card company that it had filed a bankruptcy charge against him. Serena, now described in the press as his 'agent and former girlfriend', argued that the sum of money involved was 'ridiculously small'.

In the meantime, Beth was back on the scene, with Allison said to be happily reunited with his wife and living in a house close to Selhurst Park. But their final split, after twenty-two years and four children, was just around the corner. Beth stoically acknowledged that Malcolm was simply not cut out to be the doting husband, accepting his own assertion that tuberculosis had changed him irrevocably. 'I think that while he was recovering he decided to prove himself,' she said. 'I think he came to the conclusion that he only had one life and he was going to live it to the full.'

Allison himself spoke with regret and affection. 'I cannot recall a single row between us. Not even when I disappeared one afternoon in Manchester to buy some fish for tea and didn't get home until lunchtime the following day. She was a brilliant mother and a super girl. When I was gambling I'd have £30,000 sometimes stuffed in drawers in notes and she never took a fiver.' Malcolm proceeded to kiss and make up with Serena, although their partnership would eventually dissolve for good late in 1977.

Lawton, who had moved from Manchester to London around the same time as Malcolm, had been a frequent companion during this period and together they had constructed Allison's autobiography, *Colours of My Life*. While celebrating some of its author's excesses, the work is much more than a laugh-a-minute romp through the bedrooms of blondes and bunny girls or a facile circuit of the playing fields of his professional triumphs. There are moments of sombre introspection, hints of regret over a life boisterously lived but lacking in deep-rooted contentment. The book – vastly different from most football memoirs of the time, or indeed the modern day – reflects not only the skill of Lawton as ghostwriter, but the dark alleys of depression that Allison was wandering in and out of at the time.

'I used to go up to his apartment in an old Georgian house on the Cromwell Road,' Lawton explains. 'It seems to me in recollection he was always wearing a loose Arab gown. He would sit on the settee and we would go through stuff and he would be quite sad and sober – in terms of his mood. I think things were bad with Serena and she might have gone. I don't know that I am in a position to judge Serena but I always thought she attracted quite a lot of publicity on the basis of her relationship with Malcolm and benefited from it. But Malcolm was a bit distraught when it was over.

'I remember a game around that time when they were winning 1–0 but they lost in the last seconds when the other team scored twice in stoppage time. I could hardly bear to do it, but I looked around and Malcolm just had his head in his hands. It would have made a great photograph. It was a stance I remember quite well from those days. It was as if his will was imploding.'

Jeff Powell, another friend from the world of journalism, adds, 'Malcolm was a natural depressive. So when things were bad – if he had misbehaved and was having problems in his marriage or relationships – then he would get very down about it.'

In the midst of such turmoil, even football appeared no longer to offer the certainty and stability that was so lacking in other areas of Malcolm's life. Whereas he would previously have thrown himself into training and tactical planning, those close to Allison sensed that the game had lost some of its appeal. It had needed the FA Cup run – a break from the mundane – to reinvigorate him. Terry Venables saw the phenomenon close up and felt, 'Malcolm had become bored with winning, strange though that sounds, and was looking for a fresh challenge.'

McNab puts it this way. 'At City, I always felt Malcolm had found the answer. Then he went looking for another one.' The former Arsenal man saw how uninterested Allison appeared when he went to discuss a possible move to Palace after being granted a free transfer from Highbury in the summer of 1975. 'Terry set it up for me to go and meet with Malcolm. I sat there for 45 minutes or so and he must have taken six or eight phone calls on personal matters. He was trying to get to Spain with Serena and he was on with her and the banks, and I am sitting there thinking, "The man is a disaster." We never talked about football at all. When I came out Venners asked me how it had gone and I said, "I don't know, he was so distracted."'

Meanwhile, Venables had found it was pointless waiting for instructions from his boss on the training ground, explaining that he was often 'hours late and sometimes would not turn up at all'. It is impossible to imagine the Allison who drove the likes of Colin Bell and Mike Summerbee in his early years at Maine Road being guilty of such a lack of interest. Frank Lord, assistant coach at Palace until the summer of 1975, would prepare for Allison's non-appearance by having his own training schedule ready. But frequently Malcolm would show up halfway through the session, discard Lord's timetable and announce, 'I have got this great new idea.'

Whittle's memory is of Allison being present most of the time at the training ground, but disappearing when the directors were looking for him. 'Mal used to go missing. The chairman would come asking us if we knew where he was. It was crazy.'

His friend Derek Ufton remembers urging Allison to rethink his whole career strategy. 'Frank Lord was coach at Palace and I'd had him for a while with me at Plymouth. He was a lovely guy but not the kind of coach the players had a feel for like they did with Malcolm. I used to plead with him and say, "You have got to go out and coach." He would answer, "No, I am the manager. I am going to direct it all from the office." When Terry Venables became coach they started to do better because Terry was more like Malcolm.'

Watching Venables at work, Allison admitted to recognising the same simple approach with which he himself had succeeded at City. Over the previous couple of seasons, he had witnessed his players' look of confusion at some of his own methods. Their response to Venables reminded him how he should have approached his task at Palace, although Summerbee suggests, 'When Malcolm was starting at City he had the right players at the right time. Guys like Alan Oakes and Glyn Pardoe had been waiting for someone like him and they responded. I don't think he had those kinds of players at other clubs.'

The irony is that, having begun at Palace with a group of experienced big-money signings, many of whom failed to produce, the players he left behind were not unlike the young, hungry and impressionable players he had moulded at City. If Allison had stayed at Selhurst Park and reprised the methods he employed in Manchester, the latter chapters of this book might have turned out differently. Instead it was Venables who would turn Palace into the team that was dubbed, albeit mistakenly, 'The Team of the '80s'.

To Palace fans, however, Allison's legend has outlived the bad results. When a young internet forum user asked recently why a man who had achieved back-to-back relegations was honoured in Selhurst Park's gallery of Palace greats, a wave of angry responses hit him full in the face. Among such pithy comments as 'if you weren't the snotty oik you are, you wouldn't need to ask' were a welter of tributes to the style of the man and the teams he put out on the field.

Other fans thanked him for 'turning us into the glamour side of the mid-'70s' and acknowledged the foundations he laid for Venables and the club's return to the First Division.

Allison, meanwhile, would spend the rest of his career on the move. Over the next 17 years, there would be more than a dozen jobs, almost as many sackings and a legacy of unfulfilled talent. 'It is such a terrible shame,' says Derek Ufton, who describes the vicious circle in which Allison became a prisoner. 'Having been a manager, he would never have accepted if he got offered a position as number two – which he would have been ideal at. And eventually no manager worth his salt would give him a job because he knew Malcolm would want to override him every minute of the day. But if he had gone somewhere like Lilleshall to coach he would still have a job.'

18

YOU CAN'T GO BACK

'I quite liked Peter Swales because he wore a wig, a blazer with an England badge on it and high-heeled shoes. As a man he really impressed me'

– Malcolm Allison on the former
Manchester City chairman

Malcolm Allison was out of Selhurst Park, out of a job and preparing to leave Britain. But being Big Mal, he wasn't planning to go quietly. On the day of his departure from Crystal Palace, he announced at Mayfair's White Elephant Club that he was heading to America for a three-week coaching trip, taking in Florida, California and Texas. He didn't sound like a man in a hurry to return. 'I'm going to America to weigh things up, but it will be goodbye to English football. I won't miss England a lot. It's a sad country at the moment.'

Declaring himself disillusioned with everything from the high rates of income tax to the low level of expertise within his sport, he claimed that too many clubs were 'dilapidated' and described the game as 'primitive'. He said of his fellow coaches, 'The ignorance of a proportion of them is beyond belief.' Allison was quickly brought down to earth, however, when his journey was delayed by the absence of the appropriate visa. 'He has not made it clear why he wants to go to America,' said a US embassy spokesman, who had clearly not read Allison's rant in the newspapers.

In the end, once his summer jaunt was over, it was not America that offered him a route back into full-time coaching, but Turkey, the football nation that had caused him such embarrassment while at Manchester City. Galatasaray, while not the European power they would become a couple of decades later, had enjoyed three successive Turkish championship successes under English coach Brian Birch, one of Manchester United's original 'Busby Babes' of the 1950s. After Birch moved on in 1974, club president Selahattin Beyazit persuaded Don Howe to take the job for a while – until he joined the staff at Leeds – and then appointed former Reading boss Jack Mansell. When Beyazit was looking for a new man for the 1976–77 season, he asked Howe if he could recommend any English coaches.

As Howe hesitated, Beyazit said, 'I will tell you the names I have been given,' and announced Allison and Arthur Cox, the future manager of Newcastle and Derby, who had been on the Sunderland coaching staff when they won the 1973 FA Cup. Howe replied, 'You have got two good blokes there. They both know the game but they are different personalities. When Malcolm is in work mode he is intelligent and will work hard for you, but he does like to put himself about – he likes a drink and he likes the ladies.'

Beyazit explained that his mind was made up and duly appointed Allison, with Cox as his assistant. One of their earliest assignments was a 2–0 defeat in a pre-season friendly at Huddersfield. The team, which included eight Turkish internationals, also underperformed at home, condemning Malcolm to more misery at the hands of Fenerbahce, vanquishers of his European Cup ambitions. Galatasaray qualified to meet their Istanbul rivals in the final of a tournament set up to help earthquake victims in the eastern Turkish city of Van, but were thrashed 6–1. Allison's tactics were roundly criticised, but when the teams met again in a league game, Malcolm revived his Stretford End tactic of standing in front of the opposition fans and indicating the score by holding up his fingers. This time, he played safe and indicated four goals – only to be beaten once again.

According to James Lawton, Allison seemed far from happy in Turkey. Unable to get his favourite cigars in Istanbul, he asked his agent, Richard Coomber, to pick up some Havanas on his way out to Turkey. 'Whatever you do, don't forget them,' he said. Allison was disturbed that Coomber made no mention of any package after he picked him up from the airport. Eventually, during the drive into the city, he asked, 'You did get those cigars, didn't you?'

'Sorry, Malcolm, I completely forgot,' was the reply.

Lawton continues, 'Malcolm told me, "I was so fucking frustrated I almost drove the car off the bridge." I thought that was highly significant. It was as if nothing else could go wrong – things just weren't working out at that time in his life.'

In an interview he gave in 1982, Allison reflected on his feelings of isolation during his stint in Istanbul and future foreign assignments. 'I wouldn't complain if you described me as a man of independent spirit. But that kind of freedom has its price. In Portugal, and especially in Turkey, the price was loneliness. I was happy while I was working with the players there. I am always happy when I'm working. But I often used to sit in my luxury villa or fashionable restaurant and yearn for the folks back home.'

Allison's unhappiness meant that Howe was soon receiving another call from Beyazit. 'You were right about Malcolm. He does like a drink.' With the club poised to make a managerial move, Howe suggested his former Arsenal full-back Bob McNab, Malcolm's old ITV colleague, who was flown to Turkey for an interview. McNab recalls, 'I told the owner I was uncomfortable because they still had Malcolm as coach but he said, "Don't worry. He is not going to be here long." Then I heard that I couldn't stay in the hotel Malcolm was staying in. He must have been in a mess, drinking a lot, because he was lonely out there. There were about 55,000 Galatasaray fans at the game I went to and Malcolm came out on the far corner of the field and walked all the way round with his arms up in the air. The crowd went bananas; they seemed to love him. I decided it wasn't for me, but Malcolm left anyway – I think it was his off-field activities that cost him his job.'

The next stop for Allison as he hawked his skills around the globe was a return to the United States, where the North American Soccer League was planning to build upon the foundations laid by Pelé's three successful years at the New York Cosmos by expanding to 24 teams. Various cities and their opportunistic business communities had been dazzled by the achievement of the Cosmos in attracting crowds of more than 70,000 to the new Giants Stadium. They saw the road to 'Soccer Bowl' paved with gold.

Memphis, Tennessee, was still mourning the death in August 1977 of its most famous resident, Elvis Presley, when Allison landed to take on the job of building the Memphis Rogues. He would never take charge of a single game, leaving the club 'by mutual consent' five weeks before the start of the NASL season, having signed no players for the new club. McNab, who was involved in the NASL as player and coach in the late '70s, remembers, 'He only kept that job about three months. I spent a lot of time with Bobby Moore in America and he always claimed the Rogues got the first credit card bill and saw that Malcolm had been putting fortunes on it, even though he hadn't signed anyone. That was why he went.

'Bobby used to love him. Malcolm was left-handed and when he got the credit card out his signature was like a printing machine going up and down. Bobby used to call it "the snake". I'd see him and he'd say, "Malcolm had the snake out last night. He found a card with something on it so I let him pay."'

Allison, despite his outburst of almost two years earlier, was soon back in England and returning to his first League club, Plymouth Argyle, setting in motion a pattern of unsuccessful encores on his old stages. The phrase 'you can never go back' might have been made for this phase in Malcolm's career, with one disaster following another.

On 16 March 1978, he was named as 'consultant manager' at Home Park, working with Lennie Lawrence, who had been in temporary charge for a month following the resignation of Mike Kelly. Allison had instigated his own appointment at Argyle when he called on an old boardroom ally. Club secretary Graham Little explains: 'He phoned me when he heard that the manager had gone and asked for the number of the chairman, Robert Daniel. He had been very friendly with Robert first time round and everybody at the club was delighted when he came back. I remember on his first day, he told the players they were having a practice match and the best 11 players would be in the first team. They all went out kicking each other.'

Argyle found themselves in 21st place in Division Three after a single victory in their previous 17 games, but they improved enough to finish clear of the drop in 19th place. Gary Megson, at the time a young Argyle midfielder, recalls, 'Given Malcolm's stature in the game it was a big coup for Plymouth to get him back.' But he describes Allison's return to the club as 'a whirlwind'.

The late John Craven, a versatile player whom Allison had moved on from Palace, would soon be leaving Home Park to play under assistant coach McNab at the Vancouver Whitecaps. 'John used to say that the practices were a joke at Plymouth,' says McNab. 'Malcolm was always trying new stuff. He was using them as a technical experiment. They would play one man in midfield one day and nine the next.'

The image of Allison as mad professor in front of a set of bubbling, coloured test tubes is supported by Megson. 'There was a total transformation in the training and the way we played. He tried a lot of different formations and some of his ideas were probably asking too much of the players he had. I remember two different formations he tried and at the time we weren't capable of playing them. He tried playing with two sweepers, a back four, one in the middle and two up front. The two sweepers were supposed to push forward but it didn't happen and poor old Micky Horswill was left on his own in midfield. I think we won 5–0 away from home, though, and then he changed it. Another time we played a version of 4-4-2 but without any forwards. It was all interesting but there was a tendency to use us to try out new things.'

Megson retains fond memories, however, of the individual care Allison lavished on him – the kind of nurturing he had undertaken with the likes of Bobby Moore and Joe Corrigan. 'I was a young lad who had played only a few games and he did me a world of good. If he had time for you he would make you feel a lot better than you were and he did a lot for me in a short space of time, including doubling my contract. Also I was having a problem with my back and he took me to Crystal Palace to sort it out. On the way there he took me to one of those private clubs and we ended up having lunch with Eamonn Andrews. So if he liked you, he made time for you. But I don't think that held true for everybody.'

It wasn't only young players who felt they were learning from Allison. Lennie Lawrence, an up-and-coming coach who went on to manage a number of clubs, including Charlton and Middlesbrough in the top flight, holds dear the experience of working alongside Malcolm. 'He had come with a reputation after his spells at Manchester City and Crystal Palace and it wasn't long before I saw why. I spent only nine months with him but it was the most enlightening period of my life. His coaching genius stood out. Allison was an innovator. He might not have been the best manager ever and he had many foibles but Mal was ahead of his time on the training pitch. Tactically, the man was brilliant. He introduced Third Division players to all sorts of weird and wonderful systems. His philosophy on training belonged to the twenty-first century.

'If he taught me anything it was to keep the pressure off the players when they're approaching a big game. He achieved it by being larger than life, wearing that fedora, smoking those huge cigars, being outrageous – making sure everybody noticed him. In fact people couldn't take their eyes off him. That meant he absorbed all the pressure.'

During the summer of 1978, while Argentina were winning another World Cup for which England had failed to qualify, Allison attended a coaching course at Lilleshall with the likes of Howe, Terry Venables, John Bond and Ron Atkinson. During an evening in the bar, Howe, one of Malcolm's admirers, warned him that he was squandering his talent and with all that he had to offer the game, should adopt a more dedicated lifestyle. 'You're right,' Allison responded, launching into plans to bring his Plymouth players in for pre-season training two weeks early and promising to be up at 7.30 every morning. 'I've got to start pulling myself together. I'm one of the best coaches there is and I'm going to prove it. I'm not going to have a holiday, I'm going to go to fitness camps and I'm going to do special weight training. This is a new Malcolm Allison.'

But the new Malcolm went missing sometime during the session on the booze. When Venables tried to wake him for training, it was the familiar Big Mal whose voice came back. 'Piss off. I'm too tired to get up.' He was two hours late for the session.

Meanwhile, he was back in the headlines in August after being arrested for being drunk at Paddington Station, where transport police had found him slumped on a seat. Taken to a detention room, he set out to prove he was not 'drunk and incapable'. Instead of standing on one leg or reciting the alphabet backwards, his method was to smash a light fitting and two light bulbs. He appeared in court the following day charged with being drunk and causing £28 worth of criminal damage. As he left court, having been remanded to return in October, he lunged at one of the posse of photographers awaiting his exit before, as *The Sun* put it, 'being whisked away by two blondes'. When the case was heard in October, he was fined £200, plus £49 in compensation and costs.

Allison's behaviour had unsettled the Argyle directors first time around, but at least they had never seen him in the dock. This time, though, the club, with his great supporter Robert Daniel at the helm, adopted a more tolerant approach, knowing enough about their manager's antics to be forewarned. 'It came on the radio that he had been arrested and the attitude was, "Well, that's Malcolm",' says Little. 'We knew he had gone to London and been out with friends. Apparently when they took him back to Paddington, instead of putting him on the train, they left him sitting on a bench and he accidentally rolled over onto a woman, who screamed her head off.'

Argyle's attitude was undoubtedly made softer by the decent start their team had made to the Division Three season, winning five of the first seven matches. But then they tailed off to sit in the middle of the table and were beaten in the first round of the FA Cup at non-League Worcester City.

To some, Allison appeared happy enough in his situation, having acquired a house in the Cornish town of Hessenford. Yet it was becoming clear to others that, while Plymouth might have been the perfect launch pad for Malcolm's professional managerial career 15 years earlier, this time he was, as Megson states, 'too big for the club'. Megson adds, 'I don't think Plymouth was right for him at that time. He continued living most of the time in London and we trained in the afternoons so that he could get down there. He took his girlfriend on the team bus and he always seemed to be attracted to a bigger club. It was a helter-skelter ride while he was here, but it was never a long-term thing for him.'

Maine Road had seen a number of changes since Allison's departure. His trusty lieutenant, Tony Book, had become manager after short-lived spells in charge by Johnny Hart and the dour Ron Saunders, while Colin Bell was about to admit defeat in his battle to come back from the severe knee ligament injury he had suffered late in 1975. Francis Lee and Mike Summerbee were long gone – Lee to Derby to win another League Championship medal, and Summerbee to Burnley. In 1976, Book led a City team with few survivors of the Allison era to victory in the League Cup. Form in the First Division was solid, with a runners-up finish in 1977, one point behind champions Liverpool, followed by fourth place the following year.

Yet as 1979 was ushered in by an icy blast that blanketed the country, City were struggling along in 15th position in the table. Moves were afoot to bring the prodigal son back to Manchester. Book states, 'It came about because two directors who were very staunch Malcolm fans went to the chairman and got it through. It was the last thing I wanted.'

Director Ian Niven, however, recalls that Peter Swales, who could never have been described as an Allison disciple, was the instigator of events. 'I was amazed when the chairman asked him back. I thought Tony Book was one of the best managers we had. But one day at a board meeting the chairman brought up the subject and asked, "Do we think we should change the manager?" There was a vote and it was five to four in favour of a change. I voted not to change. There were no names mentioned for the new manager, but the next thing I remember was the chairman asking me to lunch and saying, "I am thinking of bringing Malcolm back. What do you think?" He knew I was a pro-Malcolm man and I said, "If you think you can handle him then you would have my vote." I wasn't all that happy, though, because of Tony, so I phoned him and asked if he could work with Malcolm. I was out of line really but I didn't like the situation. Tony said, "You know me, Mr Niven. I can work with anyone." We had another vote and it was five-four to appoint Malcolm. It was very rare that I remember having a vote on a new manager. Normally, the chairman would decide and would tell us who was coming.'

On 5 January, with City having failed to win in their previous 11 games, it was announced that Allison was back, despite Plymouth chairman Robert Daniel's best efforts to persuade him to stay at Home Park. 'City had a special attraction for me. I would have refused any other job,' stated Allison, who would take charge of the coaching while Book remained team manager. Incumbent coach Bill Taylor, part of Ron Greenwood's England backroom team, was soon on his way from Maine Road and Book could not help but feel undermined with his old boss sitting next to him. Malcolm was hardly going to seek his blessing for his schemes in the way he had with Joe Mercer. 'He wanted to do his own thing,' Book explains. 'If you go back to the beginning, I am a bricklayer and he is the top man. All of a sudden I am the top man. It was never going to work – he came back and took over.'

As Ken Barnes, the club's chief scout, puts it, 'He was the one person Bookie would find it hard to stand up to. Especially as Swales and his pals thought Malcolm was some kind of magician who could do no wrong.'

Yet there was to be no dramatic improvement. City finished the season in exactly the same position as when Allison arrived and suffered a fourth-round defeat in the FA Cup at Third Division Shrewsbury. The most promising aspect of the latter stages of the season was Allison's familiar unearthing of young talent in defender Ray Ranson and midfielder Nicky Reid.

'The team was almost exclusively internationals, so I was thrilled to bits to get a chance,' says Reid, who was blooded in the highly charged atmosphere of City's unsuccessful UEFA Cup quarter-final against Borussia Moenchengladbach. 'Under Malcolm I went from somebody who was desperate to be a footballer but did not know if he was good enough to having the belief that, yes, I could play. Other managers I played for would speak in a derogatory way about you in the papers, saying you couldn't do this or that, but Malcolm was always very positive and showed belief in you.'

Further clarification of Allison's position at the club was forthcoming on 16 July when he was officially given the title of manager, with Book now listed as general manager. That summer saw plenty of changes on the playing side, too. Established, popular figures like Brian Kidd (to Everton), Mike Channon (return to Southampton), Asa Hartford (Nottingham Forest) and Gary Owen and Peter Barnes (both sold to West Brom) were transferred out of Maine Road, while Bell, who had managed to play ten games the previous season, finally announced his retirement.

Says Niven, 'I did have a go at Malcolm about Peter and Gary, who were popular with the crowd and were two of our brightest young stars. We didn't want the money for them; we wanted the players. He said something about their size, some stupid remark about having too many midgets. Many years later he said to me he'd made a mistake.'

Goalkeeper Joe Corrigan was one of the few old heads remaining in the dressing-room. 'Malcolm was a different person when he came back to City,' he states. 'I don't know why the decision was made to bring him back because things were going well under Tony Book. Malcolm had completely changed his attitude about the way he wanted to play. A lot of players didn't quite agree with and understand what he was trying to do and most of the senior players were sold.'

Allison embarked on a spending spree that would forever characterise his second spell at the club. He announced his intentions by paying £765,000, the second-highest transfer fee in British history, for Michael Robinson, a relatively unknown centre-forward who had played fewer than 50 professional games for Preston North End. Ken Barnes had previously recommended that City should go after the player if he was available for £150,000. A price of £300,000 was agreed for Wrexham forward Bobby Shinton and Allison paid what was considered the ludicrous sum of £275,000 for Steve MacKenzie, a 17-year-old midfielder who had yet to play a single game for Crystal Palace. Winger Stuart Lee arrived from Stockport for £80,000 early in September, but sneaked into Maine Road almost unnoticed having signed on the day that the most debated transfer of Allison's reign was completed.

Yorkshire-born Steve Daley had proved himself a valuable member of the Wolves midfield in the second half of the 1970s, without ever suggesting that he was in the game's elite. Yet he became the subject of a British record transfer when City completed his move for £1,437,500 – which comprised a basic £1,100,000 fee plus VAT and other levies. Added to the extravagances on Robinson and MacKenzie, the general opinion of the football community was that Allison had gone mad. Ken Barnes says of Allison's signings, 'They either weren't good enough or they were nowhere near worth the money he paid out for them. I think he lost the plot . . . he got so caught up in it all, it got stupid.'

Allison always maintained that it was Peter Swales who was behind the Daley deal. His version of events has a fee of £550,000 being agreed several months earlier with John Barnwell before the Wolves manager suffered a serious car accident. When negotiations were picked up with caretaker boss Richie Barker the demand rose to £650,000. Allison and Book thought the deal was dead until Swales approached Book before a game at Southampton and said that he had signed him for £1.1 million, plus tax. On hearing the news, Allison told Book, 'I'm not interested. It's nothing to do with me.'

Allison remained angry enough with Swales – who had previously assured his manager that he was 'the financial genius' – to say a decade and a half later, 'I've often been accused of spending millions on players who flopped for Manchester City. But I never spent that money. I had a meeting with the chairman and told him of a young striker called Ian Rush who was playing for Chester. They wanted £350,000 for him. I said we should buy Rush, play him in the reserves for a couple of seasons and develop him. Swales told me in no uncertain terms that he wasn't going to pay that sort of money for a reserve. He wanted instant stars and instant success.'

Book's explanation of how he, Allison and Swales constructed the transfer deals supports Malcolm's memory. 'The three of us talked about what players we wanted – guys like Robinson and Daley. When we got the figures in we said to the chairman, "Forget about it." They were asking figures that you couldn't believe. Malcolm was going to go along by bringing in youngsters and all of a sudden the chairman says he has done the deals. He got the figures the way he wanted them – he could pay for the players over a length of time, which Preston and Wolves allowed. We knew we were paying over the odds.'

Daley himself says, 'I think City were bidding against themselves. I don't think there were many teams involved in that level of bidding. The club you're leaving want the most they can get for you and the club you're going to, if they want you that badly, are going to pay the money.'

Swales later explained the motivation for his extravagance to the BBC. 'I had in my brain in those days that I wanted to be bigger than Manchester United, which really was a bit silly because I should have let them get on with their own business.' And he added, 'In those days, of course, you could pay over any number of years and that encouraged you to take ludicrous gambles. You mortgaged your future, but they were exciting days.'

Daley, hardly surprisingly, never managed to live up to the expectations created by the fee, even with Wolves quickly relieving him of the burden of being the country's most expensive player by spending the proceeds of the sale, and a little more, on Aston Villa centre-forward Andy Gray. Forced to play much of his football out of position on the left of midfield, Daley would last little more than a season at Maine Road, scoring four goals in 44 League games, before heading to America to play for the Seattle Sounders. Lamenting the sale of star players that preceded his arrival, he says, 'They were favourites of the crowd and to come in and replace them was hard. I never said I was worth the money, but it wasn't a steady ship I joined.'

Striker Kevin Reeves, who joined later in the season for £1 million and therefore appreciated the situation Daley found himself in, says, 'It is wrong to blame Steve. The fee wasn't down to him. [Malcolm] replaced a lot of experienced players and because Steve was brought in as a midfield linchpin, he was under a lot of pressure to do well. Too much was expected of him in a team that wasn't playing well and his form suffered and spiralled downward.'

Stuart Lee, a boyhood City fan who achieved his dream of wearing the sky blue shirt when Allison 'bought me with the loose change from the Steve Daley deal' adds, 'The price tag killed Steve's confidence. He was frightened.'

The first eleven with which Allison began the 1979–80 season retained only four players who featured in the final game of the previous season. At centre-half, the curly blond head of 16-year-old Tommy Caton was trusted to be wise enough to anchor the defence and he would play all 42 League games. Dennis Tueart, whose overhead kick had won the League Cup four years earlier, returned from the New York Cosmos late in the season, around the same time as Reeves's arrival from Norwich. Yet City stumbled towards a 17th-place finish. Allison at least received some praise from Liverpool manager Bob

Paisley, who said, 'Critics can crucify [him] as much as they like, but he is one of the few positive coaches in the game. At least he is looking in the right direction at Maine Road. Malcolm is constructive in his outlook when too many are not.' Paisley, of course, could afford to be generous as his collection of League Championships and European Cups mounted.

The lowest point of City's season had come in the FA Cup. Drawn away to Fourth Division Halifax, they were dumped out of the competition by striker Paul Hendrie's second-half goal after the underdogs' manager, George Kirby, had employed the services of the well-known hypnotist Romark, who claimed to have been so affronted during a previous meeting with Allison that he placed a curse on him. Kirby also took the more earthly precaution of having hundreds of gallons of water dumped onto what was already a muddy pitch.

There does at least appear to be one constantly recurring redeeming factor of Allison's managerial appointments around this time. No matter how unsuccessful the team was and how erratic his own personal behaviour and application of team tactics, individual players – especially the young and unsung – continued to feel they were benefiting from their coach's knowledge, experience and attention and therefore, advancing as professionals. Stuart Lee recalls, 'He always said that if anyone had any questions about the way things were going they should go and see him and he would explain everything. For example, he did a great job with Tommy Caton, who was a phenomenal kid at the age of 16. Malcolm coached and cajoled him through situations and made him a First Division player.'

Lee, who eventually left City for the United States, where he stayed to become a youth coach in Seattle, adds, 'In kids' football in the States now, we have a system of unlimited substitutions so if someone makes a mistake you can take him off and explain things to him right away. That is exactly what Malcolm did during training. He would pull you aside and tell you this and that instead of screaming "fucking wanker" at you. In the teams I had played in up to then, the coaches ruled by the players' fear of losing their place.'

Despite such individual endorsement, however, there was no disguising the disappointment of City's results and Allison knew that his job was in jeopardy if his team made a poor start to the 1980–81 season. No wins and only four draws in the first ten League games meant that Big Mal's return to Maine Road was about to be brought to a premature and inauspicious end. One of the most remarkable aspects of his departure, which came after a 1–0 defeat at Leeds, was that the painful, final few days would soon be seen in all their dubious glory on television. The club had given Granada TV behind-the-scenes access, allowing them to film in the boardroom, the changing-rooms and all sensitive points between. The end product, a one-hour documentary entitled *City!*, is often excruciating to watch.

Swales seems to be enjoying the limelight. Pointed features topped by unnaturally dark hair, scraped and weaved across his head to the point of ridicule, he preens across the screen like a malevolent circus ringmaster. Allison, of course, was never one to shy away from a camera – even when it had evidently turned up to record his execution – but does seem to cast several uncertain glances in its direction. Maybe he is having doubts about the velour tracksuit top he has chosen to wear for most of the programme. For the viewers, the result is like spying on the most dysfunctional family going through emotional meltdown. By the end of the piece you are tempted to start looking for bodies under the kitchen floorboards.

Faced by a lot more media than just the documentary crew, the only time Swales seems to have lost some of his smarmy self-confidence is at a press conference called to announce Allison's sacking. Unlike the sponsor-festooned setting for such modern-day events, Swales was at what appears to be a Formica-topped table in a gloomy, wood-panelled bar. His discomfort is evident when he tries to deflect the attention to Tony Book with an inane question about whether it was two hours or an hour and a half since he spoke with Allison. Reliable Book, instead of asking Swales, "What the fuck has that got to do with anything?", looks at his watch like this is important stuff and attempts to mumble an answer.

Swales finally gets round to telling the media that he has asked Allison and Book if they would 'resign from the positions of manager and coach – and that is what they have done'. Playing with his fingernails, he adds that Book has been asked to take charge of one final game, before turning to Book to ask, 'Do you want to add anything to that?' Lesser men than Book might have chosen this moment to deck the chairman rather than stoically reply, 'No. We have accepted the chairman's views,' – which one suspects was stretching the truth when it came to Allison's take on the day's events.

Book then adds, 'To be fair to the chairman, Malcolm and I always knew where we stood.'

Such absolution lifts Swales to hitherto unconquered heights of smugness. 'I'm not trying to get myself off the hook here,' he oozes. 'But Tony made that statement, not me.'

Allison is seen sitting one final time behind his desk. 'It is a very, very sad day,' he comments, wearily but still with an air that he knows a performance is required by the camera. 'I thought the joy was just coming, just developing, and I was going to get some of the pleasure. Now I am not going to get any of that pleasure. I would have gone to the end of the season. He wouldn't have had to tell me; I would have told him. If I couldn't see any light or any progress or that we were getting somewhere I would have told him. I would have said, "I am not going to make it." But I know I was on the right lines. I know that it was going to happen.'

Perhaps the most fascinating and genuine minute or so of the entire documentary then follows as Allison brings up what he describes as 'the most important book I have read', *The Master Game* by Robert Ropp. 'The most important thing in the book to me was when he said that the most dangerous thing any person can have is an ego. When I read it, I realised he was absolutely correct. I couldn't be sitting here talking to you if I had a massive ego. I have just been sacked from my job. It means I am incompetent at my job. If I had an ego that would be the most destructive thing and therefore no way I could handle this situation.'

Another way of looking at it is that perhaps only a man with an ego as massive as that which Allison projected most of the time would have had the balls to sit there and let a documentary crew record those intimate moments of shattered self-esteem. It is almost as though we are watching Malcolm wonder out loud how he ever let Big Mal put him in such a situation.

Allison's closing comment to the camera was that City's players were 'the best kids I have ever worked with', although Ian Niven now recalls the disappointment that Allison had been unable to reproduce the results of a decade earlier. 'He wasn't quite the same chap. It wasn't the same young Malcolm who got on the training field and probably the challenge wasn't as great as it had been when he first came. I think we were overburdened by paying all these players their salaries and I think that was why the chairman went against his own feeling towards Malcolm. He thought Malcolm could build a new, young team like he did before.'

After a further defeat under Book's charge, City's new manager was announced as Allison's old running mate, John Bond. The Norwich manager had been 'interviewed' in front of Granada's prying cameras. 'That was a load of crap,' says Niven. 'It was a big set-up. You don't interview the manager in front of cameras and he never interviewed him in front of us. I said I didn't want to go into the meeting, but Peter said, "We are having it, and you'd better say something." So I thought I would stir things up and said something daft like, "Who is the genius, the God, who is going to replace Malcolm?"'

Other board members seemed happy to declare, 'I will support whatever the chairman wants.' And obviously the introduction of Bond was what Swales had craved for some time.

Bond remembers, 'I'd had an interview six months previously with Peter Swales in the Royal Garden Hotel in London. Nobody knew about it, but he said they wanted me as their manager. City picked up a bit and Peter called me and said, "We won't be making a change at the moment but rest assured that when we do we will be in touch." They had just got beat at Leeds and when I got home my wife said Peter Swales would ring me at nine in the morning.'

According to Niven, one of Bond's first notions upon arrival at Maine Road had been to offer Allison the chance to work under him. 'He sat in the boardroom and said to Peter, "How about us both doing the job? Malcolm could stay with me." Peter went white and I don't think he answered. He was probably thinking, "I have just got rid of him, and now you want him back?"'

The state in which Bond found City surprised and saddened him. 'Malcolm had been in charge of everything and it wasn't right for him. Joe Mercer had been a great person for him to have around so that he could just do the football side. The club had nothing going for them and seemed a dead cert to get relegated. I watched the first game, when we got beaten at home by Birmingham, and I couldn't believe my eyes. We were taking 20 passes to get out of our own half. It was quite easy to turn things around because Malcolm was fiddling about with the game more than he needed to. I sorted out how we were playing and bought a couple of experienced players.'

Stuart Lee understands Bond's comment but feels Allison was simply trying to achieve things that were ahead of their time. 'His insight was fabulous. He was trying to get players to play the way the foreign players are playing now, but he couldn't always do it with players who were used to just hitting the ball from right-back to the left wing.'

Nicky Reid adds, 'A lot of the training methods that he tried to bring in, and which were resisted by some of the players, are standard practice now – things like warm-downs at half-time and stretching protocols. He also experimented with formations like one up front and two wingers or the diamond formation, which are widely used these days.'

With a simplified playing system under Bond – and with signings such as Gerry Gow, the extravagantly moustachioed Bristol City midfielder, and Coventry's Scottish winger Tommy Hutchison – City climbed the table to finish 12th, reached the semi-finals of the League Cup and made it to Wembley in the FA Cup, losing a memorable replay against Tottenham. Reid says, 'Malcolm should have kept the likes of Gary Owen and Peter Barnes because our young team flourished when John Bond brought in three or four experienced players. Apart from them it was Malcolm's team that reached the Cup final.'

In a remarkable turn of fate that smacked of one of the Football Association's old codgers peeking inside the velvet bag while making the draw, City's run in the FA Cup had started in January with a home tie against Crystal Palace, managed by none other than Malcolm Allison.

Less than two months after his departure from City, Allison had boomeranged his way into Selhurst Park. Once again, though, he found boardroom turmoil and recrimination swirling around him. It was chairman Ray Bloye who, having presumably got over the Fiona Richmond incident, installed Allison as manager of a team lying second from bottom in the First Division. Terry Venables had left early in the season to take the vacant job at Queens Park Rangers and Allison was originally made co-manager with Ernie Walley, who had been holding the fort and who Bloye felt needed experienced guidance. But it didn't take long for Malcolm to assume sole charge of a team that included former England captain Gerry Francis and £1 million striker Clive Allen.

The Cup draw was a dream for headline writers and documentary makers alike and the managers didn't let anyone down, taking shots at each other in the press. Allison went first, saying, 'If John Bond is so good why hasn't he won anything in his previous years as a manager?' Bond responded with, 'It's because of his behaviour, which has little changed from our time together at West Ham in the '50s, that I can never see Malcolm being a manager in his own right.'

Bond also told the *City!* film crew, 'I think Malcolm always saw me as the worst part of the Allison, Cantwell, Bond partnership. He always saw me as the one least likely to succeed. If he thinks I am just an opportunist going around taking over something he has set up at City he is vastly wrong.'

Both managers allowed themselves to be filmed in the dressing-room before kick-off, Bond warning his players not to take any notice of the psychological games Allison had been playing in the press, Malcolm himself admitting candidly, 'I need to win. I need to win.'

He didn't. Drawing 0–0 at half-time, Palace conceded four second-half goals. In the documentary, Allison, wearing a white suit and drawing on the ubiquitous cigar while seated in the boardroom, is forced to listen to Bond explaining after the game that what Malcolm needs is someone to manage him. And despite Allison's raised eyebrows, Bond is close to hitting the nail on the head for this period in Big Mal's career when he says, 'There is absolutely no doubt that he has the capacity and the ability to make players better, but I am not sure, honestly and truthfully, that he has the capacity to make teams better if he has the ultimate control.'

Allison fires back, 'I have found that man to control me. Me.'

If only.

After the defeat in Manchester, Palace chairman Bloye restated his intention not to offer a contract to Allison, explaining that he would continue to work on a week-to-week basis. By the end of January, the reason for his reluctance to tie the club too tightly to Allison was clear when he sold £600,000 worth of shares, his 75 per cent holding in the club, to Wimbledon chairman Ron Noades. Allison had been expressing his belief that he might be offered a five-year contract by Palace, but Bloye knew that the new owners had no wish to be saddled with such a burden. 'Malcolm will stand as much chance with the new board as he did with the old one,' he offered cryptically. Allison, in fact, stood no chance at all and was immediately displaced by Dons manager Dario Gradi. A spokesman for the Noades consortium expressed an increasingly commonly held view when he said that the new chairman could not work with Allison because of their differing views on 'how management control should be exercised', adding, 'Mr Noades said he had the highest regard for Mr Allison's ability as a coach.'

Allison had been in charge for 55 days, won only one game and been unable to improve Palace's position. His most significant contribution had been to bring in some cash by selling striker Mike Flanagan and defender Terry Fenwick to Venables at QPR. This time, however, there would be no post-Allison improvement and the club, for the third time in a season in which he had been involved, were relegated.

Plymouth, Manchester, Palace. The comeback tour had been an unmitigated disaster. Happily for the legacy of Allison, most City supporters have either forgotten or forgiven the extravagance and eccentricity of Malcolm's second spell at the club. Colin Bell, after whom one of the stands is named at City's new home in the converted City of Manchester Stadium, says, 'People just remember those first seven years and talk about the success he had. It overshadows the second spell.'

And one of City's highest-profile fans, Noel Gallagher of Oasis, said in an interview in 2000, 'City fans have this thing that as long as you look good in the kit or sat in the dug-out, then it doesn't matter what you're like. Howard Kendall didn't look cool and neither did Brian Horton, whereas Malcolm Allison did. He turned up at Monday morning training in a white Rolls-Royce with a bottle of champagne and some actress in the back of the car. That's football management.'

19

NORTH-EAST FRONTIER

'When I came up to North Yorkshire I thought I would find peace and contentment. Then the roof fell in'

– Malcolm Allison, 1984

By the summer of 1981, evidence of Malcolm Allison's ability to create winning football teams appeared to exist only in the pages of football's history books and the memories of older Manchester City fans. But then, in June, he accepted the job of managing Portuguese side Sporting Clube de Portugal and for a while at least, the old magic returned. Sporting Lisbon, as they are more commonly known, had been champions of Portugal four times in the 1950s and winners of the European Cup-Winners' Cup in 1964. They had turned to several English coaches as they spent the '70s trying to fight their way back to the top. But where Ronnie Allen and Jimmy Hagan had failed, Allison succeeded spectacularly.

Following his dismissal by Palace, Allison had accepted a short-term temporary posting at Yeovil, holding the reins for four games while the club searched for a successor to the sacked Barry Lloyd. The appointment offered more curiosity value than anything else, with his first game, an FA Trophy replay at Hastings, attracting five times the home team's usual attendance. Yeovil were beaten in that match and failed to win any of the three Alliance Premier League games for which Allison was in charge.

In the meantime, he had been sounded out by the Portuguese club and was duly confirmed as manager in time to lead them on pre-season visits to Venezuela and Bulgaria and strengthen the squad with the signing of Hungary's national team goalkeeper Ferenc Meszaros. When the 1981–82 season began in earnest, it was a story of almost unbroken success. Sporting went unbeaten in the league until the mid-point of the season and would lose only three games, scoring the most goals of any team and boasting the Portuguese Liga's top scorer in the veteran Rui Jordao, who finished with 26 goals. At one point their march to the title appeared to be threatened by claims of rival club Porto that Allison had fielded an ineligible player, but no action was taken and Sporting clinched the league title with a 3–0 victory against Estoril, finishing two points ahead of Benfica. They completed their version of the Double when they beat Sporting Braga 4–0 in a one-sided Cup of Portugal final.

'It was the best team performance I was ever in charge of,' Allison would say of his triumphant season. 'They won the double but then again, that was the first time I ever went to a team that was in the first three or four the year before. Usually you get a job when a team is at the bottom.'

As well as discovering how much he enjoyed coaching with the sun on his back, it is no coincidence that Allison finally rediscovered his winning touch when placed in an environment that allowed him to focus more narrowly on his area of expertise. 'I enjoy the Continental style of a coach doing what he does best – coaching,' he explained. 'To me, it is the most important part of the game, and the chance to concentrate exclusively on that aspect is far better. I have a financial adviser and an accountant who look after the financial aspect.' It was what his players at Manchester City had known all along, what the Crystal Palace players came to discover when he failed to live up to the reputation with which he arrived. Malcolm was a coach. One of the best.

When, early in Sporting's season, he returned to England to lead his team against Southampton in the second round of the UEFA Cup, he had taken the opportunity to point out the deficiencies of coaches in his native country and suggested that the administrative duties expected of English managers offered a sanctuary to lesser minds. He also predicted the arrival of the Premier League-era system in British football where the chief executive would relieve the manager of those non-football responsibilities.

'It is a far more sensible system, and it will come in here,' he said. 'It is the hardest time ever in the history of the game for managers. To ask them to handle the financial aspect is absurd. When you coach abroad, you have to prove you're a good coach otherwise the players won't respond to you. You can't get away with it, like people do in England by concentrating on the physical side. Of course some are not capable of concentrating on the game and the coaching aspect, so it's a good excuse for them to say they have too much else to do. But the demands of two jobs make it imperative two men are involved.'

Speaking from the soapbox of a 4–2 victory at The Dell, Southampton's first home defeat for a year, Allison continued his attack on the British system. 'There are not enough good teachers in England. It is all about teaching the game right through from the youth teams. When I look at some of the people working at top class clubs in this country it's a joke. When I see some youth-team coaches, some second-team and even some first-team coaches, it's a joke because they are pathetic. Several have no qualifications whatsoever. I have found one obvious advantage in working abroad to working in England. The average foreign player is much more willing to work than the average British player. Maybe it's because conditions are better but foreign players seem to enjoy training a lot more than English players. They are very receptive to ideas too and that is a major difference.'

Yet, as so often in Allison's life, it was all too good to last and again it was a mixture of off-field incidents and internal politics that led to his departure. The squad were taken, as usual, to Bulgaria for a three-week training camp before the 1982–83 season. The players attempted to add some life to their spartan hotel surroundings with a party that, according to reports, was rather more raucous than the locals were used to. Knowing that wherever a social gathering broke out Allison was unlikely to be far away, club officials held him responsible for the bad publicity. He was instantly suspended by the directors for the 'excessive behaviour' of the squad and, despite his assertion that he would be remaining in charge, his dismissal was confirmed when club president Joao Rocha returned from a business trip to Brazil.

Allison felt that the party in the Balkans was used as an excuse by a president who resented not being given more credit for his part in Lisbon's achievements. 'He was jealous of me,' he said. 'It was the club's 75th anniversary and he really wanted to win the championship. We won the league and cup and he'd paid all the debts and no one took any notice of him.'

So Allison was once again looking for a job. For all his talk of enjoying the sun on his back, for all his comfort in not having to worry about anything but coaching, when a team came around asking him to return to England's chilly north-east and to take charge of all aspects of club affairs, he was in no position to turn them down.

Middlesbrough had thought 'Big' before when looking for a manager. 'Big Jack' Charlton had led them into Division One at the end of his first season as manager at Ayresome Park in 1973–74. But when, almost a decade later, they found themselves impoverished, managerless and stuck at the bottom of the Second Division table, there was little suggestion that the club would be looking for an oversized character as their new man in charge. Newspapers speculated on the identity of the replacement for former Celtic star Bobby Murdoch, whose 16-month reign as team manager ended in September 1982, not long after Boro had finished bottom of the First Division.

The list of seven contenders presented in the *Middlesbrough Evening Gazette* was somewhat lacking in charisma, even if it did include familiar names like ex-Leeds striker Allan Clarke, former Huddersfield and Bolton boss Ian Greaves and Sunderland's FA Cup-winning manager Bob Stokoe. Seven became four, with ex-Grimsby boss George Kerr thought to be the most fancied of the candidates the club intended to interview. One man had different ideas, though. Mike McCullagh, waiting to be confirmed as club chairman following the resignation of George Kitching, quickened the pulses of local journalists by telling them that a 'mystery fifth man' – as the *Gazette* put it – had entered the running.

That man was a big enough personality to claw back some of the region's attention to Ayresome Park after a shift in the direction of St James' Park following former England captain Kevin Keegan's summer signing for Newcastle. That man, Malcolm Allison, was sitting in a Lisbon apartment preparing to launch a legal battle against the club that had fired him, but he put aside thoughts of the £92,000 he felt he was due from Sporting to fly to a meeting with McCullagh. The chairman then whetted the newsmen's appetites by announcing his intention to unveil a new manager at the following day's home game against Division Two leaders Queens Park Rangers. 'I have been able to tie everything up sooner than I thought,' he purred.

Saturday, 23 October was a momentous day for McCullagh, first confirmed by a board meeting as the new club chairman and then able to introduce Allison to excited media and fans. 'I think we have got one of the finest coaches in the world, but he is coming as manager and he'll have total control.'

Allison admitted he had not seen Boro play, adding, 'Obviously the first thing is to stop the slide. We are always looking for the miracle and it would be nice to turn it around. I regard myself as a good coach and a good manager. The problem is always the time factor.' Asked how appropriate a fit the industrial north-east was for his bright-lights image, Allison commented, 'That's not me, that's the press. They're always giving me cigars and taking pictures.'

The team's response to having Allison sitting in the stand was encouraging, beating Rangers to climb off the bottom of the table and extend their unbeaten run to four games under the interim management of former England trainer Harold Shepherdson and his assistant, Cyril Knowles. Allison's old pal, QPR manager Terry Venables, gave him a lift to London on the team bus and offered words of support for his former boss. 'This place desperately needs someone like him. There's no greater character around. It's not just that he knows football, he works hard and gives everything.'

Boro players shared the excitement that other dressing-rooms had experienced on hearing that Allison was to be guiding their fortunes. Team captain Jim Platt, the Northern Ireland international goalkeeper, described it as 'the best possible appointment'. He added, 'It will give the players and the fans a big lift. When Jack Charlton was here he often referred to Malcolm as the best coach in the country.'

Allison began work the following Monday on the strength of a handshake with McCullagh, who had said, 'As long as he is happy, we're happy.' Malcolm, who accepted that his departure from Portugal meant he was unlikely to get any money out of Sporting, explained that he would definitely be at the club at least until the end of the season, adding, 'I would like to think I am going to stay here and build a really good side.'

Before taking charge of his first game, he went on a city centre 'walkabout' aimed at drumming up support for the team. It was the kind of commitment to the club and its fans that impressed local BBC radio reporter and Boro fan Alistair Brownlee. 'I was very involved at the time with the club's young supporters association, the Junior Reds,' he explains. 'Malcolm, who had developed the Junior Blues while he was at Manchester City, was keen to play a big part in increasing the number of youngsters joining the organisation. Malcolm came with a big reputation and was what we needed. Seeing 5,000 in Ayresome Park was soul-destroying.'

Allison's reign officially began with a 1–1 home draw against Burnley in the Milk Cup,[12] insufficient to turn around a first-leg deficit. Former Burnley striker Ray Hankin had given Boro an early lead, but after the away team scored a second-half equaliser Allison observed of his team, 'They don't know how to win and I didn't do the right thing at half-time. After 15 minutes of the second half I realised they were afraid of losing it.'

Boro remained unbeaten for the first four games under Allison before a 5–1 home defeat to Blackpool and a four-goal beating at Wolves made clear the task ahead of him. Inconsistent form for the remainder of the season included enough positive results to lift the team to a finishing position of 16th and there was also the frisson of excitement provided by a 1–1 home draw against Arsenal in the fifth round of the FA Cup, followed by a battling 3–2 defeat in the replay. It was soon after the game at Highbury that Allison confirmed his intention to finally sign a two-year contract after five months at Ayresome Park. There had been speculation that once the glamour of the Cup was behind him, he would look elsewhere, but he said, 'I am very pleased to sign the deal. Another two years is about the right time to have a team really coming to fruition.'

---

[12] The League Cup was enjoying the first of its many new identities following the Football League's decision to allow the competition to be sponsored.

The biggest obstacle to achieving his ambition, however, was the club's accounts. Boro were reportedly more than £500,000 in debt and losing a further £12,000 a week. Allison was aware of the restrictions placed on his predecessor, Murdoch, but relished being given a key role in placing the club on a more solid financial foundation, including overseeing completion of a planned leisure complex. It was a strange responsibility to be given to someone so renowned for his personal and professional financial mismanagement – and one that would, ultimately and inevitably, lead to the disintegration of his relationship with the club.

'I am going to run the club with the directors,' he said shortly after his appointment. 'The most important thing, next to the team, is the financial state of the club. The understanding I have with the chairman is to sort the whole thing out. I have to know how much we have to cut back and the staff I can have. I will be looking at the books.'

He also warned, 'We have got people working all over the place and in that respect we have a big staff – although on the playing side I have only got a first team squad of 13.' Yet Boro winger Terry Cochrane recalls that one of Allison's first solutions to that delicate equation was unpopular with the players. 'He told us that he had to put the club back on a steadier footing and the first thing he did was to sack the tea man, who was on 18 quid a week. We didn't see how that was going to affect anything, so the players put their hands in their pockets to keep him.'

Money matters occupied much of Allison's time, with weekly losses reportedly dropping by £2,000 per week inside two months of his arrival. He was the driving force behind the club accepting an offer to play two friendlies in Nigeria, the schedule for which called for Boro to play a League game on a Friday, fly immediately to Lagos for a Sunday morning arrival, play games on the Sunday and Tuesday evenings and get back, exhausted, to Middlesbrough late on Wednesday night. The club justified the excursion by pointing out that it would earn them as much as a home game.

January 1983 brought news that the £1.3 million, three-year leisure centre project had been delayed by a series of building regulation defects. Allison's response was to urge local companies to effectively 'loan' his players from him. He explained, 'A company can pick a player, sponsor his wages, then he would work with them in a public relations capacity.' The expectation was to get six such deals in place, but the plan never came to full fruition.

Allison was even reduced to counting the crowd when Arsenal visited Ayresome Park. Hearing an announced attendance of 20,850, he stated his belief that at least 25,000 had been inside the ground and ordered a check to be made on the ground's 40 turnstiles. 'I am concerned about it,' he said. 'I asked for the same thing to be done at Plymouth and Manchester City and I was proved right.'

On the field, Allison's attempts to strengthen the team without significant funds ranged from the ambitious (a failed attempt to sign Liverpool forwards David Fairclough and David Johnson on loan) to the fanciful (a doomed bid to get the San Jose Earthquakes to release George Best, for whom Boro were unable to pay the £25,000 being demanded). He even took a gamble on the fitness of former Ipswich and England defender Kevin Beattie, whose battle to overcome a series of knee injuries found him playing on a week-to-week basis at Colchester. Allison installed him as captain in place of the long-serving Platt.

Unable to bring in further reinforcements, Allison put his trust in teenagers such as Paul Ward and Stephen Bell. It left experienced men like Scotland right-back John Brownlie and Northern Ireland winger Cochrane uncertain about their place in the manager's plans. 'We used to call him Big Mal the Kiddie's Pal,' says Cochrane, who was dropped as early as Allison's third game in charge. 'If you were over 19 years old you wouldn't be looked at. He got his eye in with youngsters he thought were good players. I was amazed that he thought some of them were any good, but I think he felt he could control them. He didn't like the older lads talking back to him.

'That's not sour grapes. If he wanted to go with young players, that was his decision. But he never explained that he didn't want me. He went round the houses to make it uncomfortable. Me and Jim Platt were the most experienced players he had, but he didn't know us and we didn't know him. He would just walk past us with his head down, or not look at us when he was announcing the team. It was infuriating and poor man-management.'

There was one significant addition to the personnel at Boro – someone who would remain Allison's travelling companion, close friend and valued staff member for the rest of the decade. Roger Spry, a former European kick-boxing champion and karate black belt, had been making a name for himself in football with what were considered revolutionary fitness and conditioning techniques. Having worked in Brazil with leading club Fluminense, he had been given the chance to introduce his methods into English football at Arsenal, Charlton and West Ham and was encouraged by Gunners manager Don Howe to contact Allison. 'I taught players how to disguise body feints like a fighter,' Spry explains. 'I showed how this kind of conditioning could be used to create space.'

Allison received plenty of letters like the one Spry sent him, particularly with specialist preparation for athletic contests becoming a growth industry. But he acknowledged the possibility that an outsider could offer a new perspective. After 15 minutes of watching him work with the first team, Allison had seen enough and Spry was on board – Sancho Panza to Malcolm's Don Quixote as they crossed the globe from Bahrain to Bermondsey. The parlous state of Middlesbrough's finances meant that Allison could only afford him for two days per week, but Spry insists, 'The players responded and you could see the benefit.'

Such benefits, however, brought only modest returns on the field, which Spry puts down to the lack of money for players. 'If you are used to racing a Ferrari and someone gives you a Mini it is going to be difficult and Malcolm would have got frustrated.'

Yet, given that Allison faced restrictions on his team-building, he does appear – not for the first time – to have refused to accept that his players needed a different kind of handling to the top-of-the-range models he had worked with in days gone by. Spry states, 'Malcolm was always very true to himself as a coach and to people he coached. He believed in playing in a certain way, a belief in his own capabilities.' As it had eventually been at City and Palace, that belief had perhaps become a liability.

Cochrane continues, 'I am not decrying Malcolm as a coach and I would have loved to have worked under him earlier in my career. He would have motivated me into playing better. But he was not a young man when he came to us. We thought it could be the start of the club's revival, but he couldn't get us out of the trouble we were in. In his glory days he had Joe Mercer there to help, but Mal had no one to talk to at Boro. He made decisions at times that we didn't understand. We played Bishop's Stortford in the FA Cup and he preached about how weak they were on their left. We practised all these moves down the right and come Saturday he left me out. I was the right-winger! We were 2–0 up at half-time, so it looked like he had got it right but in the end we drew 2–2.'

Cochrane is also dismissive of the unorthodox methods employed by Allison. 'He brought in Len Heppell to teach us dance moves and posture and Roger Spry, who was a black belt. As players, we wondered what it was all costing and what it was achieving.'

It just goes to prove that in football – as in politics and war – history is shaped by results. Ask the Manchester City players of the late '60s what they think of those same methods and you hear nothing but praise for Allison's innovative thinking. Cochrane continues, 'When you are with a successful team, you can try things and they are accepted. In the climate at Middlesbrough it was different. When you are doing badly you need more time to adapt to new ways.'

Having begun 1983–84 with an unbeaten run of six games, a more realistic picture of Middlesbrough's health was presented by the loss of the next five, establishing them as a lower-table team. Allison had the opportunity to bail out in October when Portuguese Division Two team Belenenses, who had just fired their manager for poor results, placed a lucrative contract offer in front of him. He turned down a deal that, on top of his basic salary, would have given him 25 per cent of all gate receipts realised by any spectators above an initial 8,000.

By March 1984, Boro had gone seven games without a win and were in 16th position. Avoiding the drop to Division Three was not much of an ambition for a club that had been in the top flight two seasons earlier. On 21 March, the day after a goalless draw against Derby had been endured by the lowest home crowd of the season, 5,735 – not enough to cover the weekly wage bill – Allison was called to a board meeting. The club, now £650,000 in debt, had to find £350,000 within a week to meet demands by the Inland Revenue.

Midfielder Mick Kennedy was reported to be interesting Brighton, while several First Division teams were said to be admirers of full-back Darren Wood. Chairman McCullagh said, 'We have tried to hold on to our players from day one, but we are not exactly breaking any records.' The message was clear: that the players were more valuable in the transfer market than they were proving on the field. Someone had to be sold before the next day's transfer deadline, but it would emerge later that an enraged Allison banged his fists on the table as he argued against the kind of instruction that had helped end his first spell at Manchester City.

The next day he publicly threatened to resign if the board sold anyone before the 5 p.m. deadline and set off to London for a managers' meeting, deliberately distancing himself from any transfer activity that might occur. Chelsea had offered £100,000 for Wood, although Allison described the same team's reported £25,000 offer for Bell as 'an insult'. He claimed, 'I want to build a team for the future but the directors told me there will be no future for the club if we do not meet immediate tax demands. I can appreciate the predicament of the directors but I must stand by my principles.'

The transfer deadline came and went. No sales were made. Allison flew back to Middlesbrough for another meeting, explaining that he would not be resigning, despite the club's attempt to offload Wood, who he claimed had turned down a £100,000 deal with Sheffield Wednesday. 'My loyalty is with the players,' said Allison. 'If Darren has decided to stay here, I will stay with him.'

Urging fans to turn up in huge numbers for the next day's game against Fulham, he continued, 'It would break my heart to leave now. I have a great feeling for the club and the area. Whichever way you look at it I am in a dilemma. I am on an each-way loser.'

After only 5,435 – Boro's poorest crowd since the Second World War – braved torrential rain to answer Allison's call, he suggested that it might be 'better for the club to die' than allow its young players to be sold off. Alistair Brownlee says, 'Even though you could understand Malcolm's frustration, it was an unfortunate thing to say. Speaking as a Boro fan, obviously no one wanted to see the club disappear.'

McCullagh declared himself to be 'shocked, disturbed and disappointed' by the stance of his manager, especially one who had been appointed partly to help solve the financial crisis. On 28 March, Allison was fired. His own version of a meeting that took all of three minutes is that McCullagh informed him that he was accepting his resignation.

'Do you mean you are sacking me?' asked Allison.

'Whichever way it is put, you are finished,' was the chairman's alleged reply.

'It's always the same in this business. It's just one of those things,' said Allison as he departed Ayresome Park to set up camp in the bar of Middlesbrough's Baltimore Hotel, owned by new Boro board member Anthony Zivanaris.

McCullagh emerged to explain, 'Over the weekend Malcolm reiterated his feelings and in one report said it would probably be better for the club to die. Obviously he has made it impossible for the board to work closely with him in the interests of the club. And no longer can he be relied upon to cooperate with us in trying to save the club. I have dismissed Malcolm Allison.'

He added that the directors could 'no longer rely on him to follow instructions and conduct himself in the club's best interests'. In that sense, Boro were merely the latest club to discover that particular truth about the man they hired. It is difficult to see what other possible resolution there could have been to a relationship that had so completely collapsed. The situation also served to highlight the danger of giving Allison fiscal responsibility when his natural instinct in all walks of life was to rail against financial constraints.

Meanwhile, Allison, still in the bar of the Baltimore, had put down his cigar and champagne long enough to sign his name to a formal statement.

The chairman of Middlesbrough Football Club fired me today. He claims my actions have irreparably harmed the club. I disagree with this. Since I have been here I have always done everything in the interest of Middlesbrough Football Club, the players and the supporters. There is much that needs to be said about the position of the club but I am too deeply disappointed to say anything else at this stage.

Irving Nattrass, the former Newcastle defender who succeeded Beattie as club captain, described the events as 'a great shock' and confessed that three players had cried when given the news. 'Feelings are running very high and we are trying to calm them down,' he said, before predicting that some might consider leaving the club at the end of the season.

Cochrane's biggest regret about Allison's reign at Middlesbrough is not the manner of its conclusion, but his belief that the club had not seen the best of the man they hired. 'It was unfortunate that he turned out not to be the Malcolm Allison that we knew as a younger man,' he says. 'He was just running up bills for drinks at hotels that he was not even staying in and expecting the club to pay.'

Once again – just as at Plymouth, Palace and Lisbon – there was a strong feeling that Malcolm had given the club a reason beyond results and his no-sale policy to remove him from office.

Following divorce from Beth and the eventual end of his on–off relationship with Serena Williams, the next woman in his life had been Sally Anne Highly, a blonde former receptionist at the Playboy Club in London. They had met in 1978 during an open-air party on Wimbledon Common and had been skating together when the ice cracked. Having been helped out of the freezing water by the chivalrous Allison, Sally had to strip out of her wet clothes, donning his trench coat while he carried her to her flat. There, so the story goes, events took a less than romantic turn: he bedded both Sally and her friend.

It was an accident on the M1 that persuaded Malcolm that Sally was the one for him. 'As we climbed out the wreckage I asked her to marry me just because I thought, "What a brave girl this is. I should marry her."' The couple were to have a daughter, Alexis, born in 1979, but motorway escapology was clearly not the basis for long-term marital bliss. 'It was the biggest mistake of my life,' Allison would admit.

While at Boro, schoolteacher Lynn Salten, more than 25 years his junior, entered his life – following a false start. 'I went out for lunch with my mum and Malcolm was in,' she recalls. 'When I left he apparently asked in the restaurant who I was and because we only lived in a small village they gave him the rundown. A couple of weeks later I was in there on a Friday evening with girlfriends and he sent over a bottle of champagne. When he joined us I thought he was chatting to my friend's sister, but then he asked if I would like to meet him for lunch. I think I'd had a few drinks – I haven't drunk since then – so I said I would meet him, but I didn't turn up. Obviously he knew where I lived and he rang and asked me why, so I said I would meet him for dinner a couple of nights later.'

As a football fan herself, Lynn knew of Malcolm's reputation, and at the age of 28, was wary of their age difference, but she admits, 'Malcolm was such a character and such a lovely man. I remember thinking on the evening we met that he had lovely hands and he was wearing a lovely jacket. He was a man – an old-fashioned man in some ways. He would open the door and walk on the outside of the pavement. He was such a generous man and that was one of the things that attracted me to him. And he had lived such a fantastic life. I used to say to him, "Tell me a story." He had so many of them.'

The early stages of what proved to be Malcolm's final long-term partnership were interrupted by his continuing on–off relationship with Sally, who at one stage had been pictured in the papers with a broken nose and teeth and black eyes after a row with her husband. Malcolm claimed in response that he had needed 26 stitches after she had hurled a tea cup at him. Only a few days before Allison's dismissal, Sally was back in the papers – taken to Northallerton Friarage Hospital with a cracked sternum after her car went off the road and hit a tree. Sally told reporters she had been on her way to confront Lynn. Even though the hacks' attempts to dig up some dirt on Lynn came to nothing – one of them told Malcolm, 'She must be a bleedin' nun,' – there was still enough material to leave Middlesbrough's directors less than thrilled with the narrative surrounding their manager's domestic disputes.

Asked for her reaction to Boro's decision to fire her husband, Sally let rip. 'I don't feel anything at all for him now and I don't feel sorry for him at all. He has made his bed and now he can lie in it. Mal's women have wrecked my marriage and as far as I can see, his career. Good luck to them now.'

Allison's immediate plans revolved around securing a £30,000 pay-off from Boro. Agent Richard Coomber, whose company had been representing Malcolm for five years, explained that there was still 13 months to run on a two-year contract and that his client would 'expect to be paid'.

Meanwhile, Boro chairman McCullagh called Jack Charlton and talked him into reprising his first managerial position, at least on a temporary basis. Charlton and Allison had been friends for a long time but the World Cup winner was disturbed to hear that Malcolm believed he had manoeuvred him out of the job. Charlton saw Allison at the FA Cup final and delivered reassurance that it wasn't the case. 'I've always had a soft spot for Allison,' said Charlton later. 'He was bold, brash and bigger than life. To a large extent he was the author of his own misfortunes, but as a football man he had the respect of us all.'

Instead of preparing on-field strategy, Allison spent the early weeks of the 1984–85 season working on the case he would be taking to an industrial tribunal to claim wrongful dismissal by Middlesbrough. The hearing was eventually staged in November, his assertion being that refusal to sell players did not constitute grounds for being removed from his post. 'Malcolm was a man of principle and I always admired him for that,' says his partner Lynn. 'Middlesbrough wanted him to sell players, but he had promised the fans he wouldn't do that and he was very conscious of what he had said.'

The club's position, which was duly upheld by the legal process, was argued forcefully by their lawyer Kevin Fletcher, who opened by telling the court that Allison had run up a £3,500 bill for champagne, cigars and brandy in the first three months of his employment. Just as damning for Allison was Fletcher's assertion that he had arrived for a meeting with the club chairman 'clearly suffering from the effects of drinking'. That had led to him being warned about his off-field behaviour, which included taking unauthorised days off. Addressing the non-sale of players, Fletcher said Allison had 'stabbed Middlesbrough Football Club in the back'. And referring to Malcolm's suggestion that the club's demise was preferable to selling its young players, he continued, 'The club's claim is that a clearer case of gross misconduct, going to the very root of the employment contract, would be difficult to imagine. His brilliance was dimmed by his off-field activities to such an extent that the chairman wrote to him expressing his concern.'

Allison insisted that he would never have signed his contract had he known he would be forced to offload members of his playing staff against his will, but not even the appearance in court of Brian Clough, who described Malcolm as 'not a man known for telling lies', could produce a late winner.

20

ROVERS RETURN

'I'm like Red Adair. People only call me when they are on fire and out of control'

– Malcolm Allison

By the time Malcolm Allison was appearing in the witness box at his industrial tribunal, a chance game of golf had led to his return to management, albeit in modest surroundings at Northern League Division Two side Willington. The club began the season under the guidance of Alan Durban, who had just been fired by Sunderland. Current chairman, and then secretary, Bob Nichols, explains, 'One of our committee members played golf at the same club as Alan, who said that, as he had some spare time, he didn't mind taking on the manager's job until something else came along. Late in September, he was offered the position at Cardiff and shortly after that we were contacted by Malcolm's agent asking if he could carry on where Alan left off.'

Willington were not one of those non-League clubs with a rich benefactor ready to buy his way up the football pyramid. 'Northern League football at that time wasn't as lucrative as it is now,' says Nichols. 'The general pattern, which we followed, was that the manager was given a fixed amount per week and he could take out of that what he wanted and use the rest on players.'

Money clearly wasn't Allison's motivation for approaching Willington. He simply wanted to remain involved in the game. During four months under his leadership, Willington continued the improvement instigated by Durban and maintained a position in the top half of the table, a satisfactory achievement after their struggles of a year earlier, especially when added to the higher profile Malcolm gave them.

Nichols continues, 'Everybody was amazed at the situation and happy to have him at the club. He generated a lot of publicity and the squad was always competitive. He mixed well and was quite genial, with no airs and graces – although we basically only saw him twice a week, at Wednesday training sessions and at matches on Saturdays.'

This brief and happily unremarkable managerial stint was ended by Allison's own volition, a welcome change after the dismissals that had ushered him out of so many clubs since the beginning of the decade. Remarkably, given his legendary love of a drink, it was the opportunity to work in the alcohol-free state of Kuwait that prompted him to bid farewell to the Northern League. Offered the job of national team coach, he set out for the Middle East in the spring of 1985. Once again, the winning instinct that had proved so elusive in England for almost a decade and a half would be rediscovered.

Kuwait had come to international football prominence by qualifying for the finals of the 1982 World Cup in Spain and achieved notoriety in their match against France in Valladolid. With the game heading towards an inevitable French victory, the Kuwaiti defenders stopped as Alain Giresse bore down on their goal, believing they had heard the referee's whistle. The sound, though, had come from the crowd and the resulting goal was allowed to stand. From his seat in the stand, the president of the Kuwaiti Football Association, who also happened to be a prince of the country, made gestures that appeared to be ordering his players from the field. Yet as they prepared to obey instructions, he arrived on the touchline and instructed them to stay, at which point the Russian referee disallowed the goal.

Kuwait would not be travelling to Mexico four years later, however. Defeat in Syria in the critical game of their first-phase group in the Asian qualifying rounds early in 1985 condemned them to an early exit from the competition. The qualifying campaign had been led unsuccessfully by Brazilian Antonio Lopes dos Santos, successor to fellow-countryman Carlos Alberto Parreira, who had steered the team to Spain and would guide his own country to victory in the United States 12 years later.

Allison was next in line. Asked to select a staff to travel with him to the Middle East, he chose Spry, to take care of the conditioning and fitness, and former Arsenal winger George Armstrong, another with whom he had worked at Boro, to help with the coaching. Commitment to the cause was a prerequisite. The coaches would be living in Kuwait full-time, with no commuting back and forth from England. It was in the desert that Spry got to know Malcolm well enough to eventually ask him to be godfather to his daughter Alexandra and saw a side of him that few appreciated. 'Malcolm is a paradox,' he explains. 'He is very studious, a real bookworm. Every time you saw him away from the field he would be reading a book, one or two every week.'

Mike Doyle had made a similar observation about his manager some years earlier. 'Most people outside the club haven't got a clue what he's really like. Mal's very quiet off the field, studious if you like. He reads books about the revolution and books by Russian authors. He's a very intelligent man.'

Spry explains that Malcolm was never tempted – or certainly not able – to break the country's strict rules of temperance. 'It was virtually impossible to sneak a drink in. You couldn't get it anywhere. But after a short while, I don't think Malcolm even thought about it. The only thing to do was focus on the football, try different things and experiment. He loved it.'

Malcolm's partner, Lynn Salten, adds, 'His mum died while he was in Kuwait and that affected him, but he was quite content there. I went to spend Christmas with him and he would just read his books and have a cigar and sit by the pool.'

The culmination of Allison's year in Kuwait was the country's participation in the Gulf Cup, the tournament held every two years among the region's nations. Staged in Bahrain in the spring of 1986, the event was a triumphant march for Malcolm and his team. They began by beating Saudi Arabia 3–1, followed two days later by a 2–0 win against Oman. A 1–0 victory against the United Arab Emirates proved to be the most important of their schedule and after a 2–1 victory against Qatar, success by the same score against World Cup-bound Iraq ensured Kuwait's place at the top of the seven-team table. A 1–1 draw in the last game, against the host country, left Allison's team four points ahead of second-place UAE, while Kuwait's Moayad Al-Haddad was named as the tournament's best player.

'To win the Gulf Cup was a big, big thing for the country,' says Spry. But not enough to keep Allison in a job. 'With most of the Arab countries, there is a flavour of the month in terms of the nationalities of the coaches,' Spry continues. 'For a while it was all British. Then at the end of a certain period they decide they want another country and it is all change.'

As has been seen, Allison was not frightened of an encore. He might have fallen foul of the Sporting Lisbon ownership, but in Portugal his reputation as a coach was an elevated one and it was back to that country that his wanderings now took him. Relegated to the second tier of the Portuguese Liga, Vitoria Setubal were in severe danger of going bankrupt if their return to the top flight was not immediate. They knew a saviour when one became available and the call went out for Allison. Once again Spry was taken along. 'He came everywhere with me,' Allison explained, touching his friend with his insistence that he should be part of the set-up at Setubal. 'Mal was a legend in Portugal. The first day I went there with him we got off the plane in Lisbon and he was stopping the traffic and being hugged and kissed by people he didn't even know.

'I was unknown but Malcolm introduced me as the best fitness and conditioning coach in the world. The club hadn't wanted me because they already had the guy who took care of the national team but Mal insisted and said that without me he would not take the job. That kind of loyalty was one of the great things about Malcolm. I have worked for a lot of coaches and they tend to look after themselves, but he put himself on the line for me.'

Allison turned to his old Sporting Lisbon players when he enlisted help for his new team – including goalscorer Jordao, former Sporting captain Manuel Fernandez, centre-back Eurico, midfielders Ademar and Zezinho and goalkeeper Ferenc Meszaros. He watched his team romp away with the championship of their division. 'Malcolm was a great teacher and wouldn't just tell you what to do,' says Spry. 'He could show you and explain why he was doing it. There were never any communication issues, regardless of nationality.'

Allison might have won nothing in England since his days as coach at Manchester City, but now three consecutive appointments with overseas teams had achieved success. In none of those positions had Malcolm's role involved any administrative functions. Spry says, 'None of the top coaches in England today are managers in the old sense. They are coaches and that is how it always was on the Continent. It was crazy to ever expect Malcolm to get involved in finances.'

It was at Setubal that Allison and Spry encountered a man who was to go on to become one of the world's highest-profile coaches, and to whom many have compared Allison during preparation of this book. Felix Mourinho was one of Vitoria's goalkeeping coaches and his son José, future manager of FC Porto and Chelsea, was often an interested observer. 'José came and watched training a lot,' Spry recalls. 'He was a young guy at university studying physical education and he became very close to me and Malcolm. He has a lot of Malcolm's mannerisms.

'They are both men who have a strong belief in their own capabilities and in what they are doing. Every player would share that same belief because Malcolm could make every player believe they were the best in the world at their position. José is the same. I don't like the word "arrogant" being applied to them – that gives the impression of someone pretending to be something that he isn't. That wasn't the case with Malcolm. He was just supremely confident, in the way that José is.'

As well as achieving victory on the field, Malcolm was finding personal contentment. 'He seemed very happy at that point,' is James Lawton's recollection of visiting him in Portugal. Jeff Powell has similarly happy memories of a trip to Portugal. 'We went to a fish restaurant and had a serious day's drinking. They had a load of live lobsters in the tank and Malcolm got quite emotional about them. "Poor bastards, waiting to die," he said. "The least we can do is give them a drink." So he started ordering vodka and tonics and pouring them on to the leaves in the tank. The old antennae were going out and eventually the bottom of the tank was all vodka. Suddenly these lobsters started getting frisky, climbing out of tanks and scuttling around the restaurant. It was chaos. Malcolm shouts out, "Leave it to us. We'll get them back in." He is organising the whole restaurant. It was mad.'

While Setubal was a somewhat ramshackle port town hit by depression, he and Lynn were settled in a picturesque house on the Arrabida hills. Late in 1987 he said, 'The boss offered me a five-year contract and I think I may take him up on it. I really like the place. I don't earn as much as in a big club but there are compensations. If you set up a relationship with a small town like this you get a very nice situation. The last time I came back from London I was pleased to be back. It was like coming home.'

Lynn, who had taken a teaching job in a local British school, describes the time she and Malcolm spent in Portugal as 'a fantastic experience'. She says, 'We had a wonderful time together and I didn't know we were so popular. It was like running a hotel because we had so many people who came out to visit. Malcolm loved that. His family and friends came out and we could take them out and show them the nice parts of Portugal.'

It was there that Malcolm forged a stronger relationship with his older children. 'He was very much on his own and I used to try to encourage him to contact them,' says Lynn. 'He was always very focused on all he did and it was me who made him send birthday cards or ring. They are all lovely children and he was very proud of all of them. He would always talk about them with great pride when he spoke to anybody about them and perhaps deep down he regretted not being there for them when they were young.'

As well as family and friends, journalists continued to be drawn to the magnetic personality of Malcolm, although Lynn soon grew tired of their one-dimensional sketches of a man in whom she had seen far greater depth. 'The press only ever wanted to portray him in a certain way and they would come and visit him with champagne and cigars and want to take pictures of him. I remember once taking them away from him and saying, "No. That's not who you are."'

Even Lynn has to admit, however, that it was at least part of who he was. 'The first time he met my mum and dad he ordered a glass of champagne and a cigar and I had to tell him, "Don't, Malcolm. I have told them you are nothing like your image." But he was very quiet sometimes. He was lovely when fans came up for an autograph, but he wouldn't say anything to them. I asked him why he didn't say something about the game or what a nice day it was and he started doing it to pacify me. They used to look at him as though he was completely mad because they weren't expecting him to strike up a conversation.'

The great Portuguese adventure could have ended in tragedy, however, had it not been for Malcolm's loyalty and stubbornness. Lynn explains, 'I started having problems with my eyesight. I thought I just needed glasses but Malcolm was brilliant. He wasn't satisfied and he really did persist with the doctors and the hospitals to find out what it was. Eventually, after lots of examinations they found out it was a tumour. When I had it removed the surgeon said it was a success, but the best way to prove it was to have a baby. I said, "Well, Malcolm has got five children that we know of so I will just take your word for it." I was 35 and loved children but didn't think it was right for Malcolm and me. Then, some time later, I was expecting Gina and she is the best thing that has ever happened to me.'

By that time, though, the temporarily smooth track of Malcolm's existence had been derailed once again after Vitoria's first year back in the top level of Portuguese football ended with an eighth-place finish. Allison, who had also managed to pick up a seven-week touchline ban for abusing referees, was out of a job. After hearing him being booed by the fans in a 2–0 home loss against Salgueiros late in the season, club president Fernando de Oliveira relieved his manager of his duties, explaining, 'He did a good job but the rift between him and the fans grew even wider after Sunday's defeat.'

Spry comments, 'In places like Portugal, you have to win something to be guaranteed your job. Manuel Fernandez was close friends with the club owners and he wanted to go into coaching, so they didn't renew Malcolm's contract.'

Lynn adds, 'The president wanted Malcolm to play a particular friend of his and Malcolm wouldn't and that was the end of that. That was Malcolm. He always had a good relationship with all the players and fans, but it was usually the chairmen he would fall out with. With the exception of Robert Daniel at Plymouth, they all seemed to be a bit jealous of him. They would possibly feel threatened and would not like it if he was more popular than they were.'

Rodney Marsh had remained close to Allison since their time together at City. It was with Malcolm and Serena Williams that he'd lodged for a while during a difficult period in his professional and personal life in the mid-'70s, although his wife Jean – from whom he was estranged at the time – urged him to move out and get his own place. She believed that Malcolm was 'the wrong sort of person' for her husband to be close to. On a professional level, Marsh had carried a debt of gratitude to Allison for talking him out of turning his back on possible England selection after Sir Alf Ramsey told him he wanted him to 'play like Geoff Hurst'. Marsh was inclined to tell Ramsey where to stick it until Allison took him for dinner and talked him round. 'I can honestly say that if Malcolm hadn't persuaded me, I would never have pulled on another England shirt,' admitted Marsh, whose meagre return of nine caps was a sign of Ramsey's reluctance to commit himself to players of Marsh's delicate skills.

Such frustrations, coupled with his inability to get on with Tony Book as manager at Manchester City, had led to him quitting England and boarding the plane for America with his famous comment about English football being 'a grey game, played on grey days by grey people'. Marsh found the colour of the North American Soccer League more to his liking and played for four seasons in the green and yellow of the Tampa Bay Rowdies. He remained in Florida after the collapse of the league in 1984 and had become chief executive of the club, who in 1988 found themselves playing in the more modest American Soccer League.

Marsh was looking for a coach after the departure of former Liverpool defender Mark Lawrenson. Allison happened to be looking for a job. Even though he didn't stay long, he enjoyed the American life to the full, as he had during his brief stay in Memphis a decade earlier. After a Rowdies team meal following one game, Marsh left Allison in the restaurant with the players. At 3.30 a.m. he received a call from the local police, saying they had a man in the cells who was giving Marsh's name as reference. It was Malcolm, of course, and he had been stopped by a patrol car while driving the wrong way down

Courtney Campbell Causeway, the vast bridge spanning the water between Tampa and Clearwater. Asked if he would stand bail, Marsh replied, 'No. Leave him there. We'll do it in the morning.'

Despite such incidents, Marsh still cared enough about Allison to put his name forward for the position of coach with the USA national team. Rowdies co-owner Cornelia Corbett was on the national team committee, so Marsh invited Allison to outline to her over dinner how he would move America into the elite of world football. On arriving at the restaurant with Corbett, Marsh was horrified to find Allison well on his way towards inebriation. His dismay grew as Allison declared that his tactics would be based on making use of all the tall people in the country by playing an aerial game. Allison then stated his case for being given the post, punctuating his speech liberally with expletives. He didn't get the job.

So instead of planning for a World Cup, Allison would soon be plotting to achieve success in the GM Vauxhall Conference. In the meantime, he had served a brief stint back in Portugal with SC Farense after being appointed towards the end of January 1989 for the remainder of the season. He was dismissed in March, having been unable to improve on the club's position of 18th out of 20 clubs. In June, he was named manager of Fisher Athletic, a small team with big ambitions, whose Surrey Docks Stadium nestled in the estates off the Bermondsey ring road in south London's docklands.

Having arrived in the top level of non-League football in 1987 as champions of the Southern League, Fisher Athletic had attracted the interest of Winners Worldwide, a trio of music and sports entrepreneurs whose Paul Crockford now admits, 'When we walked into Fisher Athletic we left our business acumen at the door.'

He explains, 'A guy called Paul Woolf, who was a lawyer, and I formed Winners Worldwide with Ross Hemsworth, a sales guy who came to us with a pitch to get involved with sport. He dropped a few names and it all seemed plausible. Originally we got involved with a view to managing athletes and being involved in boxing. Then we decided to try to find a small club in the Conference and do a deal where we put some money into the club, develop around it and end up owning a club with leisure facilities and other businesses. It would effectively mean the football club was costing us nothing.'

The group approached every Conference club and successfully followed up on interest expressed by Fisher. 'We had a deal on the table to build a health club and something for the local community,' Crockford continues. 'It was very ambitious. The local council was cooperative but wanted three years' worth of back rent, which blocked the deal. We argued that they should take it up with the previous owners.'

While that particular battle got under way, attention turned to installing a manager to replace Steve Bowtell, who had been holding the reins for four months since long-term manager Dogan Arif, part of a family that had achieved considerable infamy in the south London underworld, had been arrested for his part in a plot to import £8.5 million worth of cannabis. Crockford explains, 'We needed a high-profile managerial appointment that would put Fisher straight on the map. Someone suggested we look at Malcolm and I thought, "Why on earth is he going to want to come here?" But we made contact, had a chat and he agreed to join us. We agreed to pay him £60,000 a year, which was a phenomenal amount for a Conference club. Then we discovered that he needed Roger Spry to work alongside him as well so that was more money before we even started.'

The initial public relations return was a healthy one. ITV's *Saint and Greavsie* pitched up to film a feature, while most national newspapers were present, and looking bemused, when Allison was introduced as manager via a helicopter landing on the pitch. 'I didn't want to ask them why they did it,' he commented, although he undoubtedly appreciated the ostentatious nature of such a stunt.

Allison's first home game, at which one thousand balloons in the club colours of black and white were released into the air, attracted a crowd of 908, double the usual Fisher attendance, but ended in a 3–1 defeat, after which Allison bemoaned the bad habits his players had picked up over the years. Spry witnessed a group of part-timers revelling in being coached by such an icon in their sport and recalls, 'They all thought they had died and gone to heaven to be working with Mal.'

However, Crockford believes Allison made a serious error in his approach to managing Fisher. 'Malcolm treated the players like they were professionals. I thought he over-trained them. We had only 19 or

20 players on 50 quid a week and we lost a lot of them from training injuries. We had thought Malcolm would simply wave his magic wand and turn them into a team that would get into the Football League. Then we would use the money from the development to strengthen the team. It was a disaster. Players were dropping like flies, we were having to play kids from the youth team and they were getting battered. We were plummeting down the league and crowds were down to 200.'

By mid-November, Fisher were third from bottom in the table and according to Crockford, losing £15,000 a week. The owners' inability to move ahead with development plans because of the ongoing rent dispute meant there was no prospect of being able to recoup any of their investment in the near future. They had to tell Allison they could no longer afford him. 'Malcolm and Roger were the most expensive items on the books,' says Crockford. 'If we had felt we were close to getting promoted it might have been different but we fell out with Malcolm because he couldn't handle a club at that level. We should never have given him the job. We parted company, but it wasn't under pleasant circumstances.'

Woolf, who was club chairman, announced to the public, 'Malcolm is leaving for personal reasons and it has nothing to do with the performance of the club while he has been manager. He will be missed in many areas, especially in the junior and youth team activities.'

For one whose life so frequently seemed haphazard and lacking in any grand plan, there is a pleasing symmetry to the fact that, having made return trips to so many of his clubs, Malcolm Allison's final full-time management position was exactly where his first had been almost three decades earlier, Twerton Park, Bath. And his return to professional football in November 1992 had a familiar ring about it. Club in trouble calls upon Allison to work with incumbent manager; Allison insists on doing things his way; partnership quickly dissipates. For Bert Head or Tony Book, this time read Dennis Rofe, the former Leicester and England left-back who had been in charge of Bristol Rovers for 16 months when Allison was employed as a troubleshooter – or coaching consultant, to give him his official title.

Malcolm's return to Twerton Park, where the homeless Rovers

were the tenants of Bath City, ended a two-year period during which he had lived a largely private existence in the north-east village of Yarm, becoming a father for the sixth time. There had been some ad hoc coaching engagements and he had remained good value when the media needed a lively sound bite. He explained, 'I was doing a bit of television and radio but frankly I was bored. I wanted to be part of the game again.'

Lynn Salten continues, 'I felt he needed to be working, both financially and because he had so much to offer. I got the impression he was disappointed that some of the people he had helped along the way didn't help him out at the end when possibly he needed someone to believe in him and give him a chance.'

Rovers was intended to be a three-days-per-week appointment, assisting a club that found itself stuck at the bottom of Division One[13] following its latest defeat, 5–1 at home to Barnsley. Back in the Football League after an absence of more than eight years, Allison wasn't going to pass up the opportunity to give reporters a memorable quote. 'There are two types of people who succeed in coaching,' he said on the day of his arrival at Rovers. 'They are conmen, confidence tricksters who teach players tricks of the trade; or intelligent men who build your confidence and belief. I'm the conman. The players here are leaking a few goals and losing faith in themselves but there might not be a lot wrong. If each of them can just improve a little bit in 10 ways, the team will improve in 100 ways.'

Answering questions about how he would work in conjunction with the current manager, Allison insisted, 'When Saturday comes, Dennis is the man in charge. I know my place in a football club.' If Rofe had been reassured by the first of those comments – or even believed it – the second must have scared him. Ever since Joe Mercer had told Malcolm to 'give me two years' Allison saw his position at any club as that of head boy. Anyone else was just a prefect.

For Rovers' next match, Allison suggested various selections that were resisted by Rofe. Fielding a duo of players, Andy Tillson and Gary Waddock, bought from Queens Park Rangers for £470,000, Rovers crashed to a second successive 5–1 loss at Wolves. The Rovers

---

[13] The 1992–93 season was the first of the FA Premier League, leading to the old Division Two becoming the new Division One.

directors responded by relieving Rofe of major team decisions. Less than a week after welcoming Allison to the club, Rofe had resigned, leaving Allison to be elevated to 'consultant manager'.

Rovers vice-chairman Geoff Dunford explained that 'Dennis just wasn't prepared to listen to advice', while Rofe gave his version of events. 'Basically I was asked to relinquish control of selection and tactics to Malcolm or accept the sack, so I decided to leave.'

It was a move that shocked the Rovers players. Striker John Taylor said, 'We are all totally bewildered. We were totally behind Dennis and there were signs that we were beginning to turn the corner.'

Tillson recalls, 'I had only just joined Rovers on the strength of thinking Dennis was a good bloke who wanted me to play. I wondered what on earth was going on. Malcolm arrived in a bit of a whirlwind – and it carried on like that.'

Allison understood that his presence had made Rofe feel insecure but showed little public compassion, commenting. 'Managers have to take full responsibility and when you have had two 5–1 hidings there is really nowhere else to go. That's why I wanted Dennis to listen to me. If he had, we might still have been beaten on Saturday, but it wouldn't have been 5–1.' And he explained that, at the age of 65, there was a limit to the commitment he could give to Rovers. 'I only came here to do a consultancy job and I don't want to get too deeply involved in management,' he said. 'Football is a young man's game and I do not intend to give 15 hours a day, seven days a week. I am happy to do the job until someone else is appointed and then, who knows, he may not want to work with me.'

Allison's first act in his new role was typically unorthodox, cancelling training, calling off a practice match against local opponents and taking his players to a sauna in order to get to know them better. Once they had their clothes back on, he sat them in front of a video compilation of the 44 goals Rovers had conceded in their first 16 games. 'The players look tired out,' was his explanation. Before long he was again bringing in the old dance master Len Heppell, failing in an attempt to sign Swedish international forward Johnny Ekstrom and even suggesting that a rugby match against Bath would improve his players' upper body strength. 'But I would ask the Bath lads not to play full out,' he added.

Tillson, these days head coach of the Bath University team that has established itself near the top level of English non-League football, continues, 'Malcolm saw the value in sports science and the value of the facilities that the university had to offer and had us training there in his first week. I was looking forward to working with him. It was clear that he was trying to change things and had a futuristic approach to the game.'

But the new Rovers manager was not universally welcomed. Allison's first full game in charge, a home defeat against Derby, found a fans' petition making the rounds. 'The future for Rovers is with Rofey, not some old relic from the Seventies,' it read. His appointment finally ratified for the rest of the season, Allison's team went on a run of four League victories, only for a sequence of two wins in twelve games to leave them mired in twenty-third place in the table. One game, however, ensured that Allison won over some of the sceptical supporters, a 4–0 thrashing of Bristol City that was achieved by a series of spectacular goals. The game is still remembered on Rovers websites, with one fan writing, 'Most people were predicting a close result but then Big Malcolm Allison's shoot-on-sight training started paying off. To see Rovers score four goals like that and beat "The Shit" at the same time was one of the sweetest moments of my life.'

The draw for the third round of the FA Cup ensured headlines when Rovers were paired away to Aston Villa, managed by Ron Atkinson, who had won the competition twice as manager of Manchester United. Atkinson had managed to wrap himself in the persona of Big Ron, although where Big Mal's props were cigars and champagne, Big Ron favoured chunky jewellery, shades and a year-round tan. Allison knew a wannabe when he saw one, dubbing him 'Fat Ron' and accusing his players of 'not being able to kick a ball'.

Atkinson was affronted enough to refuse to shake Allison's hand after a 1–1 draw, offering more ammunition to Malcolm, who accused him of 'running away'. He added mischievously, 'The only time I saw Big Ron was in the dug-out. He was shrinking by the minute. I felt having a dig at him would be quite amusing. He has criticised enough people in his time and I am surprised he has not been big enough to take it. I'm certainly not bothered about the way he has reacted.'

Atkinson, who pointed out that 'half my lads are under 25 and don't know who he is', had the last laugh with a 3–0 victory in the replay. And once the dust of the contest had settled, he also made sure he had the final word. 'I feel nothing but contempt for [Allison]. I would have been quite happy to have a bit of fun with him but when he called my managerial ability into question it was all off. He has obviously forgotten who got him and his friends tickets for matches when he was skint. As far as I am concerned he does not exist.'

Within a month of arriving at Rovers, Allison's wages at the club had become the subject of much interest when he appeared at Epsom County Court to face legal action from his estranged wife, Sally, over £6,000 worth of unpaid child maintenance. Rovers were reported to be paying him only £330 a week, placing him among the lowest paid bosses in English football. It meant, Allison claimed glibly, that he could afford only one cigar a week – and only then if Lynn paid for it. The presiding judge, Simon Page, imposed a January deadline for Allison to start paying the money he owed.

Sally, meanwhile, was interviewed in the *Sunday People*, warning, 'If he doesn't honour this arrangement, then I have the right to have the money docked out of his wages.' She claimed that she and daughter Alexis, who was then thirteen, had suffered nine years of financial difficulties since the break-up of her marriage. She said she had spent the previous nine months trying to get Allison to answer her questions about the state of his finances and claimed that she was forced to scour the second-hand shops in East Molesey, Surrey. 'If you listened to Malcolm's stories since he returned to football at Bristol, you'd think Alexis and I didn't exist,' she said.

'Since Mal and I split, it has been one long struggle to get him to pay for his child and her upkeep. There have been many court appearances and many promises. But Malcolm seems incapable of keeping them. This latest court hearing was no different. Malcolm tried to explain why he hadn't paid a bean for more than a year and asked to have the maintenance payments reduced. He even brought a payslip from Bristol Rovers showing his earnings. I can't believe a man of his experience is getting only £330 a week. He has forgotten more about soccer than many current top managers know. So he must be worth more than £330. He was paying £400 a month but that stopped without explanation in November last year. I've had to scrape and borrow just to keep Alexis and me fed and clothed.'

Sally explained that her daughter's promise as a tennis player and athlete was going unfulfilled because of lack of money and accused Malcolm of having 'not responded to her pleas for help'. She added, 'I found it very hard to face him in court knowing the way he has treated his child.' With Christmas approaching, Sally added poignantly, 'Alexis is hoping she can get some running shoes from her dad. If she doesn't receive them, a little sparkle will go out of her life as well. I don't want her to grow up hating her father.'

Allison subsequently asked the court to lower his payments, claiming to have been a victim of the crash of the Bank of Credit and Commerce International, which had collapsed owing £5.6 billion in 1991 following investigations by the Serious Fraud Office into years of false accounting and financial wrongdoing. The bank, set up in the early 1970s, had operations in 69 countries. Malcolm was never one for long-term financial planning and it appears entirely in character that, while not revealing how much he had invested and lost, he should select such an organisation rather than a safe-as-houses high street building society. 'Somebody advised me it was a good bank,' he said some years later. 'Of course it was a blow when I lost the money but there's nothing you can do so there's no point worrying about it.'

What should have been a worry come February 1994 was Allison's tenure at Bristol Rovers. Vice-chairman Dunford issued a public warning about the need for improvement, while indiscreet comments from players to reporters hinted at dissatisfaction over the manager's emphasis on fitness over ball skills. Tillson prefers to remember the day Allison brought out his favoured 'wheel' theory. 'He sat down at Bath University and threw all sorts of different things at us. We had never heard of this system, never dreamed of it. But you look now and it is basically what happens at teams like Arsenal. Players take up different positions, with wingers going inside, the centre-forward drifting in. You can't really put a position on anyone. In his way, Malcolm saw that ahead of everyone else. It came a little late for him and it was difficult for us to take on board.'

Tillson, a 26-year-old central defender, was the Rovers player to whom Allison became closest. They frequently shared a train carriage when they travelled after matches towards their respective homes in Peterborough and Yarm. 'He would not talk too much about our team and what we should be doing,' says Tillson. 'He preferred to talk quietly about the time when he was a player at West Ham and all the friends he made there. He obviously had fond memories of that period of his life.'

Back in the present, Allison was losing the support of some of his Rovers players and Tillson admits, 'Malcolm gave some of the younger lads a good chance and left out some of the senior ones, which upset them.' But Allison had little time for insurrection, insisting, 'My system works and it can save the club from relegation. What I can't legislate for is the inconsistency we have displayed.'

What no one could legislate for, other than Malcolm himself, was that, removed from the day-to-day stability of home life, his alcohol intake had reached impossible levels. Tillson remembers Allison's occasional absence from training, but Malcolm at least had the presence of mind to send for help. James Lawton recalls, 'I got a call when he was struggling at Bristol. He was staying at some pub there. He had got pretty bad and he called me one day, basically saying that he needed evacuating. I was going to drive him home, but I talked to Lynn and they got him back to the north-east. It was a tough period for him, but so many have been.'

Reports circulated that Allison had been taken home and confined to bed suffering from a 'mystery chest complaint'. After missing two games he declared himself ready to return but the club had already contacted York City manager John Ward about taking over. Allison did the honourable thing and handed in his resignation, although he had enough cheek to suggest that he was now interested in the vacant York job. 'It's only an hour from my home,' he said.

But this time Allison's managerial career really was over – after eight stints at five different English professional clubs, three major non-League appointments and positions in four different countries. He had won domestic club championships in two countries, three national cups, a major European club trophy, a couple of promotions and an important regional international tournament. For many that would have been a magnificent legacy. That in Allison's case it seems an argument for underachievement and wasted talent says much for the esteem in which he was held as a coach – and continues to be by those who care to look beyond the flamboyance and flash.

In many ways, his legacy to football continues. One of his old boys, Terry Venables, enjoyed a second stint in the England set-up having previously served as manager. The list of those most closely influenced by him over the years includes the only man to have lifted the World Cup for England while many others – such as Don Howe, Dave Sexton and John Cartwright – have held important positions with the national team and earned elevated reputations in the coaching world. A family tree of those who have worked with, played for or been influenced by Allison would find numerous branches working their way throughout modern football.

That Allison himself was never invited to be more closely involved with England's national team is down to a mixture of his own misjudgements and misdemeanours and what his supporters feel is the short-sighted attitude of those who have governed football over the years. Long-time *Daily Mail* journalist Jeff Powell is well placed to comment on such a phenomenon, having campaigned for many years for his and Malcolm's great friend, Bobby Moore, to be more usefully employed in football. 'The game never made the most of Malcolm's tactical and technical knowledge. It saw him as one of the great entertainers and didn't understand his influence on the game. In the same way, it never made use of Bobby Moore's great intelligence. He should have been England's defensive coach, not wandering off to manage Southend.

'Malcolm should have achieved even more, but what he did achieve was in defiance of the old authoritarian views that ran football. The stand he took against long-ball football was pretty important to the game. He stood up for creativity and imagination. He was never going to take the results and money over the beauty of the game. Brazil was his team, not Wimbledon.'

Powell saw Bobby Moore die before the government could bestow upon him the knighthood millions felt he deserved and now believes that Allison's influence on the sport should be remembered and acknowledged by a belated place on an honours list, especially in the current climate that allows David Beckham and a possible knighthood to receive serious speculation. 'Beckham is much less deserving of being a huge personality than Malcolm Allison,' says Powell. 'His contribution to the game is infinitesimal compared with Malcolm's contribution – although perhaps that should be potential contribution. Circumstances have changed where celebrity is everything, but who would have been a bigger celebrity than Malcolm Allison? He is a very important figure in the game. Manchester City would never have happened without him and they were greater than Manchester United, where everyone gets a gong. We didn't honour Bobby Moore while he was alive so maybe we should give Malcolm something now. He deserves it.'

Even Allison's most ardent supporters would concede, however, that he has made it possible for people to disregard such claims by pointing to a career that, certainly in the later years, appeared to fall prey to misplaced ambition and the chaotic character of his private life. That career might have been over following his departure from Bristol Rovers but, as those close to him watched in horror and hopelessness, retirement was to prove no less traumatic.

21

NO MORE GAMES

'The brief span of our poor unhappy life to its final hour is hastening on; and while we drink and call for gay wreaths, perfumes and young girls, old age creeps upon us, unperceived'

– first-century Roman poet Juvenal

'Old age ain't no place for sissies'

– twentieth-century American writer Henry Mencken

Out of football management and, as usual, out of money, Malcolm Allison remained rich in those willing to offer him support. Veteran journalist Ken Jones had captured the feelings of many when, in 1991, he wrote of Malcolm, 'He made mistakes, didn't he just, and a lot of the wounds were self-inflicted. But he had, and indeed still has, the most winning disposition and manner imaginable.'

It meant that, early in 1993, there were many in the football community ready to rally round. A celebration lunch was held to mark Allison's 50 years in football, initiating a series of testimonial events. Of course, Malcolm had never laid his fedora in one place long enough to be considered for any kind of club testimonial. Among the guests at the first event was George Best, who explained his attendance by saying, 'I did it for nothing because Malcolm is the most genuine man in football. He deserves everything the testimonial committee can get for him.'

London solicitor Barry Gold headed that committee, setting up a match between Crystal Palace and Tottenham on 28 March, followed by a dinner in Manchester and a golf day in Cheshire in April. 'Malcolm has been great for football but not always clever for himself,' said Gold. 'So now it's time his friends helped him.'

James Lawton remembers, 'I went to one of those events. Malcolm was kind of embarrassed and I found it almost unbearable and upsetting, I feel quite moved now when I think about it. I remember thinking, "What a system we have in this country when a man of his ability is reduced to this." You can say Malcolm made some of his own problems but he was never paid properly.'

There were plenty of friends ready to do their bit. Jeff Powell recorded in the Selhurst Park match programme that among Bobby Moore's last requests before his death from cancer a month earlier was for 'everyone he could think of to pitch in and make sure that Malcolm Allison enjoyed a suitably extravagant and appropriately lucrative testimonial'. Many responded, some remembering the contribution he had made to their careers in football, others recalling the numerous rounds of drinks he had stood them on those nights out when no one else was allowed to dip into their pockets. He had worn like a badge of honour the fact that he would pick up the tab, whether or not he could afford it.

'He was always living way beyond his means,' says Lawton. 'If he borrowed 50 pounds off someone, as he often would, he would spend it on someone else. One night he took me and my wife to the Playboy Club in Park Lane and then we went to Tramps and had a fine meal. I remember people like Shirley Bassey being there. I made a feeble attempt to pay the bill, even though it would have been about four weeks' wages for me. Malcolm kept giving them credit cards but the waiter kept coming back and whispering in his ear, so he produced another with the same result. He got through about four or five. In the end he said, "Can I just sign for it?" The guy just shrugged and let him. Malcolm was pretty much chaos in that respect.'

Bob McNab recalls a tale from the 1980s while he was visiting from his home in California. 'Barbara and I were having dinner in a restaurant in Chelsea. Malcolm came in and he was absolutely legless. This guy at another table sent over a bottle of champagne because he was an Arsenal fan and I sent one back. Malcolm insisted on paying, but they wouldn't take his credit card so I slipped out and paid. When I came back to England three or fours years later, he pulled me on it. "Don't you ever do that again," he said. "I pay." He'd remembered, even though he had been falling asleep at the time. He was just silly with money.'

Another scheme was dreamed up on the strength of Malcolm's wit and easy ability to trot out anecdotes from half a century in football. He and Tommy Docherty, whose tongue was as sharp as Malcolm's and his managerial career as frenzied, toured around small theatres as 'The Doc and Big Mal – a frank and outspoken evening crammed with the stories they could not tell on TV'. In *The Times*, humorist Clement Freud gave the duo a less than sparkling review and left at the interval.

Meanwhile, the Child Support Agency was proving less interested in Allison's tales from the dressing-room than in his income from the testimonial committee. Little more than a year after his court appearance for failing to support his second wife, Sally, he was now reported to owe £30,000 in unpaid maintenance. Having seen tales of money-making activities, the CSA had approached Sally for an explanation and also stated their intention to question Terry Venables and Francis Lee to get a fuller picture of Allison's financial status. Sally said, 'I did warn them Malcolm would be very difficult to pin down as I have had ten years of trying to get money out of him.'

Sally claimed that she had been waiting more than three years for the £20,000 she and her husband had agreed upon and that the CSA were now pursuing him for the additional amounts fixed by the matrimonial courts. Raymond Morris, treasurer of Allison's testimonial committee, sounded as exasperated as Sally when he pointed out, 'We run his testimonial, not his domestic affairs. His matrimonial matters are his own business.'

There was another court appearance booked in Allison's diary for June, when he appeared to give evidence in former Chelsea defender Paul Elliott's case for compensatory damages after suffering a career-ending knee injury in a challenge with Liverpool striker Dean Saunders. Malcolm's appearance was far from straightforward. Originally he had been retained as an expert witness on behalf of Saunders, only to end up speaking for Elliott after claiming that

Liverpool midfielder Ronnie Whelan had suggested to him that his teammate should be found guilty. A furious Whelan denied strenuously that such a conversation had occurred and threatened legal action against Allison, whose evidence was dismissed by the judge as of no assistance to either side.

Later in the summer, Allison undertook an after-dinner speaking tour in Hong Kong, where he reminded his audience that he was, at heart, a football coach. 'I am open to offers and I would consider coming to Hong Kong. I think I can still do a good job for an ambitious side with my breadth of knowledge about the game. Perhaps even the Hong Kong national or Olympic side could benefit from me being involved. I may not be as fit as my Manchester City days but I would still have a tracksuit on.'

The opportunity for closer involvement in football than simply helping out with his local pub's Sunday League team did come Allison's way, thanks to two of his old boys achieving high office at Maine Road and the Football Association. Francis Lee and Terry Venables both stated an intention to use Malcolm in a scouting capacity after assuming the positions of Manchester City chairman and England manager respectively. One of Allison's first suggestions to City manager Brian Horton was to sign Sporting Lisbon's young midfield star Luis Figo, although the move never materialised.

Coaching might have been Malcolm Allison's natural home, but Big Mal lodged happily in the world of the media. It was only once the job opportunities on the training ground finally dried up in later life that Malcolm devoted himself – out of necessity – more completely to an area in which he could feasibly have carved himself a deep niche. Possessing the footballing insight of an Alan Hansen, the quick wit of Terry Venables and the charm, albeit of a rougher variety, of a Des Lynam, it is interesting to wonder how his life could have changed had he, say in the mid-'70s, opted to capitalise on his profile and personality rather than pursue a procession of short-lived football appointments.

Almost a quarter of a century after his irreverence and insight had illuminated many a late night during the World Cup in Mexico, he was hired in 1994 to bring a touch of colour and controversy to Century, a newly established station in the north-east that was riding the growing wave of 'talk radio' by launching a football phone-in show. Malcolm was to be one of the hosts. The somewhat low-key nature of his medium reflected the damage he had managed to inflict upon his footballing reputation over the years. For a burgeoning local station like Century, however, Allison possessed undoubted star quality and when, in 1995, it acquired the live commentary rights for Middlesbrough's Premier League games, he was the obvious choice to sit in the analyst's seat.

Meanwhile, Allison had been reported to be close to a return to League football in March 1995 when his name was linked to a consortium trying to buy Gillingham. The head of the group was Ross Hemsworth, the former commercial director of Fisher Athletic, and Malcolm was said to be poised for the role of director of football. The deal never materialised – and nor did the thief by whom Allison claimed he had been head-butted when he was pictured in Peterborough sporting a black eye a couple of months later.

When the 1995–96 season began, Allison threw himself enthusiastically into his new role alongside Century's recently recruited match commentator, Alistair Brownlee. 'The club had just moved into the Riverside Stadium, which gave it a big uplift,' says Brownlee. 'It was an exciting time and Malcolm, in his role as summariser, established himself as part of the fabric.'

Brownlee laughs at the recollection of his role in the partnership with Allison. 'Half the time he thought I was his chauffeur. I arrived to pick him up at his home in Yarm and he would come out in his trademark fedora and we would be off around the country. It was a privilege to sit alongside him in the car and listen to stories about his life in football. Wherever he went he would be recognised and there was obviously a lot of affection for him. We went to Manchester United once and he was walking in front of the stands saying, "Boro are coming to beat you", and the crowd were cheering him.

'Southampton's old ground at The Dell had a very small car park and getting a pass was a thankless task. But we simply drove up to the gate and the steward said, "Hi, Malcolm", and let us park up. One time he walked out of a game at Chelsea with a huge hamper that someone had given him and I remember a chilly night at Crystal

Palace, where they had a Malcolm Allison Lounge. Malcolm asked for a brandy and when the barman asked if he wanted a large or small one he replied, "The bottle, please." And when he said, "Will there be anything else?" Malcolm just answered, "Yes. Make sure you get that 'A' put back on my name on the sign outside."'

For a while, Allison was thriving in his new environment. Brownlee continues, 'He felt able to chip in any moment with that loud booming voice of his. He had an obvious talent for the role and people responded to him. He was very popular.'

Then came Middlesbrough's home game against Newcastle early in February. When Boro gave the ball away in a dangerous position, Allison could be heard to mutter 'fucking hell' under his breath. In the next seat, Brownlee was still worrying about whether anyone would have heard it as Les Ferdinand scored a winning goal for the visitors. 'Malcolm said, "Oh, fucking hell", again in a loud Cockney voice – very loud indeed,' Brownlee recalls. 'The listeners heard it and one or two rang the switchboard at the station to complain. It stunned me as much as anyone because I was not used to hearing Malcolm swear even in our normal conversations.'

Allison was suspended by the station for the rest of the season. 'I did use a bit of bad language on the air, and they had no alternative but to tell me I couldn't work for them any more,' he said. 'People have been kind enough to keep ringing the station asking for me to be reinstated, but I just have to accept it. I have nobody to blame but myself.'

It was not a good time for Allison. In the same month, he had his scouting role with the FA taken away from him following his public criticism of England forwards Andy Cole and Matthew Le Tissier. The *News of the World* reported that the FA had written to clubs informing them that Allison no longer worked for them.

However, believing he would have learned his lesson, and having been swayed by the considerable support from listeners for his reinstatement, Century restored him to the airwaves for the start of the new season. 'A lot of people missed Malcolm,' says Brownlee. 'It was decided to bring him back for a trial, and to make sure he would be all right on air we introduced the "Big Mal Button". He was given a microphone to work with, but it was not live at all times.

He had to press a switch to make it work and the hope was that if the F-word popped into his head it would have been consigned to the back of his mind by the time he pressed the button.'

Allison soon decided that he was not going to be silenced by a piece of crude technology. 'His way round it was to simply sit on the thing so that it was always live,' continues Brownlee, who recalls the day that his partner spoke his last on the station. 'We had a match at Coventry. The linesman gave a decision and Malcolm said, "That's a fucking disgrace." I had a call from the boss at half-time saying he couldn't continue.'

There was speculation at the time, repeated since, that Allison had been the worse for wear for drink, but Brownlee rejects that suggestion. 'Certainly he had not been drinking before the Coventry game. I drove him all the way there and we didn't call in at any restaurants. I wouldn't have allowed him to drink too much. I travelled thousands of miles with him and never saw him drink too much before a game.'

Following his dismissal by Century, the *Daily Mirror* took a voyeuristic delight in reporting that Allison, faced with the prospect of being out of meaningful football employment for the rest of his life, was 'on the breadline'. As well as having to support Lynn and Gina, now six years old, on a total of £104 per week – made up of his state pension plus other family allowances – Malcolm also admitted to a fear of losing his right foot because of an old football injury that had never healed. 'I'm having an operation in Northallerton Hospital in the next few days,' he explained. 'The foot wasn't operated on when I first broke it, and it has troubled me for years.'

Drastic measures were not required, but money still was. Allison picked up a few quid in 1997 for writing a column in a short-lived retro football magazine called *Action Replay*, but his working life was finally coming to an end. With no more encores to perform, he faded from the public eye. And without football to help keep his demons at bay, he slipped more deeply into the grip of the drink that had been a companion for so much of his life. As much as he treasured the opportunity to spend more time with his daughter, Gina, he admitted to missing the daily companionship of the football fraternity. 'When I was working my life was filled with contacts and people,' he would explain in 2000. 'But ever since I have been at home, in the past four years, I haven't really had any friends. Nobody except my lovely little girl.'

Allison claimed to have suffered from manic depression, a condition that went undiagnosed for almost three years until he was prescribed Prozac towards the end of 1999. 'I started having mood swings,' he said, describing pains in his chest and head. 'Loneliness is a thing that's difficult to explain.'

By 2000, Allison had been with Lynn for 17 years. 'We were happy. Or I thought we were,' he said. For Lynn, however, life with the increasingly erratic Malcolm had become an impossible ordeal and she'd had to ask him to leave their home. James Lawton says, 'Lynn's feelings towards Malcolm now are of sadness and she still loves him – or what he was. But she said to me that for the sake of her daughter it was impractical to live with him.'

Lynn traces the beginning of a period that she has 'only just now been able to move on from' to Allison's dismissal from Century. 'Malcolm was his own worst enemy and he would shoot himself in the foot. He had that fantastic job with Century which was ideal for him at that time in his life. He could go to the matches and catch up with friends.

'But after that he became quite dissatisfied with life and I couldn't understand that because he had Gina and me and we had a lovely home, yet he couldn't adapt to a lifestyle like that. It wasn't Malcolm I suppose. He would miss all of the things connected to football. He would still be watching on television and shouting out what they should be doing and felt he had something to offer. He would see people in certain jobs and realise that he was a lot better than they were.

'He'd had a fantastic relationship with Gina, which was the saddest thing towards the end. When Gina was tiny I'd gone back to teaching and Malcolm and Gina spent a lot of time together. They would go out for lunch and have walks in the park and I remember [one of his daughters from his first marriage] Dawn saying how lucky Gina was to have had that time with Malcolm because she didn't have that. That is why it was all the more upsetting when things went wrong when Malcolm was drinking heavily and Gina didn't want to come home to find him and didn't want him to meet her at school if he'd had a drink.'

Lurching more deeply into a pit of self-destruction, Allison returned from a three-week stint coaching junior players in Romania, determined to achieve some sort of reconciliation. He broke into Lynn's home, stayed long enough to drink a bottle of wine and was duly arrested. Lynn subsequently won a court injunction to keep him away from her home. Allison's lawyer requested of the court, 'I ask you to view this more in sorrow than anger because it is the story of a once-famous man whose whole personal life has degenerated and spiralled out of control.'

Lynn admits, 'Even now I don't know how I did it, but I had to. Malcolm changed personality completely when he was drinking and that was very hard. My friends and family saw what it was doing to me but I still defended him, which you do when you love somebody. But Gina was the reason I did what I did. I had to be quite ruthless and that was hard to come to terms with and live with.'

Malcolm's companions were becoming more aware of his problems and a group of them hijacked him at the Football Writers' Association dinner at the Royal Lancaster Hotel in London. They made known their concerns but, despite the pep talk, when he travelled home the next day the effects of a liquid lunch made him rowdy to the point of almost being thrown off the train. An acquaintance managed to calm him down, enabling him to complete the journey. But then he took a taxi to Lynn's home, demanded to enter and was arrested after he attempted to smash down the door with a paving slab. After spending the night in the cells he was found to be in breach of the injunction banning him from going near the house and was ordered to pay £300 and given a 12-month conditional discharge.

Allison's own loyalty to friends over the years had served him well. Released yet homeless, he found support from Tony Zivanaris, a hotelier and property developer who had briefly been a Middlesbrough director in the 1980s and was among those who fell under the spell of Allison's personality. He had once ordered his staff at the Baltimore Hotel to tolerate the £11,000 bill Allison had left unpaid upon checking out. Payment had later arrived via a post-dated cheque from Kuwait. Now it was Zivanaris whose intervention kept Malcolm off the street, putting him up in his hotel and instructing his staff to take good care of him.

He had a roof but still had problems. At the end of May he told a *Daily Mail* news reporter that he was 'on the verge of suicide' and living on a diet of cognac and Prozac. The article made grim reading, an unpalatable mixture of melodrama and crude, clumsy self-justification from Allison. Having done his best to make his subject's living quarters appear little more appealing than a student bedsit, the writer's description of Allison mentioned 'the faintest of tears now forming and running down his ruddy broken veined cheek'.

The sense when reading Allison's threat of suicide was of someone eager to give his audience what they wanted, perhaps to increase the monetary value of the access he had granted his inquisitor. 'We can all choose our way of life and there's no way I could be here for months,' he was quoted as saying. 'I would rather commit suicide. I won't try it, I'll do it. All those people who have said they've tried it is bollocks. I've thought about it. I won't tell you how I'll do it, but I'll do it. It's not hard to commit suicide.'

Allison's claims about his relationship with Lynn, intended to paint her as the villain, did him even less credit. He said the end of their relationship had been precipitated by Lynn's anger at him spending his money on Viagra. 'She just objects to things like that. You'd have thought she'd be pleased. I mean, we had not had sex for about six months. I asked if she was a lesbian. Of course I don't think that. But when you get no sex you think: What's going on? I don't know whether she was using the Viagra thing as an excuse or whether she just didn't want to make love to me any more anyway.' Lynn had too much dignity to respond to such comments.

James Lawton, who wrote that the *Mail* had paid Allison £600 'to ransack what was left of his life', takes up the story. 'I was very upset. Malcolm was in a bad way and Lynn had thrown him out after he had behaved pretty badly. I had sent him some money, which wasn't the smartest thing to do because he was drinking. I drove up to Middlesbrough and found him in Tony's hotel. I appointed myself as a bit of a liaison between Malcolm and anyone who could help him at all at that point. Franny Lee was magnificent. I said to him, "Obviously the drink is doing him in. From my perspective he needs to go in the Priory or somewhere, but the financial side is high there." Franny said he would talk to the PFA [Professional Footballers' Association], but said that in the meantime he would give the hospital his credit card to cover the costs.'

Zivanaris ordered his driver to put Allison in his car and head for the Priory Clinic in Altrincham, sending with him a new dressing gown, pyjamas and slippers. Several of Allison's old City players were among the visitors, taking fruit and Havana cigars. Lee also carried a warning for his old boss. 'You made Belly, Mike [Summerbee] and me do a lot of things we didn't want to do,' he told him. 'You made us work so hard we spewed up. You never stopped kicking our arses. You made us achieve things as footballers we never dreamed were possible. You were bloody incredible. I don't believe there has been a better pure football coach. You changed our lives. Now you have to change your own. We're here to help, but you have to do the real job.'

Summerbee emerged from one visit to say, 'Even now, after all he's been through, I don't believe there is anyone in football with a sharper brain, a more complete understanding of the game. I've told him that it's a tragedy he's still not involved. Maybe it is a little bit of the game's fault, but also Malcolm's. He's got to come out of that place in charge of himself, with his pride back and I wouldn't be surprised if someone doesn't say, at this late hour, "Wait a minute, this guy could help."'

Lawton, too, was encouraged to see some of the old Malcolm surfacing at the Priory. 'For a little while I was hopeful that things were looking up a bit. There was a young lad in treatment there and Malcolm was working with him. He was a footballer, not a professional but quite talented. It was quite a poignant image, this young boy who was addicted to drugs and Malcolm, the old coach, putting him through his paces. Again, the teaching instinct had emerged. He would have been a great teacher. I remember when [journalist] Ken Jones had his accident a few years ago and lost part of his arm. He was in hospital demoralised because it was his good hand. Malcolm brought him some chopsticks and said, "You do realise that the Chinese are the best ping-pong players in the world. One of the reasons is that they use chopsticks to eat with and are so dextrous. The bat is like an extension of their fingers. If you use these for half an hour every day, it will increase a hundred fold your dexterity with the hand." I thought that showed a particular way of thinking.'[14]

Lee remembers, 'In the Priory, he was absolutely the Malcolm of old – everything about him. It had been a good summer and he looked well and had a nice tan. He was lecturing people in there to stop drinking and taking drugs.'

Malcolm himself was soon announcing, 'I'm going to make a record recovery.' For a while he suggested he might be able to live up to his boast, teaming up again with Tommy Docherty to host a phone-in show on Manchester's Piccadilly Magic radio station. Yet, just like the promise of the new start he'd made to Terry Venables during the summer of 1978, it was to prove beyond his fragile willpower.

Lee continues, 'We got him right back on the straight and narrow. We got him a job on the local radio and everything was going well but all of a sudden, he pressed the self-destruct button and slipped back to his old ways. He was back drinking again and finished up creating his own problems.' Even Malcolm's stalwart friends were forced to admit that there was nothing more they could do. 'Mike and I said to his family, "Look, you have got to get hold of this and sort it out yourselves from now on because it is a family problem."'

Malcolm's plight was highlighted in May 2001, by which time he was living in warden-controlled housing. After suffering a fall outside his home, he ended up in Wythenshawe Hospital with a broken collarbone, at which point his son, Mark, said, 'He is very ill, but he's accepted for the first time he is an alcoholic. Previously he's been to Alcoholics Anonymous and has been in the Priory. But he has never actually accepted what his biggest problem is.'

Mark explained the hope that Allison would be admitted to a specialised clinic at Withington Hospital, and added, 'If he goes in a pub, which he has been doing because of his loneliness, someone

---

[14] Jones himself had related that incident in *The Independent* in the weeks after he had fallen in front of a train. 'Of all the comforting voices that have reached out to me since an accident a fortnight ago,' he said, 'predictably, it was Malcolm's that conveyed the most imaginative and practical advice.'

there will buy him a drink and then they get one of his great stories. He can't do anything on the after-dinner circuit because they are drink associated.'

Once again, Allison's public response to his predicament was to put on a brave face and crack a joke. 'Just tell people I'm in a bad way but I hope to be out of here sooner rather than later. If anyone could send me £1,000, that would be handy!'

Gradually, however, Malcolm's problems were growing beyond financial salvation. He was found to be suffering from the onset of dementia – probably triggered, and certainly not helped, by alcohol.[15] Looking back, Ian Niven believes he saw an early manifestation of Malcolm's condition. 'Malcolm would stay with me some weekends. We had got the brandy out and were reminiscing and as we were chatting he raised his voice, which he had never done in conversation between us. He started shouting, "You were one of the most brilliant directors I have known." I was embarrassed but eventually his voice subsided. That was the last time he came down and just after that he started having his troubles. I think that might have been the start of his ailment.'

Lynn also recalls that it was difficult to know where the effects of drink and the onset of illness merged. 'We would laugh about him losing his suitcase or his scarf or falling asleep on the train and missing his stop. The day we moved house he was at a game with Century and I said, "Remember that when you come back we will be in a different house." We had a house-warming party a few weeks later and some friends bought him a badge with the address on, saying, "If you find me please return me to this address." I think that was a mixture of the drink and start of the dementia.'

Malcolm's recent years have been lived out in a residential care

---

[15] Medical research has shown that prolonged excessive alcohol intake can lead to various forms of dementia, including Korsakoff's syndrome and Wernicke/Korsakoff syndrome, which are specific types of alcohol-related brain injury. Allison's condition has often been incorrectly referred to as Alzheimer's disease, although alcohol abuse is not thought to be a cause of that particular illness – in fact, moderate regular intake of wine, in particular, is thought to help protect against it.

home run by Trafford Borough Council in Sale, although in 2007 his family had to make plans to move him because of the closure of the facility. His loyal band of friends, including ex-City players Bell, Lee, Summerbee, Tony Book and Willie Donachie, have continued to visit, often taking him for days out, even though the deterioration of a man who retains such a place in their affections has not been easy to witness. Ian Niven would regularly escort him to lunch at Manchester's Midland Hotel until the levels of sedation Malcolm had to endure made it too fraught and upsetting an exercise. 'Malcolm is not instantaneous in his conversation,' says Niven, 'if you mention a certain match he doesn't remember. It is hard when that happens to a man who was never subdued, always outrageously confident and gregarious.'

In December 2001, the *News of the World* described Allison as 'frighteningly pale, grossly underweight, unsteady on his feet and needs constant care from kind-hearted nursing staff'. The reporter added, 'Even the cheeky twinkle in his eyes that once captivated women has gone.' His home was said to be a small room to which he was not entrusted with the key, being unable to make decisions about his own comings and goings. The décor featured photographs of his parents, of his successful City team and of himself as a player. Many souvenirs and mementoes of his career had been sold over the years for some instant cash. Asked about Malcolm's condition, his family were said to be 'too distraught to talk'.

Allison's son, Mark, offers a less gloomy picture, saying in summer 2007, 'He is still big and strong. There is nothing wrong with him physically and he has his better days. He goes to quite a few City games but it is difficult because he doesn't really remember what has happened because of his short-term memory loss. He has lost the ability to read books as well, which he loved.'

Malcolm does, however, retain a sense of humour, as Mark explains. 'He knows that he can't really answer people's questions so he has a set of one-liners that he uses. If someone says hello and asks him how he is, he will answer something like, "I'm better than you", or, "I am still waiting for that cheque you owe me."'

And some of the roguish Mal remains. 'We were in a bar recently,' says Mark. 'Dad can't really remember what the drinks are but he can still read, so he looked at the list and said, "I'll have that. Champagne."'

Lynn adds, 'When I call him I say, "Hi. It's Lynn here." And he always says, "Hi, Lynn-here." He always used to do that so he obviously has little things that he remembers. Malcolm is probably quite happy where he is and it is harder now for his family.'

Ironically, Malcolm's illness – and the care he requires – has brought him closer to his family than for many years. Mark explains, 'I never spoke to him for 25 years, until I returned from living abroad and went to spend time with him in Portugal. It was the same for my older brother David, who lived in Hong Kong. Now we take him to watch my son Marcus play football. I don't think he ever came to see me play. It is sad that at the time of his life when he would finally have had the opportunity to be around his family, he is not well enough to enjoy it.'

In September 2007, the Allison family staged a celebration for Malcolm's 80th birthday. Included in the festivities was first wife Beth, who has never found a replacement for Malcolm as the man in her life, remaining single since their divorce. 'She forgave him,' says Mark.

Similarly, Lynn speaks without a trace of bitterness about the man who, in their final years together, forced her to endure such emotional trauma. 'I have tried to always think about the positive things and the good times we had together,' she says. 'I have no regrets whatsoever.'

The final chapter of any biography written towards the end of its subject's life is likely to contain a degree of sadness. Yet it has needed Big Mal's own destructive touch, sprinkled with some simple ill-fortune, to create quite such an anthology of disorder out of the latter years of his own remarkable story. Echoing Francis Lee's words of mournful acceptance, James Lawton, Malcolm's friend for four decades, admits, 'I feel there is nothing left to do for him – but I feel a bit guilty about it. When I last tried to go and see him, I looked through the window of his room and he was sound asleep because of the medication he has to be given, so I left.'

Such feelings of responsibility and loyalty say something for a man whose manner of living has never allowed for compromise. Undoubtedly, he has disappointed and hurt people over the years, yet he has enriched and uplifted the existence of many others. The balancing of those columns in the ledger of life rests with higher authorities than this book. When Lawton penned a tribute for Allison's testimonial match programme in 1993, his words were intended to relate to those people who had encountered the football man, yet they could have applied equally to those whose lives Malcolm had touched in capacities ranging from friend to media contact, drinking partner to lover.

> His years were filled with controversy and only fleeting glory. But his passion, his feel for what was important in the game, has been noted and acted upon with the staging of today's game. This is where the generosity, and the imagination, lie. It is looking beyond the tyranny of results, seeing the story behind the scoreline. It is saying, 'Thanks for the memory, Mal. We didn't win it all when you were around, but we did a few things and saw some new horizons.'

No, Malcolm didn't win it all in life and those new horizons for which he was constantly striving often seemed to be at the end of a road that led to professional and personal catastrophe. To those close to him, the saddest aspect of his final destination has been the bleak inevitability of the journey. Several times after lunch visits with him in recent years, Lawton has driven away from his friend's spartan residence with the words of former Manchester City chief scout Harry Godwin echoing back to him over a distance of more than three decades.

'I used to drive to night matches and I would often take Harry. He loved Malcolm, adored him. But he used to express terrible fears about him. He had a vision of Malcolm as an old man, his friends disappeared and nothing going for him. Saying that about a young man was quite chilling. But he was spot on; that is precisely what has happened.'

Over the years, as that vision loomed larger in the future of one of the great football men, all attempts to divert him from its realisation were doomed to failure. Big Mal made sure of that. And yet, it still seems unfair on Malcolm Allison, unrepresentative of such a personality, to end his story on a note so gloomily downbeat. It is not the way his life will be remembered, even by those who have watched its deterioration.

The final paragraphs of this book, therefore, belong to Colin Bell, whom Allison considered the finest of all his footballers and who has never stopped seeing the inspirational coach behind the fading eyes in front of him, and to Bobby Moore, who, even in the final moments before his own death, chose to honour the man who had befriended and mentored him almost four decades earlier.

Bell remembers, 'Tony Book and I were chatting to Mal a few years ago and he still had his plans in his mind, breaking down the systems they play nowadays. It was wonderful. We were sat there listening to him for about half an hour.' The man Allison labelled 'Nijinsky' pauses, remembering the effect of those few prized moments when the lively minded coach of old had re-emerged. 'He made us feel like we were players again.'

The magic of Malcolm lives on in the reverence of Bell's delivery, as it does in Jeff Powell's memory of the final time he met with Moore.

'Malcolm had this long, red leather coat and when Bobby saw it for the first time he'd said, as a joke, "Love the coat." Typically, Malcolm had given it to him. The last time I saw Bobby we had lunch in the Royal Garden Hotel in Kensington. He never went out again and he had come to say goodbye. It was quite a warm day, certainly not one where you needed a jacket, but Bobby had this coat on and he sat and wore it all through a long lunch. I commented, "I see you have got that old coat on again."

'Bobby said, "Yes. This might be the last time I ever go out. I wanted to wear the coat Malcolm gave me."'

BIBLIOGRAPHY

Allison, Malcolm, *Soccer for Thinkers* (Pelham Books, 1967)
— with James Lawton, *Colours of My Life* (Everest, 1975)
Bartram, Sam, *Sam Bartram: His Autobiography* (Burke Publishing, 1956)
Bell, Colin with Ian Cheeseman, *Colin Bell: Reluctant Hero* (Mainstream, 2005)
Belton, Brian, *Days of Iron: The Story of West Ham United in the Fifties* (Breedon Books, 1999)
Best, George with Roy Collins, *Blessed: The Autobiography* (Ebury Press, 2001)
Blows, Kirk and Tony Hogg, *The Essential History of West Ham United* (Headline, 2000)
Book, Tony with David Clayton, *Maine Man: The Tony Book Story* (Mainstream, 2004)
Burtenshaw, Norman, *Whose Side Are You On, Ref?* (Arthur Baker, 1973)
Charlton, Jack, *The Autobiography* (Partridge Press, 1996)
Clark, Matthew, *Playing Away: The A-Z of Soccer Sex Scandals* (Cutting Edge, 2004)
Clough, Brian with John Sadler, *Cloughie: Walking on Water* (Headline, 2002)
Dawson, Jeff, *Back Home: England and the 1970 World Cup* (Orion, 2001)
Douglas, Peter, *The Football Industry* (George Allen & Unwin, 1973)
Doyle, Mike, *Manchester City: My Team* (Souvenir Press, 1977)
Fenton, Ted, *At Home with the Hammers* (Nicholas Kaye, 1960)
Firmani, Eddie, *Football with the Millionaires* (Stanley Paul, 1960)
Friend, Dante, *My Blue Heaven* (Empire, 2004)
Glanville, Brian, *The Story of the World Cup* (Faber and Faber, 2001)
Goldstone, Phil and David Saffer, *Champions: Manchester City 1967/68* (Tempus, 2005)
Greenwood, Ron with Bryon Butler, *Yours Sincerely* (Collins Willow, 1984)
Hewitt, Paolo and Mark Baxter, *The Fashion of Football* (Mainstream, 2004)
Hill, Jimmy, *The Jimmy Hill Story: My Autobiography* (Hodder & Stoughton, 1998)
Hugman, Barry J., *Football League Players Records 1946–92* (Tony Williams Publications, 1992)
Inglis, Simon, *The Football Grounds of England and Wales* (Collins Willow, 1983)
James, Gary, *Football With a Smile: The Authorised Biography of Joe Mercer* (ACL & Polar Publishing, 1993)

Kriegel, Mark, *Namath: A Biography* (Viking, 2004)

Lee, Francis, *Soccer Round the World* (Arthur Baker, 1970)

Lyall, John with Michael Hart *Just Like My Dreams* (Viking, 1989)

Marsh, Rodney, *Priceless: The Autobiography* (Headline, 2001)

Matthews, Peter, *Don Rogers: The Authorised Biography* (Tempus, 2004)

Moore, Tina, *Bobby Moore* (Collins Willow, 1975)

Morton, James, *Gangland: Volumes 1 & 2* (Time Warner, 2003)

Motson, John, *Match of the Day: The Complete Record* (BBC Books, 1992)

Mourant, Andrew and Jack Rollin *The Essential History of England* (Headline, 2002)

Novick, Jeremy *In a League of Their Own* (Mainstream, 1995)

Partridge, Pat with John Gibson *Oh, Ref!* (Souvenir Press, 1975)

Pawson, Tony, *The Football Managers* (Eyre Methuen, 1973)

Penney, Ian, *Manchester City: The Mercer–Allison Years* (Breedon Books, 2001)

Powell, Jeff, *Bobby Moore* (Everest, 1976)

Sandbrook, Dominic, *Never Had It So Good: A History of Britain from Suez to The Beatles* (Little, Brown, 2005)

Rhys Jones, Griff, *Semi-Detached* (Michael Joseph, 2006)

Shankly, Bill with John Roberts, *Shankly* (Arthur Baker, 1976)

Shindler, Colin, *Fathers, Sons and Football* (Headline, 2001)

— *George Best and 21 Others* (Headline, 2004)

— *Manchester United Ruined My Life* (Headline, 1998)

Steen, Rob, *The Mavericks: English Football When Flair Wore Flares* (Mainstream, 1994)

Taylor, Rogan and Andrew Ward, *Kicking and Screaming: An Oral History of Football in England* (Robson Books, 1995)

Tossell, David, *Bertie Mee: Arsenal's Officer and Gentleman* (Mainstream, 2005)

— *Playing for Uncle Sam: The Brits' Story of the North American Soccer League* (Mainstream, 2003)

— *Seventy-One Guns: The Year of the First Arsenal Double* (Mainstream, 2002)

Venables, Terry and Neil Hanson, *Venables: The Autobiography* (Michael Joseph, 1994)

Wagg, Jimmy, *This Simple Game: The Footballing Life of Ken Barnes* (Empire, 2005)

Ward, Adam, *The Official History of West Ham United, 1895–1999* (Hamlyn, 1999)

Young, Neil with Dante Friend, *Catch a Falling Star: The Autobiography of Neil Young* (Empire, 2004)

The following publications and periodicals were also of valuable assistance: *The Manchester City Football Books 1–4* (Stanley Paul, 1969–72), *Rothmans Football Yearbook* (Macdonald and Jane's/Queen Anne Press, various years), *Charles Buchan's Football Monthly*, *Goal*, *Shoot!*, *Football Digest*, *Hammers News*, *Ex*, plus numerous local and national newspapers and various team internet sites.